TWINS

TWINS

SUPERSTITIONS AND MARVELS, FANTASIES AND EXPERIMENTS

WILLIAM VINEY

REAKTION BOOKS

To George

Published by Reaktion Books Ltd
Unit 32, Waterside
44–48 Wharf Road
London N1 7UX, UK
www.reaktionbooks.co.uk

First published 2021
Copyright © William Viney 2021

Printed and bound in Britain
by TJ Books Ltd, Padstow, Cornwall

A catalogue record for this book is available from the British Library

ISBN 978 1 78914 408 6

CONTENTS

INTRODUCTION

My mother's photographs catalogue life on an English farm in the 1970s, '80s and '90s. The photos make it easy to imagine the low drone of the milking parlour, the smell of slurry and wet Labrador. All the sounds and smells that made our working and domestic lives blur as one. My mother's pictures also capture the affection she reserved for her children and for the dogs that made our home a happy chaos. But these are not the reasons my friends now want to dive into these treasured books. Each album, red and square, is fetched from the shelves and a familiar ceremony begins. I watch as my friends, with the albums on their knees, become gripped by a desire to see me at my smallest. There's something unnervingly rapid to their curiosity as they rifle through the plastic pages like a gambler nosing through a bookie's form book. Ignored are the pictures of family members with garish clothes and large hair, along with the itinerant eccentrics who would come to the farm for temporary shelter and leave years later. Instead, my friends seek a special kind of visual treasure that is discovered as we reach the first pages dedicated to 1984.

They hesitate at the sight of my mother, who has appeared from behind the camera. In one picture she stands in the old farmhouse, the serene evening light falling across a maternity dress so big it could double as a parachute. Another page is turned, and here we are, fresh from the mint. Across the next pages we grow older and enlarge, become toddlers and the children of a fluorescent decade. Here are the twins my friends have come to see. And then a multiple game of spot-the-difference happens at such a frenzied pace that it can be hard to know who are the game's eventual winners. We are a visual tease, my brother and I, and involuntary objects in a simple game familiar to other twins. Can you identify which one is which? In the discussions that follow, our bodies are broken into manageable parts and our little noses and eyes, lips and ears get scrutinized – a smile between mirth and conspiracy is judged unique to one, held in common by both, or declared an outlier in need of further analysis. 'Why didn't your mother dress you in the same clothes?' 'Is it me, or does he have a rounder face?' 'How did you make each other laugh so much?' If I can answer their questions it is because I have practised seeing the differences and have been schooled in a relationship that is both something I was born into and something that has grown and been refashioned over time, and which is still being moulded through a bewildering and occasionally painful process of public display and consultation. I am struck by how I myself cannot always tell twin from twin. Though I can look at a picture that contains the faces of two little boys, I cannot always be sure which of those faces is mine. It is a small glimpse of myself as others would have seen me in the 1980s and early 1990s, as a person put in doubt: 'So then, which one are you?' It is a game that spreads across the leather-bound albums, extends beyond their pages to the here and now. Perhaps the winners are simply those who can trace in the photographed folds of flesh a telling dimple or blemish, a giveaway sign that identifies me from him. One way or another, my development is mapped. But not just mine. No, not just me; always also him. That oblique sense of 'we' – this duo, this couple, the twins we are. We form a pair we never chose to be and live a partnership we have sometimes done everything in our power to break.

Twinning has more provocative beginnings than it does ends, because although the absolute beginning goes largely unseen it marks the wellspring of natural philosophies, religious and scientific practices, family violence and love. We are less keen to dwell on twin events of separation or terminal tragedy than we are ready to marvel at the symmetrical or sequential beginnings from which twins grow – as we did, together, two by two, first as deadweight snuffling slugs, barely able to lift our heads, then as funny little snot-nosed walruses, upright and proud, each metamorphosis entering a shared calendar and each milestone given shape as an embodied measure of life lived in parallel, anchored in time recorded by two bodies who could not know change without a corresponding contrast in the other's living hourglass.

Now, though, our lives have more distance. Our twinship has grown from a kernel shared to one scattered by the work, the people and the pleasures we do not, will not or cannot share. This is what these pictures record but cannot bring into focus: the change, the gain and the loss. Gathered round these albums, my friends bear witness to what can be seen and compared. They also engage with what has been lost or hidden. In them they recuperate something I thought had left me long ago: the twinned time of our indivisibility. It is not the children and dogs or rural landscapes that make these albums unique but their power to draw us back to a more innocent time when we, as twins, were as unaware of our union as we were of the possibility of our separation.

When we began going to our rural primary school we were surprised that some of our teachers avoided using our first names. At the age of five, we were both known among our teachers as Master Viney, like bit parts in a BBC period drama. Our teachers couldn't bear to mix us up but seemed unaware that they left us feeling like strangers to ourselves. And it wasn't just our teachers. Our maternal grandfather had a phenomenal and idiosyncratic memory, with an ability to recall detailed county cricket results from the 1950s and pages of P. G. Wodehouse, his favourite novelist, but when we spent our summer holidays with him, he'd be stumped. To tell us apart he was forced to develop memory tricks each morning, making a mental note of our clothing and keeping track of any changes throughout the day. As little boys we grew aware that not everyone had a twin and encountered these simple problems of recognition. We learned that an invisible hand could separate us from our companions. How this happened and when could take us by surprise. We were simply different for being two, different for looking alike. We tried our best to fit in. If we felt as though someone was unsure, too embarrassed to ask which person they were speaking to, we would look for opportunities to drop a hint. I found that if I was alone, announcing an inconsequential fact about him would do the trick – they'd understand I was not him. There would also be times when answering to the other's name was the simplest way to avoid causing confusion; it was not that we wanted to fool other people, it was just easier than correcting everyone who mixed us up or accepting the familiar apology. I have met twins who have impersonated each other for months, travelled on the other's passport, attended each other's classes. But I am at a loss when asked what devilish tricks we played on people, as our social world seemed constantly fooled of its own accord. Now the photos of young Master Viney leave me feeling fooled. This is the irony of these family albums. I am left unsure on whose navel I gaze.

The routine confusions, the mistaken or displaced identities, lead people to believe that twins are not all that they seem. They also give me a dose of doubt, making me think that my own experience of being a twin is not as straightforward as words allow. I have lived a certain kind of twin life. I cannot assume that what I have experienced gives me permission to speak for others; there are good reasons to think that my experience has been less than typical. I tend to be sceptical about general claims made surrounding what makes twins a community or a people who may share a set of common experiences, qualities, talents or capacities that define them as individuals, pairs or a group. Even the definition of twins as people who share conception, gestation and birth is not one that is universally accurate. We rarely give time to consider how being a twin became a category – a category of being, a category of living and a category of history. This book explores that history to show how the label 'twin' has changed, depending on the values or measurements used.

* *

WHILE OUR FAMILY photograph albums tell me a lot about my own friends' twin fascinations, they also point to the uncertainty that twins can provoke. This includes the warmly curious, largely positive response I tend to get when I tell someone I have a twin brother and extends to the mythological creation stories and religious texts, philosophies and explanations of existence that feature twins in dazzling numbers. The histories compiled in this book show how twins have been used to define and debate some of life's most intractable problems, from the nature of time and the source of good health to the nature of true love and the creation of Earth.

In the years during which I was writing this book, the national newspapers in the UK carried twin stories written in the language of the extraordinary, the unusual, the rare, exemplary or telling: twin births, achievements and transgressions, written to appeal to an enchanted and at times breathless fascination with twin people.[1] It struck me that many of these stories – reports of stage or sporting debuts, accidents, marriages, deaths and births – found national prominence because they featured twins. The events themselves are ordinary or mundane, but the involvement of twins makes the mundane magical. The lives of twins are subject to a kind of amplified significance. They are special not simply for what they do and say but for what they are taken to be. The things that twins do or say become tangled up in what their twinship represents, creating a self-fulfilling loop that keeps the world of news media revolving. In contrast to the amplification of the ordinary, twin celebrity makes extraordinary achievements an extension of the twin mystique. Popular reporting on the work of Scott and Mark Kelly (b. 1964), whose participation in the 2015–19 NASA Twins Study brought them international recognition, sought to capitalize on their twinship. Cameron and Tyler Winklevoss (b. 1981) are former Olympic rowers and Bitcoin millionaires whose twinning makes their work and fortune a more corporate mystery, and fashion designers and former actresses Mary-Kate and Ashley Olsen (b. 1986) have led careers where their twin identity on-screen secured continued celebrity off-screen. These are but recent and specific examples of a more pervasive topic explored in the following chapters: twinship ties a knot around life and vocation in ways other forms of kinship cannot achieve.

There are twins of every combination of age, gender, ethnicity, race, sexual orientation, nationality and class, and not each and every kind of twin is equally described or represented in modern media. Contemporary Europeans and North Americans seem less interested in the routine ordinariness of twinship, its banality, its everydayness. Though there are rare exceptions, the tedious and unremarkable aspects of twin life are rarely reported, yet they constitute the bedrock of many twin relationships, the drawn-out and enduring feeling of having always been twins.[2] Instead, twins appear in the media most commonly as children, who are routinely worried about for different medical, psychological and other developmental reasons and who are brought into online content, books, magazines and community support groups as examples to encourage parents to have happier, healthier twins.[3] We learn about the different ways to care for infant twins – nutrition, sleep, physical and emotional development – and the household budgets and other relationships formed in their support. By contrast, it is more difficult to learn about the social world of adult twins in this – or any other – culture, decade, century or era. One can create all kinds of optimal environments in which young twins can flourish, but it is hard to know where to learn how, why, and with what effect twin lives are transformed into objects to be optimized; how, why, and with what long-term effects twins have been placed under the strategic management of parents, teachers, therapists and others.

The twins that appear in parenting or self-help books are examples, types or cautionary figures that direct parents towards techniques of improvement. One more general effect of this unevenness in how twins reach into public life is that it is the opinions of single-born parents, psychologists and therapists that dominate this marketplace. The voices of twins themselves are largely absent. Despite all that is written about twins, there is very little that is written for twins. Despite all that is written for twins, less is written by them.

It might be difficult to imagine a time when European and North American cultures did not celebrate twins in the pages of books and magazines, on television screens and online, or at twin festivals attended by tens of thousands of people. Go back a few centuries or travel beyond these regions and it is easy to encounter many different twin cultures, displaying radically different attitudes towards twin people. Twins are seen as demonic or divine, suspicious or sensational (and a fair mixture of these extremes, too). The history of twins is a history of multiple parts, countless theories, varying debates and plural bodies. It is a history that can show not just that twins have been far from alike in their meaning, but why twins have been seen, heard, loved and feared in different ways, in different times, in different places.

Twins are not as rare as you might think, and may not be rare at all, depending on where you live. One in every thirty people you meet in Europe or the u.s. is likely to have a twin brother or sister. But don't be fooled. If you live in parts of East Asia, encountering twins is less frequent, with just one in every seventy people a member of a twin pair. The highest population of twins anywhere in the world can be found in Nigeria, where one in twelve is a twin.[4] The causes of this variation are a complex confluence of biological and social variables, linking population genetics, reproductive behaviour, and access to advanced medical technologies that are both life-saving and life-creating (such as *in vitro* fertilization, or IVF). Overall, the variation stems from how dizygotic ('fraternal') twinning fluctuates among different populations – it is relatively low in East Asia and relatively high in West Africa. Though twins are not rare, many of us have only a vague understanding of why twinning happens and what differentiates a dizygotic twin from a monozygotic ('identical') twin. Dizygotic twins occur when two or more eggs are released in a single menstrual cycle and are fertilized, often during one but occasionally through sequential acts of sexual intercourse. Monozygotic twinning occurs when a single zygote (fertilized egg) splits into a near-identical pair; this pair will share almost all the same genes, hence the physical similarities that can often be observed in so-called identical twins. The cause of monozygotic twinning is not entirely understood by scientists, but worldwide birth rates are consistent: about one in 160 babies is born a monozygotic twin.

While monozygotic twins have a very similar genetic make-up – I joke that my brother and I shared an egg – dizygotic twins share on average 50 per cent of their genes, like many other siblings. The biological categories that separate monozygotic and dizygotic twins offer comfort among confusion – two kinds, two types – but the consequences are far from binary. Biology cannot yet disentangle twins into two easily divided camps. Even if we imagine a visual spectrum that puts mirror-like identical sisters, who appear to share every possible physical and behavioural trait, on one side, and highly discordant mixed-sex dizygotic twin siblings, who seem only to share a date of birth, on the other, there is no easy way to guess at the experiences of these twin pairs. Even in a time when biostatistical measures and values make the genetic identity of twins appear generalizable and absolute, there is no guide or universal measure to twin experience. Every set of twins is different from every other, and, with time, will frequently be different to themselves, since, as the years turn, relations between twins change and tilt the twin axis of likeness or difference. Though my brother and I are monozygotic twins, we have been told that our physical likeness is a disappointment, with some saying, 'You don't look alike!' We can then be regarded with cold suspicion: 'Are you sure you're identical twins?' When my twin came to visit me at university, one unprepared friend met my eye, smiled, turned to him and then stood still, mouth open, before fleeing as if pursued by a ghost. I found him hiding behind a line of cars, laughing nervously. Too much, he said, it's just too much; you look too much alike. This sort of thing doesn't require both of us to be present, and it doesn't always turn out the same way, either. Years ago, I was trying to catch a train at a busy London train station and was chased down the crowded train platform by two men; their cheerful faces fell to Earth when they realized that I was not the person they thought they knew. I can still picture their horror, their shame, the lingering suspicion that they were being hoaxed.

The more I tell stories about twins and hear stories about twins, the more I realize that the modern numbers and the recent biological theories formed around twins give a clarity shadowed by diversity. Although statistics reveal where and when twins exist, they cannot do justice to the stories told about twins, stories that can both be scientific and take flight into realms of fantasy, artistic and religious practice, philosophy and politics. Though twins are often divided into populations according to their molecular relations, there is nothing inevitable or universal about a set of embryological and genetic categories that are scarcely one hundred years old. There exists a counter-history of twin curiosity and bewilderment, a secret history of wonder reserved for twin people that cannot be easily answered by the powerful ideas currently supplied by modern biomedicine. This is a history that highlights how those biomedical ideas are the latest in a very long story of observing, examining and making sense of twin people. For twins have been honoured as gods and destroyed as toxic dangers, viewed as essential to scientific practice and as emblems of science dangerously out of control.

* *

THIS IS A BOOK written for twins as well as for anyone interested in the historical, global, political and technological contexts of twinning. I do happen to have a twin, but I have not used my experience to judge the 'true meaning' of twinship. One of my key discoveries has been the difference and diversity that can be found among different historical periods and human cultures. This is a book about the ways other people have made twins a figure of superstition and marvel, fantasy and experiment. It is also a book about how twins continue to be these figures, how they continue to be a community or a people who are described, used, abused, studied, practised upon. That the use of twins has had a global impact is an important thread that runs through this book. Twins have transformed the world in which we live and have had a transformative impact on the ways people have thought about the significance and structure of the world, about society, about the human body and its environment. Commentators and experts in European and North American cultures tell parents how to seek the good life with their twins. They do not dwell on how twins have been used throughout history to define and refine what the good life should be.

This book avoids celebrating or promoting a particular historical, religious, scientific or artistic use of twins. This seems particularly important in an era of genomic medicine and assisted reproductive technologies, when the ability to understand and produce twins through technologies has at once reinforced, even reinvigorated, ancient ideas about twins, and challenged the accepted standards used to separate twins from others. In chapters that address these techniques of knowing and making twins, I want to imagine the subject of twins both in panorama and in the detail of specific times, places

and practices. I am guided here by the approach of the sociologist
Niklas Luhmann (1927–1998), who made the useful distinction
between observing a particular phenomenon and the business of
observing others who see that phenomenon, what he called 'first-
order' and 'second-order' observations.[5] Twins are born and made,
and their significance is not only secreted in the given orders of the
natural world but made explicit through the histories of many different kinds of observer. The challenge is always to think about the
differences and similarities across practices, between times and
spaces. One of the strangest outcomes of this book, I think, has
been to find that ancient mythology and contemporary biotechnology may be distant in the imagination but proximate in ideation,
emotion, practice, and in the common values found in twins.

The focus on practices of knowing – on how knowledge is made
with twins – means that the concepts and realities of twinning
merge with world views, what we might call the animate clines and
hierarchies that link natural and cultural, human and non-human,
biological and environmental phenomena. A history of twins that
highlights past, present and future understandings of twinning also
addresses how twins have affected these broader categories of distinction and taxonomy. Twins are people who have been made to
matter, and their bodies make matters of fact and matters of concern visible.[6] The Canadian philosopher of science Ian Hacking
has argued that human groups are 'made up' over long and interwoven durations: 'our classifications and our classes conspire to
emerge hand in hand, each egging the other on.'[7] It is important
for me that readers of this book come to view twins not simply as
a group that excites various emotions but also, and in consequence,
as a distinct group of people understood through the specificity of
both the classes and classifications in which they emerge as well as
the classes and classifications that they have helped to form. This does
not make twins a 'made-up' group like any other. Twins also make
up others – they have a double role that engages scales that distrib-
ute agency and power. This book argues that twins have occupied
multiple stations in the hierarchies of value, prestige and visual recognition that still shape European and North American cultures

– twins are or continue to be gods, beasts, spirits, monsters, animals, signals and signs, instruments, molecular assemblages, fungible communities, textual and filmic devices. They can be found at several stations simultaneously, inter-animating between human and non-human, biological and environmental, and so on. This vibrant and metamorphic capacity involves them in a broad sweep of investigations and experiments, as they are enrolled into novel formulations of what humans were, are and might yet be.

Each chapter of this book explores how twins have been thought about, admired, feared, studied and schooled, in a bid to bring together the different histories of observers and their interests in twins, and to recognize the different powers, materials, tools, methods and intentions that are their legacies.[8] In the later nineteenth and early twentieth centuries, the emergence of academic disciplines such as genetics, epidemiology, psychology, sociology and anthropology meant that new grounds for comparison, new forms of likeness based on different human sciences, could facilitate the demonstration of new 'epistemic things' that twins helped to reveal.[9] Disciplinary identities can be made and lost according to who has access to and can claim authority over canonical texts, artefacts, archives, spaces, places or bodies.[10] The approach adopted in this book is broadly interdisciplinary in spirit, one that seeks to pass across or between disciplinary partitions to bring them together for comparison. As the following chapters show, twins have touched and are touched by many different kinds of thinking, and research disciplines are a recent example. Though interdisciplinary approaches like the one taken by this book often focus on the decision-making agency of individual people or groups of people, more attention needs to be paid to how interdisciplinary approaches are formed in relation to restless objects of study. Some objects of research, like the things we use to make thought more material, cannot and will not stay indoors.

History of the kind composed in the following chapters may not follow linear patterns of cause and effect, pressure and consequence. Nor does each chapter progress from the uneasy valleys of indeterminacy to the upland plateaus of enlightenment. This history's beginnings are as uncertain as the unknown location of its conclusions. Just as twins emerged in tandem with the practices of knowledge that use them, their lives as individuals and as groups of individuals are held in the tumbling rivulets, braids and tributaries of collective thought. The modern cultural critic Rita Felski has observed that human groups gain recognition according to 'distinct histories, rhythms, and temporalities quite apart from the traditional forms of periodization. History is not one broad river but a number of distinct and separate streams, each moving at its own pace and tempo'.[11] Felski's criticism of one traditional metaphor of time and history, as a kind of river, helps us to imagine how human groups may not flow together at consistent velocities or in common currents.[12] Working with the same fluvial metaphors, the philosopher Michel Serres (1930–2019) wrote that time itself 'descends, turns back on itself, stops, starts, bifurcates ten times, divides and blends, caught up in whirlpools and counter-currents, hesitant, aleatory, uncertain and fluctuating, multiplied into a thousand beds'.[13] Twins are enmeshed in complex ecosystems of atmospheric and material change.[14] Rather than a history of twins that is confident of neat beginnings and satisfying ends, this book traces change in torrents and pools as well as in meandering offshoots, whirls and cross-currents.

There are many ways in which this book can be read. It has been organized into a numeric sequence, but it need not be read that way. Readers may enjoy particular chapters for the windows they open onto the human practices that have been affected by twinning. Each chapter has an approximate theme or idea that has been pinned to twins and tries to explain the effects this has on twin people and on the category of twins more generally. Each chapter follows a statement about what twins have been said to be: myths, monsters, dangers, worlds, birds, experiments, manufactures, performers, words. The list is not exhaustive. The things twins are described as being are multiple.

1

TWINS ARE MYTHS

Light pours over Rome's buildings, touches palaces and churches, museums and restaurants, ruins and homes as I climb the steps to the square, with its winter shadows thrown before me. I can't remember how I first heard about Rome's twin myths, since the only classics that mattered to us when we were young were sold by rappers, publishers and sports brands, but when I began spending time in Rome I started to notice twins everywhere – as heroes, icons, victims, founders and villains – and their stories, close to Rome's present but also woven into its distant past, made the city an unsettling, unnatural and extraordinary place to me. Rome, I realized, is a place that has been born with twins, a city of people born together with others.

As I climb up the Quirinal Hill, the highest of Rome's seven hills, puffs of breath leave me in clouds. The winter is unusually cold this year and there are just a few sunglassed couples taking selfies, cut by a line of French teenagers marshalled by nuns in dark habits. Ceremonial guards stand motionless in brown and red uniforms near the door of the Quirinale – proud *corrazzieri* who safeguard the residence of the President of the Italian Republic. A short distance away, members of the military see to Operazione 'strade sicure' (Operation Safe Streets) in their green battle fatigues, machine guns slung over their shoulders. These once temporary figures, used to satisfy a local political crisis, are now semi-permanent features of Italian anti-terror policy. In the absence of a crowd and surrounded on three sides by palaces, the guards secure an empty space, dwarfed by two colossal twin statues: Castor and Pollux. Flanked by rearing horses, they rise through the light, restrained, as if poised to leap from their columns and smash through the streets. The reason twins occupy these plinths rather than two unrelated persons is not made clear

1 Giovanni Battista Piranesi, *Veduta della Piazza di Monte Cavallo* (View of the Piazza di Monte Cavallo [now the Piazza del Quirinale with the Quirinal Palace]), etching of the statues of Castor and Pollux, the Dioscuri, 1750.

by any inscription or official guidebook. What, then, in the history of this city, has made icons of these twins? And who has placed them within its most politically significant public spaces?

Twin history is larger than life, larger than one life, and more than the sum of individual parts: wondrous, monstrous and unreal. Many stories about twins, whether fictional or historical or some combination of the two, turn on powerful beginnings and extraordinary events – their presence is transformative for the places and the people they describe. They embolden particular versions of the past and allow new kinds of future to be forecast. Strange, mysterious or surprising things can make twins different from those who are not born in a pair. The dramatic beginnings and ends formed by these stories make twins toe lines that separate fact and fiction, legend and historical truth. Ancient Greek traditions are full of disagreement about what twins are, what they do and why they do what they do. This variation has to be managed, and, often, a particular version of a story concerning twins becomes more popular than others. While twins are imagined to be unusual or even strange in these stories, the ways they are described can become routine, even ordered. Despite being treated as extraordinary, making make-believe with twins is neither unusual nor strange.

In Homer's *Odyssey*, Castor and Pollux are said to be 'two sons, intrepid twins', but not gods.[1] For the Theban poet Pindar (*c.* 518–*c.* 438 BCE) they are both twins and gods of a particular kind: quasi-twins, demigods. It was Pindar's version that became popular in medieval and Renaissance Europe, when the twins were depicted in paintings by some of European art's great masters and absorbed into Italy's most famous art collections (see illus. 10). According to one traditional telling, the twins were born to Leda but have different fathers: Pollux is the immortal son of Zeus, while Castor is the mortal son of a Spartan king, Tyndareus. Pollux was conceived when Zeus took the form of a swan and had consensual sex with or raped Leda – accounts vary on this and many other details, and later Catholic depictions took pains to focus on Leda's motives, her bestial lust. Shortly after this union between deity and animal and human, Leda conceived with her husband, Tyndareus. The 'heavenly twins', as they became known, are what modern biologists now call 'superfecundated' – that is, resulting when two or more ova from the same menstrual cycle are fertilized by sperm from separate acts of sexual intercourse. Already sexually metamorphic, with a god taking the lustful form of a swan, the twins' form of conception is analogous to the superfecundation that is now a common phenomenon via assisted reproductive technologies. Of course, Pindar's tale of the queen, the god-as-swan, the king and the twins brings a different intensity. This is a bombastic story: a transgressive jumble of sex, fantasy, and violence to bring worlds of gods, humans and animals together. Twins, rather than single-born people, rise out of this jumble. They are emblems of a new settlement between the heavens and the earth. The heroes are inseparable adventurers and heroes. Then Castor is mortally wounded. Their tale ends with Pollux choosing whether or not he can bear to live without his twin. Zeus explains the conditions of their afterlife together:

> '. . . if you fight for your brother,
> And are minded to share with him in all things alike,

You may live half beneath the earth,
And half in the sky's golden palaces.'
He spoke, and Polydeukes set
No double counsel in his heart,
But freed the eye and then the voice
Of bronze belted Kastor.[2]

Pollux decides to share his immortality and joins Castor in death, whereafter they alternate their days in Hades and on Mount Olympus. Pollux's decision not to be separated from his brother collapses all the differences that their birth may have created; their life of unity is perfected in death. In Pindar's account, 'Polydeukes' (Greek for 'many doubles') is in no doubt. The twins enjoy cosmological status in the 'sky's golden palaces' as Gemini, the heavenly twins.[3]

The simultaneous birth of twins can put two beings into lifelong comparison, caught in the extremes of difference and sameness. But twins can also figure as composites and models for thinking about, comparing and melding people into transgressive images. Twins may make it easier for others to see similarities and differences between people, as peculiar binoculars for complex problems, and they often get recruited, over and again, to serve the interests of others. Castor and Pollux are not unique for being twins who are celebrated for what they reveal about relationships, social interactions, the world and the cosmos, but they do not act alone as twins; they are part of a large company.

The power of gods to intervene passionately and generatively in the world of humans is often expressed in twin-making fecundity. Zeus fathers at least three sets of twins and Poseidon four, while the twin god Apollo, when tending the cattle of Admetos, is given the unusual power to create twins among other species: 'causing all cows to deliver twins at every birth'.[4] Distinctions between deities and humans are not simply reproduced through twinning but are often reworked or revised.

The large number of twins in Greek legend means that it is difficult to give them a single meaning. The Swiss archaeologist Véronique Dasen has observed that all the different things that twins do mean that generalizations about them are difficult to uphold. There is a 'complex range of twin relations', she writes, 'from intimate union and concord to rivalry and deadly hate'.[5] A further distinction can be added to this particularly active spectrum of mythic twin relations: what should we say about the many twins in Greek myths who seem to have little or no impact on the greater tale of Greek origins? They are not given a transformative position within the social, geographic or political development of the ancient world; they do not go to war with one another; nor are they bonded by unusually strong feelings of sibling devotion. Some mythic twins seem to 'do' little. Being a twin is not a free pass into a pantheon of greats. Though Eurysthenes and Procles are said to jointly rule Lacedaemon, and marry the twin sisters Anaxandra and Lathria, it is their sons who found the royal Agiad and Eurypontid dynasties of Sparta.[6] In these inconsistencies, which are underpinned by the variety of storytelling and written traditions, a middle ground opens between the stereotypes of active collaboration and violent murder. Twins of ancient Greek cultures and the cultures that have adopted Greek models, such as those of ancient and modern Rome, continue to have many roles and meanings.

These motionless twin figures have a cultural, historical and material life that is nevertheless far from static. There are inconsistencies in the way that twins are imagined between pairs, just as there are uncertainties in the way twins are valued within pairs. Castor and Pollux, heavenly twins, Gemini, Dioscuri (*dios* meaning 'god' and *couros* meaning 'male youth'; the twins are literally 'sons of god') – they have many names and multiple histories, magical and violent. Half-blinded by midwinter light, I squint through my fingers at these carved blocks of stone. It is strange how statues and the stories attached to them get mixed up, especially when, as in this case, what is being celebrated as uniquely Roman turns out to be a serial copy. The Romans believed that the legend of the twins had a Greek origin. They speculated on these origins in a way that left those of the medieval era attributing the marble sculptures to Greek artists (hence their fanciful inscriptions *opus Praxitelis*, the work of Praxiteles, and *opus Fidae*, the work of Phidias). But the attribution is a later Roman invention. The statues have been traced to the fifth century CE, dating from the restoration of the Baths of Constantine in circa 443 CE, and were later moved and restored by Pope Sixtus V in 1585, and again by Pius VI in 1786. Their current position in front of the Quirinale is ancient, medieval, early modern, and formed in more recent centuries. In turn, they have been copied.[7]

Heroically divine, horse-riding twins – of which Castor and Pollux are an example – can be found in many Indo-European languages and cultures. Throughout Indic, Greek, Baltic and Celtic mythologies, twins are routinely viewed as celestial and godlike, and they represent forms of fraternal as well as martial union. From the Isle of Man to Sri Lanka, from Anglo-Saxon settlers and warrior heroes Hengist and Horsa to the Welsh brothers Brân and Manawydan, to the Hindu Aśvins, divine twin horsemen of the Rig Veda – 'heavenly twins' have travelled in word, image, ritual and rite. Castor and Pollux are myths of mobility; twins on the go. Both now and in the past, Rome's Castor and Pollux are given a global as well as astrological pedestal. Iconoclasts of the present and past have understood that public monuments like these, especially when mediated by the modern photographic lens, appear as fixed things rather than changeable figures of history. And statues, mute and muting, stand as symbols in whose name bold authority can be stamped. Not all twins are born equal; not all twins become icons. Castor and Pollux occupy the third sign in the astrological zodiac, Gemini, after the constellation that bears their name. Their elevated position in this city is achieved in matter and mind, written into stories and carved in stone in ways that have tied twins to weird biologies and spectacular acts of violent heroism.

* *

I PASS THE Dioscuri, walk on down via Ventiquattro Maggio, and enter the area of Rome known as Monti as traffic swirls about the cobblestones in a chaos of sound and light. Seduced by a sense that things are not as they appear in this city, I blunder through each quarter, half hoping I may find myself standing before something new, something never told. And now, as I walk south through Monti,

I find myself with what first-time visitors come to see, their minds whetted by a thousand books, postcards and films. At one edge of the Forum, with the Colosseum to my left, Trajan's Column to my right, and the ruins of one twin myth giving ground to the others; stones and stories share common space. I avoid the queues forming in front of the remaining columns of the Temple of Castor and Pollux, built to commemorate an early Republican victory when the twins were said to have fought for the Romans. I turn left, off the street that connects the Forum's many visitors with the Colosseum and the brilliant white Altare della Patria. I enter the basilica of Santi Cosma e Damiano, one of Rome's oldest Christian churches, dedicated to the twin saints and medics Cosmas and Damian, victims of and accessories to religious conquest.

The building has an unusual architectural and archaeological pedigree. It formed part of the Templum Pacis (Temple of Peace), a series of public buildings and spaces initiated by Emperor Vespasian in 71 CE. Serving many uses – a meeting place, a library – it was rebuilt in the early fourth century. Pope Felix IV (r. 526–30) established the church to honour the physician saints Cosmas and Damian, and it was the first Christian church to be sited in the Forum.[8] The building's modern entrance opens into a gloomy peace and a small courtyard flanked by colonnades that lead to the main door of the church. Leaving behind the hubbub of tourist Rome, I am met with an immense rush of gold, green, blue and red. Though the main hall is relatively small, with seven Renaissance-built chapels and a spectacular panelled ceiling, the fifth-century Byzantine mosaic apse is one of the finest examples in Rome. It portrays the martyred twins being presented to Christ. In contrast to the tendencies of modern biographies, whose writers limit themselves to earthly sayings and doings, hagiographers – the biographers of Catholic saints – make life elastic; they gather the sayings and doings of individuals as they affect the lives of others in life and in death. The miraculous accomplishments that picture Cosmas and Damian make them as body blenders, life makers, grafters and healers. Their twinship forms an integral aspect of their iconographic power; one that extends powers of healing beyond the grave.

While they were alive, Cosmas and Damian are said to have healed the sick without charge. Like Castor and Pollux, they were celebrated with many names: *i santi medici* (the medical saints) or Anargyroi (Greek, 'the silverless' or 'unmercenaries'). The twins died in about 303 CE in what is now Syria, martyred during the persecution of Christians by the Roman emperor Diocletian. Serving a system of belief in which pious suffering may shock believers into rejecting a pagan world and inspire them to strive for more spiritual riches, the brothers' deaths are described as being both long and gruesome – they were stoned, shot by arrows and placed on a rack. All proved miraculously ineffective. Beheading marked the end of their mortal lives.

For Catholics around the world, Cosmas and Damian are the patron saints of doctors, nurses, surgeons, pharmacists, dentists and barbers. Saints attain their divinity through records of miraculous intercession. The twins owe some of their modern popularity to the depiction of one striking episode. They are said to have appeared, long after their deaths, before a Roman deacon who was suffering with a severely cancerous leg. They performed the first interracial limb transplant, amputating the deacon's leg and attaching that of a recently deceased Ethiopian man, saving the deacon's life. This, their most celebrated miracle, known as the Miracle of the Black Leg, serves as a powerful and powerfully racial, ecclesiastical and geo-political icon: Christians have the power to bring life to the dead, to make the dead serve the living, to rejuvenate and restore one body with another.

The Miracle of the Black Leg entered Europe's well-known religious works. In 1275 Jacobus de Voragine published his hugely popular *Legenda aurea* (Golden Legend), and the story was widely read and translated:

Felix, the eighth pope after S. Gregory, did do make a noble church at Rome of the saints Cosmo and Damian, and there was a man which served devoutly the holy martyrs in that church, who a canker had consumed all his thigh. And as he slept, the holy martyrs Cosmo and Damian, appeared to him their devout servant, bringing with them an instrument and ointment of whom that one said to that other: Where shall we have flesh when we have cut away the rotten flesh to fill the void place? Then that other said to him: There is an Ethiopian that this day is buried in the churchyard of S. Peter ad Vincula, which is yet fresh, let us bear this thither, and take we out of that morian's flesh and fill this place withal. And so they fetched the thigh of the sick man and so changed that one for that other. And when the sick man awoke and felt no pain, he put forth his hand and felt his leg without hurt, and then took a candle, and saw well that it was not his thigh, but that it was another. And when he was well come to himself, he sprang out of his bed for joy, and recounted to all the people how it was happed to him, and that which he had seen in his sleep, and how he was healed. And they sent hastily to the tomb of the dead man, and found the thigh of him cut off, and that other thigh in the tomb instead of his. Then let us pray unto these holy martyrs to be our succour and help in all our hurts, blechures and sores, and that by their merits after this life we may come to everlasting bliss in heaven.[9]

The power of a good story needs the influence of strong storytellers (see illus. 11). The legend of these twins also entered into a different kind of renaissance, one that was both socio-economic and geo-political. Throughout the late medieval and Renaissance periods their popularity grew, partly thanks to their close association with Italy and Europe's most wealthy dynasty: Cosimo de' Medici (1389–1464[10]) and his twin brother Damiano were named after the saints. Though Damiano did not survive infancy, subsequent Medici would produce numerous popes and royals (the name de' Medici means, literally, 'of the medics'), carrying the legend of the twin saints visually and geographically as icons of earthly and divine power. There is no simple explanation for why their popularity spread across Eastern Orthodox and northern European churches to colonial settlements in the Catholic Americas, where they continue to be venerated in the twenty-first century. Such a story would have to follow the ways that beliefs in twins have been exported through colonial systems of conquest and capitalist development. This might best be seen on the west coast of Brazil, where, in the mid-1530s, Duarte Coelho sailed from Portugal to colonize and settle. This he did with military violence as well as commercial, nationalist and religious self-belief. In the state of Pernambuco he founded the village of Igarassu, where he established sugar plantations. In 1535 Coelho built Brazil's first Christian church, Igreja Matriz de São Cosme e São Damião, dedicated to the twin saints. Later, millions of people in Africa were enslaved and taken to Brazil, where they were forced to work on Portuguese coastal sugar plantations. They would cultivate and reinterpret the ritual veneration of twin deities of their own traditions. A rich set of West African rites and rituals around twin-ship were grafted onto and mixed with Christian beliefs and calendars. Meanwhile, Cosmas and Damian remain prominent among Afro-Brazilians and Portuguese Brazilians, standing for multiple infusions of African and early Christian divination beliefs and visual, religious and cultural practices.

The modern medical historian Jacalyn Duffin has traced the cult of Cosmas and Damian to Brazil and elsewhere. She detects a 'universal Dioscurism' – a tendency throughout the world to use, think about and venerate twins. The human condition, she argues, is expressed in an unwavering psychological model formed of opposites, and thus twins help to acknowledge 'the permanence and significance of dual archetypes in the human mind: the supervitality of the double birth and the natural harmony of primal opposites, uniting earth and sky, day and night, disease and health, life and death'.[11] Divine twins like the Dioscuri or Cosmas and Damian help people think through irreconcilable differences and manage life's chaos. This is one explanation – twins pull together and unite the elemental – but it says little about what twins do and think or how the violence of colonial rule and plantation slavery met with indigenous twin beliefs. Or why it is that the twins that travel and are translated are often male rather than female. Cultures, like the stories they produce, are not reproduced without being transformed.

* *

JUST MINUTES FROM Santi Cosma e Damiano rise the Capitoline Museums, where twins form another part of Rome's tangled heritage. Despite their place in a museum, twin myths are not buried in the city's past. The history of these twins is as neat as it is confused, as foundational as it is contemporary – a vision of the past that has helped to form many different Roman futures. This is why I did not begin my tour of Rome's twins in the place where some may have expected me to, with the legend of Romulus and Remus – because they have not always been imagined as 'the first', and their use as a wellspring for Roman renewal, self-importance and bloody self-determination has been inconsistent and opportunistic.

Like the Dioscuri and *i santi medici*, the story of Romulus and Remus has been whipped together in time's blender, composed at different times as a confection rather than in a single telling. Canonical versions found in the accounts of Livy, Dionysius of Halicarnassus, Plutarch and Ovid tell of two princes abandoned on the banks of the Tiber and nursed by a wolf.[12] The twins are said to have been adopted by a shepherd and his family, growing up tending sheep. As adults they learn of their past and support their grandfather's claim

2 Capitoline Wolf bronze sculpture, 5th century BCE (with twins added 1471–3 CE).

to the throne before setting out to establish a city. They cannot agree, however, on which of the seven hills to build this new settlement, and so they seek divine guidance. After waiting for auspicious birds to pass by, to help them resolve their dispute, they still cannot agree and, as they argue, Remus is killed and Romulus becomes the first king of his namesake city.

The Capitoline Museums have a bronze statue of the wolf with the infant twins suckling beneath her. Myth and material entwine, but not in the way we might like to believe. Materially, archaeologists have dated the bronze wolf to approximately 480–470 BCE. The figures of the twins were added much later: around 1500 CE.[13] Just as the myth of Castor and Pollux and the canonization of Cosmas and Damian took centuries, so the legend of Romulus and Remus has grown and has been stitched together from many sources. In its earliest incarnations, there are no brothers but rather an abandoned child born to a virgin. Sometimes an animal rescues them and together they found a city called Rome. Various elements of the story are added and redacted by different tellers, ancient and modern, and the twins are added at different stages, too. The classicist T. P. Wiseman has pieced together many different variants of the story to show how Remus is a sacrificial victim in a way quite unlike many other foundational twin myths in the Indo-European pantheon. He argues that the death of Remus is an invention, the result of a plebeian power-share of the fourth century BCE. The myth is an elaborate form of propaganda wherein historical fictions served contemporary interests.[14] Many other political explanations have been suggested to make sense of the twinship that became central to Rome's foundation narrative: the unification of Latin and Sabine people; a power-share between two patrician councils; an agreement between patricians, plebeians and the aristocracy that needed to accommodate a narrative of conflict and resolution. The debate continues. But the legend is not merely an elaborate fiction but a malleable foundation, an imaginative source that has allowed different groups and individuals to project their power and desire for change. Whatever its origins, the continued appeal of the myth is partly served by the flexibility of the story – a flexibility that continues thanks to the unresolved question of what twins are supposed to mean in a society of those born as one. In the time of Augustine of Hippo (354–430 CE), for example, the outrageous idea of Rome's first king being a wolf-suckling murderer was reason to renew and regenerate the city's Christian faith – the twins, and Romulus in particular, were an abject pagan screen against which a Christian Rome could be reborn. Centuries later, Mussolini used the twins to signal Italy's original, uncompromising and primeval strength, a symbol ripe for a Fascist state.

Children in this city must be registered with the authorities under the vengeful and protective gaze of a wolf. Those registering births at the city's civil registry office, just minutes from the Capitoline Museums, can consider Rome's ongoing attachment to twins. I have been twice, with my second-rate Italian and my post-partum nerves jangling, carrying the birth certificates of my singleton children. I was wholly unprepared for the experience and unnerved by the absence of the corporate veneer common to British bureaucracies. The offices were stale with cigarette smoke and cluttered with paper, and staff chattered among themselves while filling out the record by hand in an enormous ledger. At the door hangs a bronze relief of the twins and their wolf mother. They preside over the reception area, imposed upon a map of the ancient city that spreads out around them, the streets and buildings carved out in relation to the twins, who act as a kind of spatial and temporal compass. These parts of the registry office's interior are of Fascist vintage, relatively unchanged since Mussolini sought to make the twins the zero point of Rome's foundation – the centre of Italy's creation, its regeneration, its destiny. They became model citizens for an anciently new national spirit the Fascists called *romanità*.

In order to nurture a nation of Romuluses and Remuses, the young were captured. When the Fascists formed the paramilitary youth faction to bring party doctrine to Italy's children, the youngest section, for boys and girls aged six to eight, was called Figli della Lupa (Children of the Wolf). Young members were prepared to fight and die in Italy's colonial campaigns before and during the Second World War. When my Italian father-in-law was born in occupied Athens in 1942, Mussolini's government sent his mother a simple message: 'Italy welcomes children of the wolf.' He and his peers were imagined to be twin descendants – pioneers, fighters, founders – brothers prepared to kill and be killed, and maybe even kill one another, for the sake of Rome's glory: 'Believe, Obey, Fight'.

Further up the river Tiber, at the northern end of the Piazza Augusto Imperatore, is the former building of the National Institute for Social Security, the office used for administrating Fascist welfarism and the apparatus of state power that sought to influence how the people lived, how they believed and what they valued. So while the registry office's statuary envelops new life within the state, one's subsequent relationship to the state's authority also took place beneath bombastic images of the wolf and twins. Designed by Ferruccio Ferrazzi (1891–1978), the murals on the National Institute for Social Security sought to connect the modern buildings at the perimeter of the piazza to the ancient mausoleum at its centre. Ferrazzi was delighted by the invitation to create the work, claiming that he was 'fascinated by the idea of a fabulous narration . . . of a *fantastic Roman reality*'.[15]

The propaganda of the Fascist period and its images, symbols and metaphors repeatedly called on the twins Romulus and Remus to be icons of change, rooting *romanità* in people born together and prepared to kill one another for the sake of the Italian state. The appearance of twins in these places does not fall upon straight lines of influence or into neat periods of time. And next to the fridge magnets and postcards, the miniature figurines and T-shirts on which the twins appear and which are sold throughout the city's gift shops, AS Roma, one of the city's two top-flight football clubs, brings Romulus and Remus to global sports audiences. The club was formed in 1927 when smaller clubs merged under the direction of the Fascist state, which wanted a Roman team that could rival the more successful clubs of the north. The Roma club crest carries the twins and their wolf mother.

I cross to the other side of the river and walk along the riverbank. The day's weather now feels unrelenting, dry and cold. I find a contemporary image spreading along the walls of the riverbank, an artwork by the contemporary South African artist William Kentridge, a monumental, 500-metre-long frieze called *Triumphs and Laments* (2016). At its beginning is a version of the Capitoline Wolf. But instead of the twins, two vessels take their place. Such an image is a helpful way of thinking about how history has treated twins in this city and in others. It might be possible to do the historical detective work and claim that the process of myth-making is guided by particular political, religious, economic and geographical necessities, such as the harmonization of multiple myths into a ritualized narrative or the celebration of those martyred by rulers of the past. It takes a different kind of imaginative and emotional work to understand how twins are understood in more recent times, or why it should be twins that are reused and refashioned over successive generations – from the fabric of Proto-Indo-European twin myths of which the Dioscuri are a part, to the modern reimaginings of the Romulus and Remus legend. The study of myth tends to focus on how such stories were crafted in the past, now understood as historical artefacts. But twins are not simply, or only, historical objects. And history is not something that occurs only in the past.

The appeal of one version or variant of a myth over another is telling – it tells us that myths are actively produced and that they express desires about the future as well the past. In ancient and modern imperial conditions, one account can become attractive to a community, and a particular story is thus reproduced and canonized. Myths, in this view, are expressions of politics by a different name: the thoughts and battles of others, seen through an opaque lens, intrinsically connected to social contradictions and struggles for power.

How might we connect the twins who live and breathe in this city, or who tour its monuments, with twin legends cast in bronze, chiselled in stone, illuminated in mosaic or, as in the case of Kentridge's vessels, power-washed around a stencil to leave the wall's patina of pollution and biological matter? It doesn't all fit and connect together, and perhaps it need not. But the myths and legends gave shape to a past that still resonates today in terms of what myths are and how they are reformed over time. Their legacies have not yet run their course, and speak to the ways in which twins are treated as radically different from other people. The mythology of twinning continues to place twins in other worlds, real and imagined.

Ideas about twins stand on various kinds of plinth. This tells as much about twins as it does the lengths to which historians, theologians, artists, philosophers, politicians and others will go to reckon with their image. As my journey across Rome has shown, time cannot be resolved in the sweet linear sweep of historical storytelling. Twin myths start and stop, they shape-shift and they blend. Twins, in this sense, can never be contemporaries; their time is put forever out of joint by the adaptations and interpretations that have gone before. Their significance gets revised and reversed in ways that put legends into temporal eddies, whirls, great troughs and cascades of change. The writer Penelope Farmer has argued that an encounter with twins in myth reveals 'the seemingly universal need to give twins a special status, special rituals, mental or actual, in order to regenerate the society that their very otherness divides'.[16] In her view, the meaning of twinning arises from a universal need for conceptual, spiritual and societal clarity about what twins are. But things are rarely so even or predictable, not least for those twins who help to form new stories of foundation by busily collating and comparing stories about twins. Dona Lee Davis, a twin and an anthropologist of twinning, has warned against universalizing the meaning of twins out of a limited and limiting group of narratives, especially one from such a specific part of the world. She also notes that by focusing on myth, scholars circumvent any examination of how actual twins think and feel, and their agency becomes 'limited to discussions of divinity (twins as gods), or analytically engaged as imaginary characters in myth and folklore'.[17] But the myths encountered in these streets are not culturally or geographically located in a single space or time; they are neither simply secular nor routinely spiritual. Myths – however unreal modern North American or European scholars may judge them to be – have real effects on the world.

It is not necessary to choose between timeless and episodic experiences of twinning. Nor do we need to categorize stories according to whether they are universal or specific, past or contemporary, fictional or real. After all, such categories are not neutral, and nor are

3 William Kentridge, *Triumphs and Laments*, 2016, detail from a large-scale 550-metre-long frieze along the river Tiber in Rome.

they universal. The telling of fantastical stories about twins happens in many times and places, and it frequently folds time and stretches space in unexpected ways. Narrating any kind of twin life can create new ways for the real to be fictionalized, for new matters of fact to emerge and for new forms of creative matter to be made flesh. One purpose of this book is to highlight how meanings get attached to twins in multiple and sometimes contradictory ways, not just in the stereotypes we may be familiar with in our current times and cultures but also in the temporal and geographical differences that are the basis for the mythic and the lived, the fantastical and the real, the collective and specific, the natural and cultural responses to twins. The meaning of twins is not static but is globally ambiguous, mixed and confused. With a more historically convolved perspective comes an opportunity to reflect on how twins do not simply appear in a prefabricated idea of linear time but constitute and embody time's many possible rhythms.

2

TWINS ARE MONSTERS

In 1897 workers constructing the Trans-Siberian Railway came across a burial ground near Lake Baikal, in southern Siberia. Discovered at the confluence of the Irkut and Angara rivers, within the modern city of Irkutsk, the cemetery was given the name Lokomotiv. Over the next one hundred years the site at Lokomotiv would become the focus of a series of archaeological projects, uncovering 59 graves found to contain the remains of at least 101 individuals. The site has been dated to the early Neolithic period, with some of the burials more than 7,500 years old. They reflect various funerary practices: a quarter show signs that the heads of the buried were removed before interment; and there were a number of dogs and one wolf buried at this cemetery.[1] In 1997 the body of a woman was excavated. She was judged to have been 20 to 25 years old when she died and was buried approximately 7,000 years ago. In 2015 the archaeology team reported further findings. Like others at Lokomotiv the woman had been buried in a prone and extended position, and was found with fifteen marmot teeth that are likely to have once been threaded into her clothes. She was also buried with others in a way that makes her exceptionally rare. The Lokomotiv site is geologically stable, meaning that the woman's bones had scarcely moved in the thousands of years that had passed between her interment and her excavation; as a result, the team, led by Canadian researchers, was able to DNA-test some bones that appeared lodged in her pelvis and abdomen. She was found to have been pregnant with twins at the time of her death. The twins are the earliest materially confirmed set of human twins in the world.[2] The size of the twins suggests they were near full term, between 36 and 40 prenatal weeks, and the archaeologists analysing the remains identified one twin positioned in a breech position, with its feet or bottom first, and the second in the normal, vertex (head-down) position, making it likely that their mother died while delivering them. The remains found at Lokomotiv are significant for archaeologists for two reasons: they are among the oldest evidence of death in childbirth, and they are also the oldest confirmed case of human twins worldwide.

Finds such as those at Lokomotiv tell us about the presence of twins in prehistory. This is important because, as the archaeological team at Lokomotiv note, the birth rate of twins in prehistory is 'virtually impossible to establish' because in other known cases the status of twins is only possible or probable, 'inferred from circumstantial evidence'.[3] Maternal death was common in prehistory, but evidence of twin birth being its cause is often difficult to confirm – no mark is left if a woman died after her children were born, or if she died while pregnant or during childbirth itself. Equally, some funerary practices, such as the Roman practice of removing the child from the womb of any woman who died during childbirth (known as *Lex Caesarea*), make archaeological records unreliable. It is striking that the other documented archaeological instances of suspected twins are historically more recent, and come from geographically diverse sites, such as at Olèrdola in Catalonia, Spain (*c.* fourth–second century BCE) or Khok Phanom Di in eastern Thailand (settled *c.* 2000 BCE).[4] Archaeologists at these sites reflect on the difficulty of establishing how twinning affected humans and human bodies in prehistory. In place of material evidence there remains an abundance of ancient legend and clues to be gleaned from ancient science.

* *

TWINS ARE MALLEABLE models for thought, fear and belief. They appear in ancient as well as modern myths and so often seem to be lifted out of history, detached from archaeological records like reality's shadow or rival. But this characterization of myth, which makes it an adversary and opponent to rational knowledge, is a relatively recent way of dividing fiction and fact. When rendered in stone or told in text, whether figured in image or formed by performance, myths about twins have invited engagements that reflect, elevate, exult, question and rebuild social realities between humans, environments, non-human animals, gods and the cosmos. Plato (*c.* 429–347 BCE) recognized that myths can be simultaneously true and false, and observed the following paradox: 'we begin by telling children stories [*muthoi*]. These are, in general, fiction [*pseudos*], though they contain some truth [*alethes*].'[5] Education, for Plato, depended on spoken stories, legends and myths: the imaginative fictions that could instruct and entertain at the same time. It is these that tended to describe processes of nativity, origination, formation and genesis – stories about human and non-human beginnings. As the modern classicist Penelope Murray has written, the Platonic view of myths also made them an essential instrument of rational persuasion.[6] For Athenian philosophers of the fifth and fourth centuries BCE, reason and myth interacted in ways that made them not opposites but compatriots or companions. In the previous chapter, a walk around Rome showed how this can be experienced on the streets of a European city, one that has repeatedly reinvented its relationship to the past and to twin people. When used for political or religious purposes, twin stories cannot be only *muthoi*, in the sense that they are tall tales full of fiction; they tell us about how societies use certain kinds of people to project power and influence.

Mythologies about twins – as heroes and kings, gods and monsters – are intimately and unexpectedly connected to the history of how human reproduction has been studied. We can try to dig up and analyse the bones of ancient twins. But we know that writers of ancient natural philosophies (physics, biology and other natural sciences) viewed human twins as exceptional. This is clear in the natural philosophy of Plato's most famous student, Aristotle (384–322 BCE), in whose writing myth, observation and medical orthodoxy combine to make twins particular kinds of humans that deserve a special form of attention, now labelled 'research'. Different types and kinds of twin populate Aristotle's work, types and kinds that are directly comparable to those that feature in contemporary works of biology and medicine. Before we reach those comparisons, it is important to make clear that Aristotle did not consider twins to be special or exceptional for their visual, physical or behavioural similarities or differences. Pollux's decision to share in his brother Castor's mortality made their relationship supernatural, fantastic and spiritually bound, but all this was underpinned by the fatalistic consequences of their having different fathers. Their mixed parentage was viewed as their most important difference, a difference neither chose; they were conceived apart but born together – one of the few consistent elements of the various narratives of their lives. Thus ancient empirical thought converged on a mythical tradition: specifically, the myths of ancient Greece and Rome feature many examples of superfetation, the fertilization of two different ova from two different menstrual cycles, as well as superfecundation, the fertilization of two different ova from the same menstrual cycle.[7] Like the monument given to the Dioscuri on Rome's Quirinal Hill, the ancient natural philosophy of Aristotle found a different kind of plinth for twins, raising them to a state of exception. Likenesses within or between pairs, or across statistical populations – the signature code that differentiates twin from twin in contemporary times – are nothing to Aristotle compared to the social and biological structures that he says twins help him reveal.

Aristotle was not a mythographer, but his descriptions of superfecundation and superfetation in animals use a combination of sources, of which myths about human twins are one. His writings on twins involve three kinds of source: abstract theory about how twins are created, as a set of biological processes; instances of twin births reported as anecdote ('there has been actually the following evidence'[8]); and the appearance of twins in mythological stories. To an ancient philosopher like Aristotle, there was a rhetorical relationship between each element: twinning as a theory, specific and empirical reportage of historical examples, twins as a mythological trope. Each combines with the other to show where the *phainomena* of twins – how they appear to us – and *endoxa* – the different opinions about them – contrasted. This 'endoxic method' is based on gathering many different beliefs, theories and stories, and includes some accounts called 'myths' that are put alongside empirical observations.[9] For example, Aristotle says of the theory of superfecundation and superfetation that they 'deliver them like twins from one seed', to which he adds for clarity: 'as in the myth of Iphicles and Hercules'.[10] Evidence follows in the form of three accounts of women who conceived superfecundated and superfetated multiples: an 'adulteress' who gave birth to a child that bore a physical similarity to her husband and another child who looked like her 'adulterer'; a further case describing a woman who gave birth to twins but also a third child, born four months premature; and the report with which Aristotle concludes, describing another case of triplets, the first child delivered two months premature and the other two following at full term. He organizes his evidence for superfecundation and superfetation based on two forms of reported narrative: myth and case history (observed or reported). Half of Aristotle's examples involve twins whose mothers were raped or had sex with men other than their husbands. And so, contrary to modern belief, twinship is not only a relationship shared by two people from birth. It is a state of being produced by the (sometimes violent) sexual behaviour of adults.

Rather than separating out the fact from the fiction of twin life, Aristotle's treatises on human and animal biology rely on blending together different sources. This has big consequences for how different kinds of twin story get valued in early works of Western natural philosophy, as well as how twins weigh upon the idea that knowledge should be divided into different disciplines of thought and practice. As a rhetorical resource and as a form of evidence, Aristotle uses a minimal account of the Heracles and Iphicles myth that relies on his audiences being familiar with how they were conceived. Those audiences were sufficiently acquainted with it not to need the following details: as children of Alcmene, Heracles is the twin brother to Iphicles, but they do not share a father. Like Castor and Pollux, they are not 'ordinary' people or even 'ordinary' twins. One night, Zeus disguised himself as Alcmene's husband, Amphitryon, and had sex with her, whereupon Heracles was conceived. Later that same night, Amphitryon returned from war to his wife, and Iphicles was conceived as his son. Heracles was celebrated as one of the most awe-inspiring Greek deities, while Greek and Roman sources characterize his brother Iphicles as human. Their human and divine characteristics are often separated at birth, with stories telling of how the infant Heracles fought and killed a serpent while his brother fled.[11]

The separation of 'myth' from 'knowledge', the irrational from the rational, has become popularly celebrated as one of Aristotle's major contributions to the history and philosophy of science. Particularly over the course of the twentieth century, Aristotle became viewed as a foundational figure who led philosophical practice away from archaic *muthos* and its cults and superstitions towards rational *logos*, which would help shape future principles for scientific inquiry.[12] This view of Aristotle as the 'founder of scientific reason' is a modern invention. It is true that Aristotle is at pains to counter myths and folk beliefs with observed details, being dismissive of those who 'purvey mythical sophistries'.[13] He also uses the word 'myth' to dismiss rival explanations. But Aristotle harnesses his audience's familiarity with the Heracles and Iphicles story to his explanatory advantage. It is in this way that imaginative, religious and empirical ideas about twins have mixed, despite subsequent modern attempts to drive them apart, and it is for this reason that empiricism and mythology about twin life, in some of the formative texts of Western philosophy and science, mingle together.

Having observed the relative abundance of multiple births in other animals, Aristotle returns to the mechanisms of biology that, for him, made twinning possible: 'if ever too much [material] is secreted, then twins are born. Hence such cases seem rather to be monstrous because they are contrary to the general and customary rule.'[14] Twins, argues Aristotle, are unnatural for sharing in the material processes that generate physical mutations:

> The reason why the parts may be multiplied contrary to nature is the same as the cause of the birth of twins. For the reason exists already in the embryo, whenever more material gathers than is required by the nature of the part. The result is then that either one of its parts is larger than the others, as a finger or hand or foot or any of the other extremities or limbs; or again if the embryo is cleft there may come into being more than one, as eddies do in rivers; as the water in these is carried along with a

certain motion, if it dash against anything two systems come into being out of one, each retaining the same motion; the same thing happens also with the embryos.[15]

If there is a history of thinking with human twins – as totems and models, as examples and as bodies of evidence – then it can be found in the long historical tradition that has made human twins unnatural or quasi-monstrous beings, people contrary to observed nature, and subjects who can be trangressively mixed and separated from an established norm. One explanation for why Aristotle describes superfecundation and superfetation in humans in detail, doing so by accommodating myth alongside comparative methods of scientific empiricism, is that he already viewed twinning as an unusual process that is best understood as an abnormality. This is a tradition that Aristotle helped to popularize by couching his observations in the indifferent and dispassionate language of *epistêmê*, likened to more modern uses of the term 'knowledge'.

Twins are *téras*, 'monstrosities', to Aristotle because they do not follow the rules of matter or form. Instead they are materially *mal*formed, *de*formed or *dis*abled. If biology is guided by rules of formal and material necessity, as Aristotle suggests, then twins are human kinds made by physical excess. Aristotle understood the phenomena of twinning to be aberrant, resulting when the human body makes a mutation whose cause is comparable to that which generates an extra limb or digit. Twins do not only represent an exception to a norm. Twinning is also a material manifestation of rules and customs being broken, a sign that the norm of single birth has been overthrown.

If twins are monsters for Aristotle, then it is not because they are horrifying or awful. For ancient Greeks, *téras* are signs, wonders and marvels, the portents of natural and magical worlds that may otherwise be hidden. Commenting on modern Gothic expressions of the monstrous, the modern theorist of gender and queer identity Jack Halberstam has written, 'the monster always represents the disruption of categories, the destruction of boundaries, and the presence of impurities.'[16] In the pre-modern writings of Aristotle, twin monsters are numerous rather than singular. They emerge from natural orders of observed frequency as creative and destructive figures. In ancient Greek myth and science, the monstrosity of twinning stands as the basis for the deification of gods and their mingling in the worlds of men. Situated on an axis of wonder and horror, it is this elastic blend of scientific and imaginative difference that will both elevate and denigrate twins for the next two millennia.

The twin conceptions found in Aristotle's writings are naturalized outliers. They are physical abnormalities clinging to a natural norm. They are created from an unnatural abundance but associated, thanks to Aristotle's 'endoxic method', associated by tales of adultery, unwanted pregnancy and the birth of gods. He was not alone in this reasoning. Other natural philosophers and physicians linked twin conceptions to the strength of reproductive 'seed' – an idea that Aristotle is likely to have taken from the Hippocratic tradition. The Hippocratic writers claimed that twins are born when 'the seed secreted from both parents be abundant and strong'.[17] Parental strength, particularly the strength of the male seed, has two functions in the work of Aristotle and Hippocrates. Twins may indicate the power of parental fertility and sexual potency, but they are also seen as irregular, monstrous, potentially threatening births that compromise norms and ideals of perfection.

While Aristotle conflated superfecundated or superfetated births and other twin births as the equal products of biological abundance, the Hippocratic Corpus claimed that twins were the outcome of a single act of intercourse.[18] Aristotle thought that twins were created whenever there was an abundance of male and female seed. The Hippocratic writers thought that there was also another, anatomical explanation: a woman's uterus was believed to have 'sinuses' in which multiple offspring could develop. According to the fifth-century BCE author of the Hippocratic treatise *Generation*:

Twins arise from one act of intercourse: the uterus has sinuses that are curved and multiple – some farther from the vagina, others nearer to it – and animals that have many births at the same time have more of these than animals that have fewer births at once. This is how it is in cattle, wild animals, and birds: when the seed happens to be divided and to arrive in two of these sinuses, when the uterus receives it, and when neither of the two sinuses opens into the other one, then the seed is separated off in each of the sinuses, forms membranes, and grows in just the same way I have described for a single (sc. fetus).[19]

As it was with Aristotle's writings on natural biology, there has been a tendency to see Hippocrates as an early champion of modern science, with physicians of later periods promoting him as the precursor to the dispassionate, rational, scientific individual celebrated in modern times. But modern classicist Jacques Jouanna warns, 'our knowledge of the embryology of the pre-Socratics is very indirect and fragmentary' and argues that the Hippocratic Corpus presents knowledge that is as much cosmological, mechanical and material as it is medical.[20] So we find Greek gynaecology resembling some ancient origin myths, insofar as generative seed is cast into and nurtured within cavities, leading to a theory of reproduction that emphasizes the internal environment of a passive host. Connections like these, between ancient cosmology and gynaecology, pre-date Aristotelian and Hippocratic writings: Pherecydes of Syros, a sixth-century BCE mythographer, claimed that Chronos (the personification of time in Greek mythology) made fire, wind and water from his seed, and these were 'distributed into five recesses' to generate the older gods.[21] The Hippocratic tradition, by contrast, became foundational to more secular, mechanistic medicines structured around a power hierarchy of doctor and patient. In an era when systematic human dissection was forbidden, twins were taken as a symptom for many phenomena that were not always visible to the human eye: human development and population increase, fecundity and sexual difference. As malleable, vital models, they were kinds of people who proved and reinforced cosmologies and mythologies as well as established reproductive norms.

Gynaecology in ancient Greece provided a medical corollary to the masculinized, plentiful and supernatural powers attributed to twins in ancient literatures, myths, religions and folklore. The bodies of women are seen in fragments, the uterus given the mechanically passive capacity to 'receive' the more active male seed and foster multiple births.[22] This reinstates stereotypes of female sexual difference found in canonical myths about women that made them late arrivals to the world of men, a separate 'race'.[23] This is an explanation of twins that begins or passes not through one myth but through many; it is a story of cause and outcome, a narrative that seeks to explain the unexpected through female sexual difference.

Hippocratic and Aristotelian theories had lasting effects on how twinning was seen as an expression of sexual differences between men and women. For instance, when explaining the genesis of mixed-sex – dizygotic or 'fraternal' – twins, Hippocratic authors stress the action, strength and power of the male contribution:

> in any sinus where seed happens to arrive thicker and stronger, a male arises, but in any one where it arrives more watery and weaker, a female arises. If the seed enters both sinuses in a strong state, in both males will be engendered, but if it arrives in both in a weak state, both offspring will be females.[24]

The Hippocratic tradition nurtured the view that women are physically and temperamentally weaker, cooler and damper than men (who are stronger, warmer and drier). After centuries of mythological remaking and refashioning it is noticeable how ancient Greek and Roman gods who are twins are men or quasi-gods. Female twins enter the canon of Greek twin myth rarely – Artemis, Phoebe and Hilaeira, occasionally Helen and Clytemnestra are depicted as twins born with the Dioscuri – and they are not readily associated with the godly, heroic or foundational stories celebrated in ancient literatures. It is not unreasonable to view the authors of these ancient medical treatises as developing multiple arguments via the birth of twins: they establish the 'proper' formation of the embryo and they also try to situate that discussion within a speculative philosophy that could explain, in Hippocrates' words, 'how man and the other animals are formed and come into being'.[25] They do this by making twins the product of a certain kind of biological world view; and they do that by making twins people born to certain kinds of men and women.

* *

BY WHAT FORCE, thought or feeling did I become a twin? I cannot say it was because I or anyone else in my family learned about ancient Greek philosophy, medicine or myth. And in any case, how I became a twin may now seem like an odd question to ask, since explanations about what makes me a twin tend to be handed to me fully formed, as if they are self-sufficient facts of life. Fields of biomedical science such as human reproduction, psychology and human genetics provide interactive models that have separated 'nature' and 'nurture' and pieced them back together again. During the nineteenth and twentieth centuries, these models were created and exported globally from northern European and American centres of research, becoming some of the dominant ways of explaining what twins are and how they come to be called 'twins'. The answers to the question of how I became a twin were filtered through these sciences and came to me through all manner of media – television shows, films, magazines, newspapers and scientific reports – and in daily interactions with friends, family members, colleagues and others. Twins, I was and I continue to be told, are those people who are conceived, gestate and are born together, and can be classified according to their genetic and interpersonal relatedness.[26] From conception, the stages of gestation, birth and perinatal development provide the relation of likeness felt between me and my brother, and measure the beginning and end of our twinship: the germinal and terminal states of being a twin rest, primarily, between two people.

There have been dramatic changes in the biological knowledge about twins. And yet processes of nomination and classification are as important as ever to the formation of group identity, exception and norm, and how twins continue to be understood. People are routinely sorted and placed within categories and collectives; the strange thing about twins is that, over the centuries, the categories have changed, and so too have the persons included in those collectives. Such processes of nomination guide how people are categorized: Lina is an *x* because she has *y*; Miguel is like Lina because he also has *y*; thus they are both an *x*. Now, rather than sorting and classifying me based on the monstrosity of my birth, the strength of the seed that bore me, or the anatomical structure of my mother's uterus, we might say that 'William is a monozygotic twin because the egg his brother and he once shared split, so he is genetically "identical" to his twin.' Ian Hacking argues that the formation of people into groups of this type, into human 'kinds', occurs through dynamic interactions between different classifications, institutions, fields of knowledge and experts. Hacking suggests that individual and social identity does not pre-exist in a natural state but develops and emerges thanks to our interactions with, and responses to, how and why 'we' become designated as certain kinds of people. Institutional classifications are formed, managed and reproduced by experts; experts whose classifications identify people, he says, 'that would not have existed, *as a kind of people*, until they had been so classified, organized and taxed'.[27] Hacking gives a special role to modern science for galvanizing various 'engines' of discovery – engines that count and quantify, normalize, medicalize, correlate, geneticize – that create human kinds that can then be organized, administered and resisted by those who are the object of new labels. Technologies are developed and powered by institutions – medical, educational, legal, military, financial and governmental – that help to place human individuals into collectives, slotting and sorting people into different kinds.[28] These institutions, such as markets made to develop and accelerate the meeting of 'like-minded' people, also facilitate the recognition, inclusion and exclusion of twins, according to the ways they fit or fail to fit. As we will see in later chapters, technologies offer different modes of sorting individuals into one kind of person or another, and they allow for new ways of making twins as kinds of persons.

Though medical and other forms of research may have accelerated the 'engines' that have made twins a kind of person, the structures of thinking that have recognized, taxonomized and made sense of them have a long history. Classifications, institutions, fields of knowledge and experts all existed in the ancient world, working to produce 'twins' in ways that rendered them monstrous and their parents sexually different from one another. Supplementing these categories with what they valued in terms of personhood – exemplified through myth, religion and the gendered structures of social organization – ancient Greek philosophers and physicians developed their nominations, classifications and categories based on what they knew of human life. 'There has been making up of people', concedes Hacking, 'in all times and places, but only in the past two hundred years have the sciences been so central to the human understanding of who we are.'[29] Twins may have always been a kind of person, but they are different from the kinds of people that Hacking focuses on – people with autism or multiple personality disorders, or so-called 'obese' people – because twins, when studied by the sciences, have had a long and enduring relationship to the identification of 'who we are'. It may be true that it is only in more recent centuries that the intertwined personalities of twins have come to matter a great deal to the sciences of the body and mind, making twins a different kind of person from the kind indicated in previous times and in other places. Yet the fusions of natural philosophy, myth and religion that surface in the work of Hippocrates and Aristotle suggest that twins have also been central to classifying, mixing and purifying what gets called empirical 'science'.

There are philosophers who maintain that myth-telling has an enduring role in the formation of contemporary culture. In response to the notion that rational, scientific practice is free of mythic thinking, the modern philosopher Mary Midgley once said that myths and science are kindred practices. Both possess 'powerful imaginative patterns [and] networks of powerful symbols that suggest particular ways of interpreting the world. They shape its meaning.'[30] Midgley's conception of myth would not compare the birth of Heracles and Iphicles to the epistemological structures implied by the laboratory work of the biological sciences, but it may highlight how the stories told of twins as heroes, monsters and gods produce ways of interpreting taken-for-granted patterns. Both are models for understanding what Midgley calls the 'huge, ever-changing imaginative structure of ideas'.[31] This may drain myths of some of their specificity, as stories and narratives formed under historical pressures, but it is useful in resisting the illusion of a discrete kind of scientific knowledge as a clean, hygienic practice into which fictions never enter. Works by Hippocrates and Aristotle show how twin stories, recruited in the name of biological explanation, have tangled roots that concern how twins are valued and how information about the world can be learned through their example.

3

TWINS ARE DANGEROUS

There can be no human history without a history of twins, the torchbearers of hopes and dreams, fears and suspicions. Twins disclose things hidden or forbidden within human life, and those secrets reveal the concerns and worries of people through time. Odd stories about twins are woven into European history – philosophies and religions, medical practices and military conquests have taken hold of twin people and, in so doing, divided them from their single-born kin. That rich tapestry of beliefs has often left twins and their parents marginalized and stigmatized: twins have been treated as a danger to communities or to themselves; a threat to natural order and a threat to social orders. We know this history not because comprehensive studies of twins were conducted in, say, medieval Europe – there were no extensive studies into what twins experienced – but because twins in all periods have been used as evidence for a wide range of different beliefs. They are treated as gateways into the secret or forbidden realms of life, and as figures of art and entertainment.

At one end of an incredible library of stories about twin people are the folk tales and ballads, court poetry and prose, that testify to how twins were thought about in Europe during the medieval period (traditionally given as lasting from the fifth to the fifteenth centuries). Reading imaginative writing as evidence of the feelings and experiences of a mostly illiterate society is fraught with problems. In medieval times, imaginative writing was for a privileged few, and those thoughts and feelings of society remain caught in literature's hall of mirrors. This notwithstanding, medieval stories entertained and instructed some people about twins, and they can help to put a spotlight on the beliefs of those who wrote, read and listened to those stories. But we also need to feel for the other threads of the twin fabric – threads that are philosophical, medical and religious

– which can give sight to a more comprehensive tapestry of what it meant to be a twin living in past centuries. To understand what it meant to be a twin in the past we need to put fiction and fact together. Then and now, fact and fiction's constant and unerring collision is one important part of being a twin.

Perhaps the most famous story – and certainly one of the most celebrated – about twins in the early medieval period is 'Le Fresne', a romance written by Marie de France (*c.* 1160–1215).[1] Born in France, she was a poet active in the English court of Henry II, and 'Le Fresne' was one of Marie's most popular *lais*, a form of short narrative poem. The story unfolds in a tense atmosphere of anxiety, suspicion and social fragmentation, providing clues as to how the birth of twins may have been valued by some medieval audiences. It shows that twins may have been viewed as dangerous, at least to the extent that these stories – like modern-day thrillers – stirred an entertaining variety of social and sexual anxiety. It begins with the marriage of two knights and the birth of twin sons to one of the wives. On hearing about the twins, the other wife makes a strange accusation: the newborns are not the sons of one man. She accuses her neighbour of adultery:

> And tell of shame to this end,
> That his wife has had two children.
> Well may man write therefore
> That she has had two men in an hour
> That is her double dishonour.[2]

A twin birth is instantly shameful because it signifies that the mother must have had sex with someone other than her husband. The twins are sufficient proof that this is true. But in a dramatic twist, the woman who makes this accusation conceives twin daughters of her own. She becomes incriminated by the judgement she dished out to others. Now pregnant with her own twins, she seeks to protect her reputation. She considers killing one of her twin daughters – leaving a child to die of exposure was a common response to unwanted births during this period[3] – but instead gives one daughter to a servant, who leaves the baby in the branches of an ash tree that grows in the grounds of an abbey. As is common in medieval romance stories, the baby is left with items that will later identify her. In this case, she is wrapped in expensive cloth and has her mother's ring. She is discovered by the abbess and is named after the tree in which she is found (*le fresne* in Old French, *frein* in Middle English), and Fresne grows to be a beautiful young woman.

One day she falls in love with a wealthy knight called Gurun. Sadly, he is under pressure to marry someone rich and noble. Seeking someone with Fresne's qualities, and ignorant of the connection between the sisters, Gurun decides to marry Fresne's twin sister. Fresne is sorry but accepts her low-born status. She adorns the matrimonial bed with the cloth in which she was first abandoned, and when this garment is recognized by her mother, Fresne also produces her ring. A scene of recognition and reconciliation unfolds, and Fresne finally marries Gurun, while Fresne's twin is married to a suitably wealthy knight. Over the course of the story, all manner of sexual and religious dangers – so damaging that a mother would abandon her daughter – find harmonious redemption in the ideal of Christian marriage.

Marie de France's 'Le Fresne' is packed with the stuff of courtly romance: knights, maidens and chance encounters leading to marriage and harmony. It might then be tempting to dismiss Marie's treatment of twins as a one-off, just part of a tall tale. But a writer like Marie drew on many narrative traditions and reworked stories made by many hands. Scholars have noted that 'Le Fresne' bears similarities to traditional Anglo-French ballads, such as 'The Man with Two Wives' and 'Fair Annie',[4] and it also followed broader patterns when it came to the depiction of twins. In stories of this period, the arrival of twins frequently provided an opportunity for one woman to accuse another of adultery and for those twins to then be separated from their parents and from one another.

Twins are almost always a tragic event in medieval literature.[5] 'If one thing becomes clear,' writes the historian and literary scholar Erik Kooper, 'multiple births do indeed lead to numerous kinds of disaster, both for the mother and for the children.'[6] Of the twenty or so examples he gives, only four of these stories leave mother or child protagonists untainted by accusations of adultery or monstrosity. Tragedy, suspicion and horror pile up in the others. Consider *Octavian*, a popular fourteenth-century romance that begins with Emperor Octavian and his empress desperate for an heir but struggling to conceive. They even build an abbey in the hope that this might bring them divine favour. Their prayers are answered when twin sons arrive. First, the text stresses the physical exertion and exhaustion of the delivery: 'Full grete scho wexe with paynnes sore' (full and large she grew with sore pains) (l. 86).[7] But then more difficulties arise. The empress's mother-in-law claims that the lowly kitchen servant is the twins' real father – again, the presence of twins is sufficient evidence for the mother to be accused of adultery. The emperor exiles his wife and the children. The family splinters. Each twin is then abducted and brought up by wild animals. Further abductions, adoptions, killings of giants, battles and romantic quests ensue. The twins display valour at court, and their true identities are finally revealed both to each other and to their estranged parents: 'full joye there was also / At the metyng of the brethir two' (ll. 1898–9). The emperor's mother is sentenced to be burned to death and takes her own life to avoid the flames. Narratives like 'Le Fresne' and *Octavian* took for granted that their audiences understood the threats posed by twin births. So, in these medieval worlds, the moral facts of twin birth speak for themselves: twins are an incriminating kind of evidence that cannot simply be hushed up. Their mothers deserve to be shamed and their twin children hidden or abandoned, families divided and bonds broken.

Was it possible for one woman to accuse another of adultery solely on the basis of her having twins? Medieval court poets did not write in a bubble, and they were not divorced from the wider ideas of their era. Many were keen readers and translators of ancient medical and philosophical texts, and so read what ancient philosophers like Aristotle, Hippocrates and Galen had to say about human reproduction. Medieval writers could adapt and accommodate ancient ideas about human biology to their Christian beliefs. In their commentaries on classical authors, medieval scholars could focus on both the anatomical environment experienced by foetuses and the moral behaviour of sexual partners. As a consequence, women became much more responsible for the fate and formation of twins – if anyone was held to be at fault, it was them.

Concerns about the medical dangers of multiple births can be found in ancient medical texts. Some medieval interpretations of these writings are illustrated, and these images are a fascinating visual record of how the phenomenon of twinning was explained and imagined *in utero*. Illustrated gynaecological tracts exposed the female uterus in cross-section, visualized as a vessel and disembodied from the surrounding organism. A good example can be found in a tenth-century image used to illustrate a copy of Muscio's *Gynaecia* (see illus. 12). The image illustrates a text that was originally composed in Latin sometime in the fifth or sixth century CE, and its reinterpretation and translation thus stand as testimony to the enduring and international value of centuries-old gynaecological information about the hidden prenatal world of twins.

Curiously gargantuan, the foetuses depicted in this image are caught, twisted and entwined together. These earlier fifth- or sixth-century CE images of twins *in utero* display a profound and long-lasting influence on how medieval and later, early modern writers imagined twin pregnancies. Some of the most influential show hundreds of years of use and reuse.[8] Muscio's *Gynaecia* was itself a translation of an ancient Greek gynaecological text by Soranus of Ephesus (98–138 CE), and both would become important sources for Eucharius Rösslin in his *Der Rosengarten* (The Rose Garden, 1513), one the best-selling medical books of its day.[9] *Der Rosengarten* went through sixteen editions in its original form and was revised into three different German versions, each given multiple printings, and was translated into Czech, Danish, Dutch, English, French, Italian, Latin and Spanish.[10] Rösslin's work also reproduced those familiar globular, disembodied wombs, a place of nurture and conflict for their rugged-cheeked twins.

Between ancient sources and medieval reinterpretations, pious northern Europeans may have recognized the Bible's most influential pair of twins, Jacob and Esau. They are said to have 'struggled

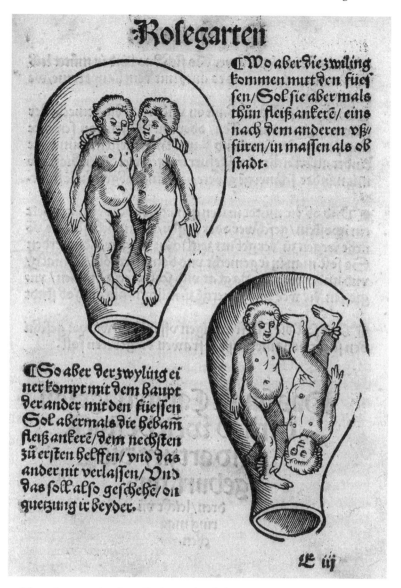

4 Obstetrics engraving from Eucharius Rösslin's *Rosegarden for Pregnant Women and Midwives* (*Der schwangeren Frauen und Hebammen Rosengarten*, 1513).

together' in Rebekah's womb (Genesis 25:22), one twin clasping the other's ankle – similar to how Jacob 'took hold on Esau's heel' (25:26) – to signal the dramatic and foreboding sense that physical conflict in the womb is what causes postnatal conflict or struggle in infant and adult life, especially in monotheistic cultures dominated by systems of primogeniture. The arrival of twins was met with a medical and moral foreboding: twins may bring lifelong discord.

Medieval illustrations in works of gynaecology provide a visual record of twin pregnancies in the context of births that were routinely categorized as 'difficult'. The help and advice some books gave to midwives sought to mitigate the severe risks that were attached to twin births. These texts may, at first appearance, take us away from the imaginative worlds of 'Le Fresne' or *Octavian*. However, they show how twins were frequently seen as dangerous in ways that were not only medical but social. One fourteenth-century Hebrew writer encountered 'difficult births' whenever one of the following occurred:

> the foetus is dead, or when his head is very big, or when he has two heads, or when there are / twins, or when the birth is unnatural, or when it occurs before time, or when the woman is very old, or as a result of the uterus's diseases etc.[11]

This litany of problems is telling for its organization. Twins find their place among the congenitally malformed or 'unnatural'. Here, as in the writings of Aristotle and other ancient philosophers, twins fall into the same category as those who suffer from a physical mutation and are similar to disabled, abnormal or very ill people. Twins are difficult, unwanted and potentially deadly. In one of the earliest obstetric works in Middle English we find the idea that twins are 'vnkyndely' or 'unnatural'.[12] The 'Trotula Manuscript' is a fifteenth-century CE translation of the most influential compendium on women's medicine in medieval Europe. The advice it gives provides some insight into the challenges faced by mothers and midwives; when delivering twins, a midwife is instructed to put:

> one back again with her fingers while she brings out one of the children. And then afterward, another, so doing that the uterus is not constricted nor the children brought to grief, as often happens.[13]

Elsewhere in the handbook, a constricted uterus is said to cause blood retention, the build-up of 'corrupt and venomous uterine humors', feverishness and fainting.[14] The risks are not only multiple but, predictably, malignant.

Theories of health and well-being promoted the idea that good health was achieved by balancing the four humours: yellow bile, black bile, phlegm and blood. To remain healthy, individuals should try and keep these humours in equilibrium, since even a temporary imbalance could lead to sickness or disease. In a manuscript dating from the early fourteenth century, a *figura infirmitatum* (see illus. 13) – a teaching device shown to students of anatomy and medicine – shows the locations of different illnesses and diseases said to afflict the human body.[15] The image shows a woman's body with its many possible pathologies: tumours, swollen feet and skin conditions. Perhaps one of the more unexpected of these ailments appears at the right side of her abdomen, where two faces look out at the viewer.

This image has a bearing on how twins relate to the overall health of their mother and how the birth of twins reflected her sexual and therefore her social reputation. In contrast to the disembodied images found in the gynaecological tradition, the more holistic view presented in the *figura infirmitatum* puts the uterine vessel back into the female body, although one that is profoundly ill. It also shows the uterus of this afflicted woman to be in two parts. And so reproductive health is connected to medieval ideas of balance, proportion and equilibrium, and provides further clues about how twin pregnancy and twin birth were valued.[16]

According to Galen (*c.* 129–*c.* 216 CE), the influential Greek philosopher and physician, a woman's uterus has two sinuses, in proportion to the number of children she is capable of conceiving. His argument follows Hippocrates, whose ideas were explored in the previous chapter, but it develops the additional belief that all animals give birth to the number of offspring they are able to rear: 'just as the whole body is double with right and left sides, so too there is one sinus placed in the right part of the uterus and another in the left . . . all other animals too always bear the same number of foetuses as they have teats.'[17] Galen believed that the uterus had two cells and that each side was responsible for forming the gender of a child: females developed to the left and males to the right. We see this theory reflected in the *figura infirmitatum*. But in the medieval writings of the alchemist Salernus (*c.* 1140–1167), this ancient belief was extended to seven chambers, to account for multiple births of higher numbers, and this theory remained popular well into the late medieval period.[18] The doctrine of the seven-celled uterus was adopted in its complete form by anatomists at Salerno and Bologna, and by those scholars who visited these centres of anatomical thought, such as Michael Scotus (1175–*c.* 1232) and Mondino de Luzzi (*c.* 1270–1326).[19] As a consequence, a mechanistic theory was established that could explain different kinds of birth according to the foetus's place of development, with three chambers on the left for females and three to right for the males, and another in the middle where it was thought that intersex people ('hermaphrodites') were gestated.

The biological responsibility for twinning fell on 'natural' capacities, but it also made twins a woman's secret, something that was naturally stored or harboured within her and exposed in the event of a twin birth. This fantastic pile-up of scientific and theological misogyny means that theories of the seven-celled uterus, whose origins can be placed in the Galenic tradition but whose influence developed over subsequent centuries, reappears in popular court poetry of the late Middle Ages. It is here that we get the clearest fusion of sex, biology and morality, with the birth of twins shown as taboo and as reliable proof of a woman's sexual behaviour – her babies were an evidence that could speak far louder than her words.

This extract from an early medieval poem, translated from French by Hugh of Caumpeden (or Campden) in the 1530s, sees literary, biological and philosophical ideas converge in a single text:

May any woman bear mo
Children in her at once but two?
A woman may ber kindly
Seven at once in her body,
For the matrice of woman,

If that thou understand can,
Hath seven chambers and no mo,
And each is departed other fro,
And she may have in each of tho
A child and with seven go,
If God's will be first thereto
And the kind of woman also.
If hot of kind be the woman
And great liking hath to man,
One chamber or two or three
Of thilike that in matrice be
Of great will open there again
When that a man hath by her lain.[20]

Hugh's text describes the anatomical structure of a woman and how it is matched by her 'great liking' – her sexual desire. Adopting and extending Galen's theory of reproduction and humours, the poem also claims that women are naturally warmer than their male counterparts. So, when women became 'hot of kind', higher-order multiples become more likely. The birth of twins was a measure of an enlarged sexual and reproductive potential in women, serving to reinforce stereotypical male fantasies about female sexual energy and desire as being boundless and in need of surveillance and repression. Threads converge, then, on the idea that twins are a dangerous extreme for a moral order expressed in natural terms.

The fusion of ancient, natural philosophy and medieval Christianity is especially evident in the writings of the thirteenth-century theologian Albertus Magnus (Albert the Great). Albert did not fully endorse the Hippocratic or Galenic view that it was the shape of a woman's uterus that caused twins. He did, however, regard multiple birth as a clear sign of an unbridled and animalistic sexual desire.[21] This is partly because Albert compared the sexual behaviour of humans to that of other animals: 'The human is an animal lying midway', he writes, 'between two genus, one of which naturally generates many young and the other which naturally generates one young.'[22] Twins are evidence of people at a threshold, a midpoint between two kinds of animality – human and non-human. Female humans and mares, says Albert, are the most likely to conceive through separate but sequential occasions of copulation, and so generate twins in a single gestation. Whereas Aristotle said that superfecundation and superfetation were rare events, alluding to the Greek myths familiar to his peers, Albert linked these processes to female desire. He thought that women

> desire copulation more than do others. It is the toughness of their flesh which creates (or rather gives indication of) this appetite. All animals which have tough flesh have full flesh because blood does not flow out from them and the last food is poured into the members. They thus desire a great deal of copulation, especially woman and the mare.[23]

Albert surpassed Aristotle. Women can emit a material excess of 'spermatic humor', as Aristotle believed, but they are also naturally predisposed towards an increased sexual appetite.

Reflecting the deep connections between northern European scholars and philosophers from the Middle East, Albert's thesis on the generation of twins borrows from the Persian philosopher and medic Avicenna (*c.* 980–1037). Albert mimics Avicenna's understanding of twin birth and its departure from the more mechanistic theories championed by the Greeks. Thanks to Avicenna, Albert stresses the deep emotion involved in human reproduction to show how the pleasure and heat that people may feel during sex contribute to the generation of twins. This pleasure is said to occur in three stages – at the moment of ejaculation (*eiectiones spermatis*), during the movements of the vulva when it draws in semen (*Motus orificii matricis in sugendo*) and in the movements of the womb throughout pregnancy.[24] But again the focus is on the various kinds of pleasure women feel during and after intercourse, especially where it may encourage movement. A woman who enjoys sex will absorb abundant *sperma* and cause it to settle into different parts of her uterus. In these writings, morally and anatomically, the birth of twins is directly linked to female pleasure. The twin-making pleasures of women reinforced Albert's belief that they should be held responsible for their creation. When compared to other animals, women were judged to be sexually insatiable, and the generation of twins was used as evidence for how the abundant nature of their sexual appetites directly affects human reproduction.

Twins were factored into arguments about the anatomy of human sexuality and gender, and the social roles ascribed to different genders. Assessments of twins that stress the sexual behaviour of women meant that twins were drawn into moral debates about the state of nature, the ideal size and composition of populations, and the true path to Christian salvation. For women of the medieval period, reproduction was inextricably tied to their salvation. Their physical and spiritual health depended on bearing children, viewed as both a punishment for the original sin of Eve and as a means to attain salvation.[25] Though theological treatises on human reproduction do not always mention twins explicitly, the moral imperative that encouraged women to have children makes the arrival of twin children a fulfilment of a cosmological duty. This puts the birth of twins at the juncture of female pain brought on by the difficulty of multiple birth and the expectation that they must atone for their original sin. Nicholas of Gorran (1232–1295), a Dominican monk and contemporary of Albertus Magnus, argued that a woman's source of Christian salvation lay in her ability to 'generate children continually until her death'.[26] Where twins are mentioned in Albert's writings we find him taking a more cautious view towards multiple birth and towards human population growth more generally. He acknowledges that reproduction may lead to salvation but, if pursued, multiple birth harboured the threat of *over*production. In an image from an illuminated manuscript of his treatise *De animalibus* (On Animals), a continuum emerges (see illus. 14), from a single pregnancy at the top of the page, to a twin pregnancy inset directly below, to a woman at the bottom corner pregnant with quintuplets, to a figure occupying the right margin, pregnant with 28 foetuses. Though Albert says that such outcomes are unlikely, the depth he ascribes to female desire makes overpopulation through multiple birth a real and possible danger.

Anxieties surrounding the birth of twins not only touch on individual health and well-being. Twins mark the start of a social descent into monstrous abundance, the thin end of a wedge that may lead to an unsupportable multitude: a threat to the ideals of what society should be, to match those ideals that are levelled at what an individual should do. As a Christian monk, Albert was a surprising advocate of abortion, as a means of controlling population levels: 'he who strikes a pregnant woman [in a way] which brings about abortion of a not yet formed foetus,' he writes, 'should not be guilty of homicides.'[27] We cannot tell if this practice was widespread. Latin writers had noted the mortal threats posed by twin pregnancies: 'when twins are born,' wrote Pliny the Elder (23–79 CE), 'it is rare for the mother or more than one baby to live.'[28] It was considered even more risky to have twins of mixed sex, with infant girls viewed as more vulnerable and more likely to suffer. The death of at least one twin during pregnancy was sufficiently common that, Pliny said, the ancient Romans gave the surviving twin a special name, *Vopiscus*.[29] As the historian Robert Wood argues in *Death before Birth* (2009), infant and early neonatal mortality rates, as well as the frequency of stillborn or 'deadborn' children, were significantly higher than they are today. Despite the challenges associated with calculating mortality rates in periods when standards of documentation and categorization were inconsistent, single-born infant and maternal death rates were at least three times higher prior to 1550 compared to later periods.[30]

From death return the lives that began this chapter, and tight-knit relations between sexuality, difficulty and danger. Twin pregnancies, with their added range of developmental, nutritional and obstetric risk, as well as low birth weight and increased rates of premature delivery, were (and continue to be) more hazardous than single pregnancies. Having twins and being a twin in medieval times were fraught with moral risks, too. The sexual agency that court poets and theologians like Albertus Magnus gave women made the birth of twins a threatening sign of a fallen animality, imperfection and sinfulness. This is why twins continued to be absorbed into categories of monstrosity, which, following Aristotle, placed them in the taxonomic company of those born with extra digits or extra limbs, for example. But in the hands of medieval writers, anxieties about female sexuality became linked to twins too. In other words, writers looked to account for how pain and physical abnormalities ('physical monstrosity') were linked with aberrant ethical behaviour and customs ('moral monstrosity').[31] Twins were recruited into scholarly debates as evidence and as an omen: proof of parental and moral error and the sinfulness of mankind.

4

TWINS ARE GLOBAL

In 1651 the astrologer William Lilly (1602–1681) published an engraving in his book *Monarchy or No Monarchy in England* that depicted twins dangled over a fire. London, according to astrologers of that period, was a 'Gemini' city, born under the sign of twins. Other images in the book showed corpses plagued by illness and a large city in flames, and these contributed to Lilly's reputation as one of the country's most notorious astrologers – a science considered of great importance by many of his contemporaries. Few expected the catastrophic fire that destroyed large parts of London in 1666, least of all Lilly, who, after the fire, stood accused of either starting the blaze or knowing those responsible. The prediction images he had published fifteen years earlier had become forensic. He was brought before the authorities to explain his strange forecast. To Lilly's admirers and accusers, the pictures suggested forewarning, foreknowledge or even direct involvement on his part. After a flamboyant defence he was acquitted of involvement in the devastation, and his reputation as among the country's pre-eminent men of astrological prediction remained largely intact. The twins were taken as portentous wonders rather than as signs of misfortune. However, their publication before the fire was enough to intrigue learned men who followed astrological fashion. The signs were not strong enough for Lilly to lose his head.

England's seventeenth century witnessed a tumult of natural and unnatural events – the passing and murder of monarchs; a civil war; the growth and dispersal of religious, scientific and political sects; and the gross and violent enlargement of colonial territory. Whether in the name of philosophy or faith, moralists of the ancient and medieval periods sought to control the potential harms posed by twins and their mothers. But by the sixteenth and seventeenth centuries that negativity, reserved for twins in medical, philosophical, literary and philosophical works, was at once challenged and enriched. Twins became newly magical, wonderful and visually exciting. The imaginative space reserved for classifying how twins think, feel and desire was also enlarged in a global context. But this took place unevenly; white Europeans explored new twin interiors while identifying newfound twin inferiors. Religious, moral and political individualisms were being formed through the violent subjugation of others around the world.

5 William Lilly and other astrologers thought London was a 'Gemini' city. This 'hierogliphick' from *Monarchy or No Monarchy in England* (1651) pre-dates the Great Fire of London by fifteen years.

Though little is known about the life of William Shakespeare (bapt. 1564–1616), an industry has grown to explore the worlds contained in his work. We do know that he was the father to a daughter, Susanna, and to twins, Judith and Hamnet (bapt. 1585). The twins were probably named after Hamnet and Judith Sadler, bakers in Stratford who were family friends of Shakespeare and his wife Anne Hathaway. Though this much is known, modern literary scholars and historians dispute the passing likeness and uncanny resemblance between Hamnet and Judith Shakespeare and the characters in their father's plays. Hamnet died in August 1596, at the age of eleven, while his sister Judith lived to see her father achieve celebrity, the king decapitated and the country torn apart by civil war. And since many Shakespeare plays revolve around fatherhood, loss and mourning, audiences have been invited into biographical readings of his work, focusing for example on the Danish prince as Hamnet's namesake,[1] or Constance's description of grief so strong it 'fills the room up of my absent child' (*King John*, III.4). Unsurprisingly Shakespeare's plays about twins seem to sharpen attention on Hamnet and Judith more than his others do. *The Comedy of Errors* and *Twelfth Night* feature three sets of twins, each separated from one another, from their parents and from the lands that they call home. Both also centre upon what it means to lose and regain a twin, what it means to lose one's sense in the world, what it means to find a new home in a new land and build a place to live. It is in this context that they portray twinship in the terms paramount to Shakespeare and his contemporaries – the early modern era of European conflict, conquest and expansion.

Theatre can be closer to dream than documentary, and historians of twinning should approach the appearance of twins in art with some measure of caution. Still, the looking glass of art remains useful for glimpsing twins as they were created by, and enjoyed by the audiences of, writers and artists of the early modern period. *The Comedy of Errors* was written during the period before Hamnet's illness, and it concerns the reunification of two sets of lookalike twin brothers: the brothers Antipholus and the brothers Dromio. Both pairs of brothers are separated early in their lives by the 'unjust divorce' of a storm (1.1.104).[2] Antipholus of Syracuse and his servant Dromio of Syracuse go in search of their twin siblings: 'reft of his brother, but retained his name' (1.1.128). They journey to Ephesus, known to English Protestants as a city synonymous with paganism and witchcraft. They find people possessed, who appear to 'speak by inspiration' (11.2.167). The audience understands that the brothers are being mistaken for their twins, but Antipholus and Dromio of Syracuse believe themselves to be sucked into a terrible pagan land: 'There's not a man I meet but doth salute me', worries Antipholus of Syracuse, 'As if I were their well-acquainted friend' (IV.3.1–2). Even common speech no longer holds, and the twins begin to fear they are going mad: 'Every word by all my wit being scanned,' exclaims a bewildered Antipholus, 'Wants wit in all one word to understand' (11.2.150–51). Meanwhile, their twin siblings are equally confused by the peculiar assumptions and expectations of others, generated by their lookalike siblings. Finally, and according to comic convention, the twins meet one another at the end of the play. What happens before that final act dramatizes the uneasy space between the known and unknown, recognition and metamorphosis, the consolation of being with your twin and the tragedy of losing them.

As with many of Shakespeare's works, *The Comedy of Errors* is based on earlier stories. The commonly recognized sources are two plays by the first-century BCE playwright Plautus, *Menaechmi* and *Amphitruo*.[3] What Shakespeare adds to these sources is revealing. First, he doubles the number of twins from one to two sets. Then he significantly increases the number of mistakes that these and other characters entertain.[4] As a consequence, the play overflows with twins and the abundantly unnerving, tragic, joyful and hilarious things that befall them. Second, Shakespeare's play allows his twin protagonists to meditate upon the composition, location and substance of their twin selves in ways that depart from the cosmologies described in the previous chapters of this book. This play contains multiple twins, but it also considers what twins contain – it wants to say who and what twins are, and to find an adequate language for that desire. When Antipholus of Syracuse sets out to find his brother, he tries to articulate this desire, framing it as an absence. By doing so, he provides a way of framing a relation – ideal as much as feared – that he compares to other, ideal forms of intimacy:

> He that commends me to mine own content
> Commends me to the thing that I cannot get.
> I to the world am like a drop of water
> That in the ocean seeks another drop,
> Who, falling there to find his fellow forth,
> Unseen, inquisitive, confounds himself.
> So I, to find a mother and a brother,
> In quest of them, unhappy, lose myself. (1.2.34–41)

When spoken onstage, these words give a canny sense of double entendre. They express the character's discontent and also highlight the theatre of twin life as play, as performance, a thing without content; the falling metre invites readings that both stress the ceremonious artificiality of Antipholus's 'content' and his blunted fatalism, his existential desperation, at that which 'confounds' him. Without his twin, Antipholus of Syracuse cannot be content, he cannot be happy. Without contentment, he cannot be himself and he cannot possess the thing, the relationship, that would ground him. Coppélia Kahn has argued that 'the image of one drop falling into a whole ocean conveys the terror of failing to find identity: irretrievable ego loss.'[5] But Antipholus is not a person but a persona. He is an actor and a player playing a twin: an imitation of a figure that is seeking a likeness. His is an ironic complaint, and his failure to be 'contented' without his brother – to have content or be content – is linked to the failure to possess himself both as a player and as a twin, and to be his playwright's true twin son.

One of the comic moments in the play is when Antipholus of Syracuse meets his brother's wife, Adriana. She's aggrieved that her husband acts like a stranger. Her loss is expressed in a similar language of immersion that Antipholus of Syracuse used to question his content:

. . . thou art then estrangèd from thyself?
Thy 'self', I call it, being strange to me,
That, undividable, incorporate,
Am better that thy dear self's better part.
Ah, do not tear away thyself from me!
For know, my love, as easy mayest thou fall
A drop of water in the breaking gulf,
And take unmingled thence that drop again,
Without addition or diminishing,
As take from me thyself and not me too. (11.2.120–29)

Her marriage, she says, is a union. Her husband's 'self' is already hers. Christian belief made marriage a rite that unites two people in one flesh (Genesis 2:23–4; Ephesians 5:28–33). But pagan traditions had already made twins materially mixed. In one source for Shakespeare's play, the *Menaechmi*, Messenio observes: 'Never have I seen two men more similar than you two men: / Water isn't more like water, milk's not more alike to milk / Than that man is like to you' (ll. 1088–90).[6] What is striking in *The Comedy of Errors* is that pagan and Christian images of material infusion agree on the figure of twins. Shakespeare imagined some twin relations to be marked not by distinction, by difference, but by the threatening sense of indistinction.

Twelfth Night is also a play about a twin, Viola, who is shipwrecked and loses her twin brother, Sebastian. On arrival at Illyria, she disguises herself as a man, Cesario, and begins working for Duke Orsino. She gets herself (and her unsuspecting brother, Sebastian) caught up in all kinds of tangles until, at the end of the play, the twins are reunited and many misunderstandings are resolved. The play also measures a transition in the history of twinning that we are still living through: the movement from a fear of twins as signs of sin or monstrosity to viewing them, instead, as wondrous products of the natural world. The play is a message in a bottle with respect to twin history. By the end of the seventeenth century, writers of medical and anatomical texts were increasingly interested in twins as benign wonders rather than signs of sin or biological monsters. The modern

historians Lorraine Daston and Katharine Park have observed that
the seventeenth century marked an important break in the history
of how physical deformities and abnormalities were understood.
Instead of interpreting deformations in cosmological, spiritual or
moral contexts, physicians now sought norms: 'a normal function
either disrupted by malformation . . . or served by extraordinary
means'.[7] By 1752 the pioneer of midwifery William Smellie could
make this frank, categorical distinction: 'When two children are distinct, they are called twins; and monsters when they are joined
together.'[8] Audiences and readers are not made to fear but invited
to marvel at Viola and Sebastian. On seeing his sister, Sebastian
recalls that upon his soul or 'spirit' there is a body with whom he
was born:

> A spirit I am indeed,
> But am in that dimension grossly clad
> Which from the womb I did participate.
> Were you a woman, as the rest goes even,
> I should my tears let fall upon your cheek,
> And say 'Thrice welcome, drowned Viola!' (v.1.229–34)

Distinct from the theological tradition in which twins pose mortal
or moral dangers, *Twelfth Night* finds a mirror image in Platonic
delight: 'How have you made division of yourself?' asks the Duke
at the end of the play, 'An apple cleft in two is not more twin, /
Than these two creatures. Which is Sebastian?' (v.1.215–17). Sebastian
is not sure himself: 'Do I stand there?' (v.1.219). The Duke sees the
twins in two bodies and as host to two beings, with 'One face, one
voice, one habit, and two persons, / A natural perspective that is
and is not' (v.1.208–9). The play's non-twins now gather about
Viola and Sebastian and twinning becomes the focus of their collective scrutiny. Audiences may be wary of the allusion being made
to Aristophanes' speech in Plato's *Symposium*, where the first humans
were imagined to have 'four hands and the same number of legs,
and two identical faces on cylindrical neck', until Zeus decided to
'cut every member of the human race in half, just as people cut sorb

apples in half'.[9] Aristophanes claims the source of romantic and erotic experience is based on this original severance, since separate beings seek an archaic whole. While audiences may take this as implying an incestuous attraction between Viola and Sebastian, the play's text is diverted towards more contemporary concerns about the status of conjoined twins, to which Viola and Sebastian are compared. The company invoke the possibility that Viola and Sebastian were once conjoined – not as a 'difficult' birth or the outcome of an adulterous act, or even prodigious beings, but a 'natural perspective'. Fundamentally and finally, Olivia does not express horror or even dread of spiritual abomination at the sight of the twins but instead declares them 'most wonderful' (v.1.218).

* *

COLLECTIVE EXPERIENCES OF striking likeness and identicality, the mystery of identity lost and found, show that Shakespeare's twin plays flirt with the kind of monstrosity that can be diverted towards pleasure and entertainment. By assuaging a threat, by regulating and containing moral, religious and intimate dangers, twins are brought to order by institutions of theatrical comedy, while audiences can enjoy marvellous and wondrous conclusions. One effect of performing twins on the early modern stage was to toy with the possibility of this supernatural force, without giving those forces the authority to confirm twin people as a threat.

Whereas works of medieval theology, philosophy, literature and medicine may have depicted twins as a problem – especially during pregnancy and birth – Shakespeare's plays develop a different set of pleasures and problems that concern the interior and social worlds that twins face or, in some cases, may find themselves excluded from. Despite entertaining all manner of unseen twin spirits, *The Comedy of Errors* grounds its mayhem in versions of twin experience, in loss, confusion, recognition and reunion. *Twelfth Night* concludes with avoidant allusions to the monstrous. In this way, it is possible for theatregoers to view powers invested in twins – competing ideas of spirit, fate, error and personal sovereignty. Twins could be spectacular for dramatizing the competing understandings of what guides and derails human life, presenting a view of twins that can be playful, ambiguous and experimental. But this emerging sense that twins are 'good to think with' – that they make known social and individual powers – also occurred on a broader, international stage, one where certainty and fate, error and personal sovereignty were not questions of entertainment but of life and death.

One of the central legacies of Roman law dramatized in Shakespeare's twin plays concerns what makes a 'person'. The plays suggest that the 'person' is valued, beheld and known according to what he or she is able to command – the things, the stuff and the relations that they may own. Slaves are not persons, in Roman law, not because they are not 'free' in the modern liberal democratic sense, but because they cannot own anything. To have ownership over things was the precondition of being a person, which began in the identification and possession of objects, and then extended to the formation of citizenship and the protection of law.[10] The power to assert oneself over other persons involves possessing them as things. The slave was relegated to being a non-person by being unable to own and by being owned.[11] Without the ability to make, use or own things that give contentment, Antipholus of Syracuse lacks the autonomy of sovereign personhood. He cannot attain himself – 'the thing that I cannot get' – and so he cannot become who or what he is without first coming into possession of *his* twin thing, his brothered self. Such talk was the stuff of entertainment in early modern England. Elsewhere, however, the question of who could be a person was being played out with appalling violence.

The sixteenth and seventeenth centuries marked a period of intense colonial expansion. The competitive nature of European colonial projects transformed the way twins were valued as Europeans sought to impose their culture, language, religion and science on those they considered inferior. They also took twins, the families of twins and the communities that valued them and transported them around the world. While it is impossible to detail the full effects of this global catastrophe in all its personal, interpersonal and environmental consequences, it is possible to identify colonial tendencies in the form of both purposeful coercion and incidental legacy, and to show how the value of twins continues to be shaped by this era of European colonialism.

When European naval ships began to land in the Americas to settle, colonize and extract natural resources, they encountered indigenous communities with intricate systems of belief that, among other things, elevated twins as a focus of custom, rite and history. After the Spanish landed on the Yucatán peninsula in 1519, for example, Hernán Cortés and his troops swept through the region. After the Spanish took the Aztec capital of Tenochtitlan in 1521, Pedro de Alvarado led his forces south throughout what is now Guatemala, Honduras and El Salvador. So foundational was the character of twins within post-classical Mayan and Aztec belief systems that the way indigenous communities treated twins became an important way for Spanish conquistadors and church missionaries to organize military, religious, ethical and moral challenges against them. Here and elsewhere, white European settlers used twins and twin beliefs as a way to understand, transform and dominate indigenous societies.

Evidence for Mayan and Aztec traditions around twins can be found in the texts composed just after the arrival of Spanish conquistadors in the 1510s and 1520s. Hunahpú and Xbalanqué are miracle-born twins of the ancient Maya religion. They were conceived when the severed head of their father, Hun, transformed into a gourd and his spittle fell upon the hand of their mother. Magically conceived, these trickster twins devoted their lives to avenging their father and uncle (also twins by some accounts), who were murdered during a ball game with the death gods. After playing loud games above Xibalba, the underworld, the twins are summoned there. They are set numerous tasks and they outwit the gods of Xibalba and get revenge. One enduring story involves their final test, during which Hunahpú is decapitated by a bat, symbol of death in Maya cosmology, and his head is taken by the death gods to be used in a final ball game. But Xbalanqué fools the death gods during the game, replacing his brother's head with a squash, and puts his brother back together. When the gods learn of this ability to resurrect the dead they ask the twins to do the same for them; the twins agree but do not bring the lords back to life. They reveal their true selves to the rest of the underworld and give the terms of defeat to the lords of Xibalba. Having avenged the deaths of their father and uncle, they speak with them at their burial place before ascending to earth and beyond, to their apotheosis as the sun and the moon. Not only are Hunahpú and Xbalanqué tricksters, capable of overcoming death – the power monopolized by Jesus Christ for devout Catholics – they are the reason night follows day.

Christian missionaries followed the armies of Cortés and Alvarado. They sought to use the beliefs of indigenous peoples like the K'iche' Maya had about twins as a justification for setting up missions to Christianize local populations. Their aim was to transform the lives of the K'iche' in every possible way – every practice, belief, custom, thought and soul became a target. In 1524 the Spanish allied with the Kaqchikel to defeat the K'iche' Maya in the Quetzaltenango valley. As a consequence, literate K'iche' nobility translated their sacred texts using the European alphabet for the first time. The *Popol Wuj*, which began as an oral tradition, may have been written down for the first time in the mid-sixteenth century, and a Spanish translation was coordinated by the Dominican priest Francisco Ximénez in the early seventeenth century. It is one of the few indigenous accounts of ancient Maya belief systems, history and religion that survived the widespread practice of Spanish erasure and destruction. In 1562 the Spanish bishop Diego de Landa destroyed many texts written by the Yucatán Maya, but, Landa having no jurisdiction in the southern region of the K'iche', the *Popol Wuj* was spared. It remains one of the earliest and most important written documents of mytho-historical stories in pre-Columbian Mesoamerica. Nevertheless, Ximénez's recording too was an attempt to understand and evangelize the K'iche'. The process of colonization was motivated by a desire to understand – and erase – the *Popol Wuj*'s twin stories.

Texts like the *Popol Wuj* empowered their twin heroes with abilities to hunt dangerous animals, overpower the lords of the underworld, trick death, transform and shape-shift and compose the sun and moon. Mesoamerican peoples tended to view twins as dangerous or malevolent. The Aztecs considered their birth to be an omen and a threat, a sign of misfortune. In a striking parallel to European theological and medical traditions, the Aztec god Xolotl was the patron of twins, monsters and the deformed, which suggests that Aztec twins were categorized as a physical as well as spiritual disaster. In the Nahuatl language, which at the time of the Spanish conquest in the 1500s was the Aztec administrative language of chronicles, arts, documentation and codices, the word *xolotl* meant both 'twin' and 'double maize plant'. Linguistically, poetically, the figure of Xolotl signifies fertility, deformity and abundance in ways that resonate with some European perspectives on twins in the Middle Ages. However, their independence from the European well-spring of Judaeo-Christian religious practice meant these theories were also viewed as heretical. In the early 1600s the Spanish missionary Pablo José Arriaga witnessed the fear of and contempt held for twins by the Inca people of Peru. Failed harvests and cold winters were associated with the birth of twins.[12] The pseudoscience of medieval European folklore also placed twins among the extraordinary, connecting them with omnipotent powers that meant that they were viewed as sinful, and their parents were made to seek penance.

The emotions felt by missionaries like Arriaga towards the indigenous peoples of Mesoamerica and South America included horror and compassion – the evangelist conviction that the Christian faith must save these 'heathen' people. One less common but important reaction was to wonder why their Christian God had abandoned the Aztecs, Maya and Inca and not provided them an earlier opportunity to hear about salvation by Christ. In seeking signs within Mesoamerican culture of a prophecy – some indication that the arrival of Christians to the New World was their god's desire – the figure of Quetzalcóatl became pivotal. Catholic priests noticed he was venerated by the Aztecs as a strong, chaste and noble person, frequently depicted with a cross on his head. The persona of Quetzalcóatl was at some points seen as a deity that could become Christian, or interpreted as in some ways already Christian in character. In *El Fénix de Occidente: Santo Tomas descubierto con el nombre de Quetzalcóatl* (The Phoenix of the West: Saint Thomas Discovered with the Name of Quetzalcóatl; 1675), the Jesuit priest Manuel Duarte became convinced that Quetzalcóatl was not actually an Aztec myth but the transmogrified figure of St Thomas the Apostle. The idea that Quetzalcóatl was St Thomas circulated among Franciscan and Dominican missionaries as a heresy, but Durate argued that Quetzalcóatl and Thomas were one and the same. His evidence was partly linguistic: Quetzalcóatl means 'precious twin', and the deity can be often found alongside Xolotl, the god of twins. Meanwhile, Thomas derives from the Greek form of the Aramaic name Tā'ōmā', 'twin', which corresponds to the Greek *didymos*, also meaning twin. In some gnostic traditions described in the apocryphal Acts of Thomas, the apostle is 'twin' to Christ, who carries the Word to subcontinental India.[13] To the learned priests of 'Old World Spain', this was a sign to guide and motivate them into the 'New World' – an ancient twin familiar, an apostle commanded by Christ who had travelled before them. The men and women of this New World should be brethren; their ancestors had encountered twins in faith. The task of Spanish missionaries was to reignite a fire – *el fénix de occidente* – by taking the heretical and reviving a latent potential.

If white European missionaries made explicit attempts to impose their belief systems in the Americas, first by proclaiming indigenous beliefs idolatrous and then by reinterpreting those beliefs as pseudo-Christian, European colonial projects elsewhere in the world brought other judgements on twin life. From 1520 to 1870, more than 12.5 million Africans were captured and sold to slave traders, loaded onto ships and taken across the Atlantic.[14] They were forced to work on plantations in North America, the Caribbean and Latin America. Opportunistic as well as brutally systematic, the capture and redistribution of human life led to economic, industrial and political changes that stripped individuals from their families and communities from nations in ways that continue to shape the social, economic and political inequalities of the twenty-first century. European empires were fuelled by slave labour and the extraction of raw resources that powered trade and industry.[15] The world's different beliefs about twins were caught in the sails of these violent conflicts. Although twins may appear marginal to the story of European imperial expansion, the links made possible between twins and cultures that celebrate or demonize twins have shaped the practices of both colonized and colonizer. As in Mesoamerica, the presence of rituals around twins gave Europeans opportunities to exploit not only the physical labour of African societies but their cultures, histories, spirits and souls.

From West African ports came Yorùbá, Ìgbò, Kongo, Fon and Ewe people (from modern Côte d'Ivoire, Ghana, Togo, Benin, Nigeria, Cameroon, Equatorial Guinea and Gabon). Millions of slaves, thousands of twins, were taken from these diverse ethnic communities and kingdoms with sophisticated and varied systems of custom and belief. These cultures still exist, albeit in hybrid forms, throughout African-Caribbean and Latin American diasporas. Yorùbá brought *òrìshà*, or *orichá*, to Cuba, *orixá* to Brazil and *orisha* to Trinidad – the polyvalent and polytheistic systems specific to Yorùbá-Atlantic religion. Among Brazilian Candomblé, those twin deities became known as 'saints',[16] because 4.8 million West African people were enslaved and transported to Brazil between 1520 and 1866, with rites centring on *ibejí*, African twin deities important to the Yorùbá religion, which then merged with religious figures present in colonial Brazil: the Catholic cult of saints Cosmas and Damian. The fusion that resulted is what scholars of religion and culture call 'syncretism' – the ongoing combination of beliefs, cultures, languages and political systems.[17] Today, it is difficult to disentangle the traditions from which the Afro-Brazilian Candomblé practices emerged. Candomblé is not only Yorùbán: it is a composite or creolization of diverse African, European and indigenous practices that celebrate twins. These practices attached to twins are prominent expressions of mixed histories and adapted rites and performances. In the northeast state of Bahia, on 27 September, the feast day recognized by the Roman Catholic Church, small twin figurines are brought into *terreioros* (houses of worship) and special Afro-Bahian meals made of okra are offered. The figures are ceremoniously washed and may receive animal sacrifices. These figurines can in the richest households be dressed in silks and given glittering jewels, like *ere ibejí* (twin statues) found in Yorubaland, painted and adorned with cowrie shells. There is no perfect symmetry between American and West African practices.

Syncretism partly occurs because the different parts of the puzzle are not identifiable or simplified in time and place; European beliefs about twins were changing as a consequence of colonial contact with West African communities, so West African beliefs about twins throughout black Atlantic cultures are neither uniform, homogeneous nor unchanging.

The last slave ship left Porto Novo on the African west coast for Bahia, Brazil, in 1851. Slave smuggling continued up the coast of Africa throughout the 1850s and 1860s.[18] One man, Samuel Àjàyí Crowther (c. 1809–1891), was captured in 1821 and put on a Portuguese slave ship that was later intercepted by an abolitionist British naval ship. Like many 'freemen' Crowther was taken to Freetown, Sierra Leone, where he was incorporated in a growing British empire.[19] He studied local languages and went on to translate scriptures into indigenous languages, particularly Yorùbá, in order to share the Christian religion as widely as possible.[20] Bishop Crowther, as he became, tackled every aspect of indigenous traditions, including twin beliefs carried out in the lives of twin people, their parents and the people who celebrated them.

European and African missionaries viewed traditional West African religions negatively. African agents with their foreign money and influence became increasingly powerful agitators and negotiators within the Niger delta. Crowther's English contacts, his education at Oxford and his European religion made him an important broker for British colonial interests. In places where Crowther's Church Missionary Society found resistance, they focused their attention on women and children who had been cast out of their communities. The mission station at Bonny, for example, was typical of how Christian missionaries approached their work of evangelizing indigenous people – they established their mission station near a 'bad juju bush' where locals would abandon newborn twins.[21] Crowther railed against twin infanticide in all walks of life and would exhort locals in Yorùbá to consider Rebekah of the Old Testament, whose God tells her that 'two nations are in thy womb' (Genesis 25:23), a fittingly violent metaphor for an unfolding colonial project. For if the British had decided that stripping children from their families

6 Kossola O-Lo-Loo-Ay (known as Cudjo Lewis), one of the last survivors of the Atlantic slave trade between Africa and the United States. Pictured in 1927 with his twin great-granddaughters.

and communities was no longer possible across the slave Atlantic, then the occupation of their lands, the erasure of their culture and the patriarchal separation of favoured from less favoured 'sons' became an alternative system of political, economic and spiritual reproduction.

The first converts to Christianity in the Niger delta tended to be the mothers of twins and their twin children.[22] Missions such as the one at Bonny strengthened, a school was founded, and powerful chiefs came to support and ally themselves to African agents. The killing of twins was declared an offence not to Christian beliefs but to local deities: 'there shall be no more destroying of twins,' decreed Chief Oko Jumbo in 1867.[23] As the historian T.J.H. Chappel has written, this was part of a general shift in the delta region that moved from twin rejection to deification.[24] Chappel explains that among the kingdoms of the Niger delta it was once thought that twin births were a form of spiritual retribution, a curse, a precursor to an epidemic and a sign that the mother was morally corrupt. 'A twin birth', writes Chappel, 'was an unequivocal sign that the mother was morally degenerate: the twins themselves a form of supernatural curse.'[25] In what might be a surprising echo of early medieval views of twins, the mother of Yorùbá twins was believed to be guilty of having sexual relations with spirits: she was ostracized and her children killed. The twins, then, had issued from a category of irregular or 'unnatural' birth, the children the product of a corrupting proximity to the spirit realm. Gradually, attitudes have changed, but this process has been slow and uneven. For example, Yorùbá groups to the east, such as the Ekiti, Bunu and Ondo, continued to practise twin infanticide into the early part of the twentieth century. Oyo Yorùbá are thought to have changed their practices when they came into contact with their Fon and Egun neighbours after witnessing how good fortune seemed to meet families of twins.[26] Alternative traditions emerged and came to replace practices of infanticide, traditions that celebrated twins as a special gift from god, or Olorun, to be treated with care and reverence as a deity in miniature, one of many sacred deities (òrìshà) that are the focus of Yorùbá religion.[27] Across this comparatively small region, the ways that twins were treated were at opposites. Over time, and under the influence of European missionaries, the region came to adopt more positive views of twins.

* *

THE PAGAN EPHESUS encountered in Shakespeare's *Comedy of Errors* appears to be a supernatural realm, a place of dark magic. It is 'the fairy land', says Antipholus of Syracuse; 'we talk with goblins, oafs, and sprites' (11.2.189–90). His companion Dromio agrees: 'There's none but witches that live here' (111.2.154). By the play's conclusion there, the land's confusion has been exorcized. Antipholus finally found his referents, his name, body and content, and with them his hopes to relocate his body within another. The play is a comedy of colonial error and restitution. And so Dromio does not necessarily lose his identity as a consequence of being mistaken for his twin, but he comes to know his body in novel ways. When he meets Nell, the kitchen maid and presumably the lover of his twin, he is shocked to discover that she knew

> what privy marks
> I had about me, as the mark of my shoulder, the mole in my
> neck, the great wart on my left arm – that I, amazed, ran from
> her as a witch.
> (111.2.140–43)

Dromio of Syracuse has already described his confusion and transformation, making him feel 'besides myself' (111.2.78) – mad, absent, adjacent, humoured, strangely reduced or belittled – but by the final scene Dromio of Ephesus can turn to his brother and observe, 'Methinks you are my glass and not my brother: / I see by you I am a sweet-faced youth' (v.2.419–20). By being mistaken for his brother he has come to feel paralleled by the person he took himself to be, while the other Dromio can see by the other the person he fancies himself to be. The historical underside to this scene of recognition was being seeded throughout the world, in white European refusals to value people of other cultures and belief systems.

While twins were being recognized in new ways in northern Europe, evolving systems of racialized violence meant that twins were categorized as significant others. In limited ways, the medical and moral anxieties attached to twins eased in northern Europe, and they were also recognized and absorbed upon stages of popular prophecy and entertainment. But in their colonial encounters, people from northern Europe built systems of rule that transformed where twins were born and how they were valued. Colonial legacies continue to influence how different cultures are understood and compared. The next chapter will show how social scientists give twins an anthropological visibility and significance that is at once a response to, and expression of, colonial pasts. There I want to show how twins and the study of twins have afforded occasions to note the wide range of meanings that twin lives embody, while also demonstrating the usefulness of twins in the science of social description as enduring models for thinking about what constitutes a culture. This second aspect – the usefulness of twins for doing anthropology and sociology – is not always an explicit interest of those who have devoted their energies to studying human culture. But the gift of twins is that they appear given like an objective and natural fact of life, to be interpreted in different ways, even when the meanings that get gifted to them are revealed as a process determined by changes that are never natural or simply objective, but the results of negotiation and struggle, achieved with skill, time or coercion.

5

TWINS ARE BIRDS

'Nowhere is the real or fantasised relation between two partners as emotionally charged', reported the anthropologist Jane Belo in the 1930s, 'as in the Balinese reception of the fact of a boy and a girl having been born together at the same time and from the same mother.'[1] Belo (1904–1968) travelled to Bali and stayed for nine years. She encouraged some of the most influential anthropologists of her generation to join her.[2] While living in small villages and conducting studies of Balinese kinship structures, she was particularly interested in the ways that children were treated and became socialized. The people she met were deeply concerned about the birth of mixed-sex twins, and she describes what she calls the 'veritable bombshell of concern and agitation was dropped when twins were born'.[3] This bombshell befell some members of society more than others. For the *jaba* or *sudra*, the common caste that constitutes the majority of Bali's population, mixed-sex twins were highly unclean and polluting. They posed a threat to the families and communities into which they were born. These twins were categorized as *manak salah*, or 'wrongly born'. By contrast, high-caste twins were celebrated. Belo was told that the birth of high-caste twins was as if 'the prince had brought his bride into the world'.[4] These twin siblings might even marry in later life. One reason for this is that only gods and kings should have mixed-sex twins, while those of a lower social rank were thought to be transgressors who had entered an intimate and incestuous marriage while in the womb. More so than the other practices that the Balinese thought were abominable, such as homosexuality or infidelity, twinning was considered a challenge to sources of personhood, tied to spirits, land and family. As Belo found, there was a deep-lying feeling that to bear more than one child at a time was to have children as animals do, in litters. To atone for their sins, parents and twins were banished from their villages for 42 days. They were forced to live in the most unholy places; their homes were burned and their possessions destroyed. It was not only that twinning was viewed as extreme, in need of an extreme response; for different people of different social class, newborn twins crossed the thresholds that kept humans, animals, kin and different sexual partners separate. But for the anthropologists that observed them, something different was at stake: the real or fantasized relations between two partners, and the rites and rituals required to manage bombshells of concern and agitation, were local problems for the Balinese but also anthropological questions of totem and taboo.

Reports like Belo's began in the Dutch East Indies and other colonial trading locations. They travelled in print and, thanks to Belo and her colleagues, in photographs and film, reaching societies that had either forgotten or never acknowledged that they, too, had once considered the birth of twins a moral, medical and religious misfortune. While academic attention focused on the value of the facts produced and the methods underpinning those facts, reports of twin infanticide, rituals of public shaming and the religious punishment of twins and their families induced concern and agitation, curiosity and fascination among European and North American readers. Such stories continue to galvanize strong emotions in those that hear them.[5] What European and North American people view as the 'abnormal' treatment of twins stands in contrast to the elaborate ways that those same people treat their twins, with a mix of psychological fantasy, secular enchantment and scientific adulation.

In the first part of the twentieth century, Belo's work on Balinese culture had a market and was part of an emerging genre – the anthropology of twins and twinning supported new social scientific theories of culture. At the beginning of the twentieth century, British anthropologists such as W.H.R. Rivers (1864–1922) could report, in a style that is typical of its period, that for the Toda of southern India 'it is the custom to kill one of them, even when both are boys. If they should be girls, it is probable that both would be killed, or, at any rate, would have been killed in the past.'[6] These studies note that twins were considered spiritual and material misfortunes, burdens of shame and sentinels of social disharmony. Their research was politically underpinned and financially sponsored by colonial governments, and reports about twin rites and rituals in Africa, India and the Pacific were considered a matter of fact rather than concern.[7] Missionary work of earlier colonial periods had already cultivated pious horror among believers and sought to capitalize on the treatment of twins for evangelical purposes. Late nineteenth- and early twentieth-century research on twins was no less didactic: it hoped to reveal the forces and structures that shaped different cultures, to understand the minds of people, and to teach others how to do so.

European and North American anthropological research on twins in the colonial era sought to document the variation, dynamism and apparent contradiction in how twins have been treated. Within relatively small geographical areas, one community could kill or abandon twins while another revered them. Despite these differences, twins are frequently thought to be at odds with conventions of personhood – wrongly born, spiritually abominable, too godly or too animal. Because twins are treated differently in different global locations, anthropologists have been remarkably consistent in forming twins into a lighthouse group, using them to shed light on different cultures and societies. Their being used in this way does not happen because individual twins, pairs, or even their parents and communities wish them to be recognized as 'twins' in the manner that social scientists want to recognize them. The values twins attract in different cultures, when studied by European and North American scholars, are filtered through assumptions based on likeness and difference that are not always thought through or even acknowledged, assumptions that are specific to European and North American customs and beliefs in rational behaviour, gender, ethnicity and race that remain fundamental to the commercial and competitive life of academic study. For twins to be recognized as a group in a way comparable to those observed in European and North American societies, aspects of their nature must be held as a universal constant. Meanwhile, their culture – religious, historical and linguistic in life – is made to whirl about them. The anchor of twin nature, separated from twin culture, provides grounding for their global comparison.

Later chapters in this book will show other uses of twins that have led to the diametrically opposed approach, where standardized twin cultures are a ground on which different biological categories are made. Yet for social scientists, especially anthropologists, it is culture that makes twins visible and various; whether made spontaneously or by technological assistance, in poverty or wealth, twins participate in common, natural and constant twinness, bound to a category called 'twins' that is varied but fundamentally shared.

Researchers use twins to raise questions about particular societies and about human life in general – the origins and structure of kinship, violence, sexuality, rite and ritual, animal life and spiritual existence. When twins are already there, found, living through and appearing to animate these problems, and because twins pre-exist and outlast the interventions of social scientists, some responsibility for posing these problems shifts from ethnographers to twin subjects and their companions. Twins are animating and animated kinds of evidence for these cultural detectives, imagined as listening posts, 'monitoring instruments' and the beacons and vectors for a variety of messages that signal society's reality.[8]

One case study can show how twins have been treated in one particular place in the world. Generations of European and North American commentators have analysed the significance of twins in the Niger delta, especially among the ethnic majority known as the Yorùbá, whose capture and dispersal during the era of transatlantic slavery was described in the previous chapter. The rate of twin births in this region is significantly higher than in other parts of the world. Approximately 4.4 per cent of all maternities result in twin births, the highest dizygotic (fraternal) twinning rate globally.[9] As also noted in the previous chapter, Yorùbá once killed their twins, and now they are largely celebrated.[10] This knowledge is not entirely natural or neutral. The reasons we know so much about traditions concerning twins in this region are geopolitical and ideological. The historical entanglement of high twin birth rates; the dispersal of twins and twin customs into colonial systems of plantation slavery in the Caribbean, Latin America and North America; and the sustained colonial and post-colonial interest in West Africa in the period in which anthropology became professionalized as an academic discipline, have meant that Yorùbá twin rites are among some of the most studied and most frequently discussed by European and North American scholars. It is for this reason that they provide a way of considering the enduring colonial legacies of slavery and exploitation, from the competitive traffic in human bodies to the competitive scholarly evaluation of human life and culture.

The sacred status of twinship in parts of northwestern Nigeria is multifaceted – active when twins are together and influential even when they are separated. Yorùbá twins are thought to share a common spirit. This emerges from a cosmology founded on a universal division between body (*ara*) and spirit (*èmí*) as the visible and invisible parts of the cosmos. The special intimacy enjoyed by Yorùbá twins is both intergenerational and prenatal. Since all humans are said to have a spirit double, a twin is the spirit double of their twin sibling. They are *ibeji*, from *ibi* meaning 'born' and *eji* meaning 'two' – the Yorùbá for 'twin' indicates their double birth in body and spirit. In the early 1970s, one Yorùbá explained to Marilyn Houlberg, an art historian: 'we do not think of each twin as having its own spiritual counterpart in heaven; they are the counterparts of each other.'[11] Whereas single-born people are assured reincarnation through their absent spirits, twins are thought to be spirits in human flesh, or *adámí édá*. They inhabit one another in matter and spirit.[12]

Some Yorùbáns report that twins are born directly from the god of thunder, Shàngó, and share his destructive power. It is impossible to tell their mortal from their heavenly parts. 'Individuality is not a solitary existence as in the Western tradition,' observes Philip M. Peek, a modern specialist in African divination and folklore, 'but a uniting of diverse elements.'[13] And so twins do something that few others are able to achieve: 'the birth of twins is, for many, the actualization of that imagined ideal – the self and the other coming forward at once, together.'[14] Yorùbá twins unite and are united; they are the living confluence of spirit and body, one and another. The religious status of twins lies not only in their being bonded to others but, because they are so bonded, they must be also treated as distinct, unique. If religions (or concepts of 'individuality') are comparable then it might be in their common structural capacity to separate things sacred and profane, even while promising the resolution between or revolution of one upon the other. Many world religions describe participation in faith as a promise of wholeness, an incorporation into a One, so that political philosophers such as Giorgio Agamben contend that religious practices should be defined by their powers to divide: 'defined as that which removes things, places, animals, or people from common use and transfers them to a separate sphere'.[15] Yorùbá twins are a sacred commonplace and a form of living sacredness. Their religious nature requires careful management; since they course between the sacred and profane, they affect the fortunes of their parents as well as the moral and spiritual merit of the wider community.

In Yorùbá culture, both twins are treated with equal reverence. Their sacred twin status is attended to through a complex set of occasional and routine rituals.[16] For example, at the birth of twins, shrines (*objubo ìbejì*) may be built where votives and other offerings, sacrifices of food and oils, are regularly laid.[17] Irrespective of their sex, Yorùbá twins are given the same special names that stress perinatal co-development, union and cooperation, as well as birth order: the name Táíwò is given to the first born, and Kéhìndé to the second and more senior of the two. According to one Yorùbá saying: 'Kéhìndé sends Táíwò to be the foreigner for him, to see if the world is a good place.'[18] Despite this difference, maintaining equality between the twins is important well into adult life. It was common for twins to marry on the same day while wearing identical cloth, even if the twins were of the opposite sex. These rites of passage, which mark the identical separation of twins, were accompanied by particularly lavish expenditures on food and drink and further observances to recognize the importance of twins.[19] Rites are performed as acts of reverent gratitude because twins are considered to be spiritually gifted beings, capable of bringing good fortune to their parents and others. This is achieved neither through a process of acquired social status nor according to a system of caste; being born a twin is sufficient, though the nature of twins is not simply an event of birth. As one divination verse states:

Twins, beautiful egrets, native of Ísokún town,
You entered the house of the poor.
Twins turned the poor into the rich.
You turned the beggar into somebody with food to eat
You turned the wretched into the wealthy . . .[20]

Addressed as equals and as a single beneficial entity, twins can make their parents wealthy. In these traditions, Yorùbá do not distinguish between twins according to biomedical conceptions of zygosity or genetic similarity; their meaning at birth is not coded according to shared or divergent genetic identities, but their status is forged through the circumstances of their gestation and their shared entry into an established set of religious practices. Twins are recognized as more than human, as persons of abundance.

The magical influence attributed to twins and exercised over one another and their families extends beyond death. Should one twin die, then a small wooden twin statue, *ère ìbejì*, will be commissioned (see illus. 15). These memorial figures can also be found throughout communities in Niger, Benin, Mali and Sierra Leone, as well as in Cuba, Haiti and Brazil and other parts of the African diaspora. They are placed as part of a shrine inside the home and treated as if the child were still living: symbolically fed, dressed and played with, these objects express a mutable series of relations between twins, things and spirits. These statues are not revered with a sacred status because of the personalized, affective representation that a deceased person may have with an object; instead, they have an impersonal function. This is partly achieved through styles of adornment. The statues can be decorated with camwood powder, clothed, draped in cowrie beads or protective bracelets, their hair coloured, and reflect the age and sex of their subject and carry their *ila*, or lineage marks, on the face. They typically do this by showing the twin at an age that the dead child did not reach, as a fully mature adult, reflecting an age hoped for when the dead twin is reborn.[21] In this respect, the statues indicate the past, present and future of the deceased; so skewing the time of the living and the time of the dead. Imagined in an age that the child has not achieved, *ère ìbejì* amplify a supernatural conception of twinship.

They act as substitutes and models for people who are understood to be spiritually conjoined. If a statue is not placed on a shrine, a mother may carry it with her, tucked into her wrapper and kept where her departed child would have been held. It is carried as a public sign of a spirit that remains, a testimony to her bereavement, and in respect and fidelity to her people's traditions. So *ère ìbejì* do not mark a twin child's absence but recognize an enduring influence, one that does not measure a finite passage between life and death but the extension of the living as it penetrates and is penetrated by non-human life.

Though the high infant mortality rates that affect twin births in this region may have contributed to customs surrounding *ère ìbejì*, insofar as the loss of one infant twin would be more common than in single pregnancies, dead twins are active agents with the power to negatively influence the lives and fortunes of the living. According to one Yorùbá woman, the statue is cared for with the understanding that anything 'done for the living twin would be done for the dead twin statue as well, in part to prevent the latter from enticing the living twin to "leave" (die), in part to protect the health of the parents'.[22] The costs of not honouring the spirit of the departed twin can be severe. The surviving twin is believed to be haunted by his or her departed sibling, while their mother is threatened with infertility.[23] Corroborating this finding, the scholar Marilyn Houlberg also observed:

> Whether living or dead, twins supposedly have the power to cause sickness and even death to parents, siblings, their counterparts, and to themselves. If they are not properly honored, a woman may not be able to bear more children or a twin may die of his own accord.[24]

In this respect, *ère ìbejì* are not simply examples of memorial or funerary art but spiritual hosts and the conduits of fatal powers, the vectors for fortune and misadventure. The development of an international market for these objects, combined with the expense of commissioning handcrafted statues, has driven down local demand for handcrafted *èrè ìbejì* in recent years.[25] However, the continued adherence to these traditions can be seen in their substitutes – mass-produced plastic dolls or photographs of the deceased.[26] The statues themselves constitute just an expression, but not the essence, of Yorùbá customs surrounding twins. That they have been substituted for plastic or photographic alternatives partly reflects the dynamic twins have in time, space and material, between the physical and spiritual.

Yorùbá beliefs about twins resonate with others in West Africa. Many have treated twins with caution. In colonial-era Ontisha, a southeastern Nigerian town, twins were viewed as abhorrent pollutants and some Igbo speakers continue to view twins with caution; the Win of Burkina Faso believe twins can be dangerously ruled by the spirit world; and Hausa-speaking Mawri communities of Niger stress the perilously supernatural capacities of twins.[27] Interpreted as signs of luck and increased fertility, Mawri twins are also thought to be intensely sensitive to comparisons between one another. Prone to jealousy, the twins can seek violent retribution should one gain favour over the other. According to anthropologist Adeline Masquelier, the Mawri believe that the effective management of twins begins by recognizing that 'they are, above all, dangerous children' with powers of invisibility, flight, intimidation and the ability to cause sickness:

> They can fly like witches and birds, and are fond of nesting on the roof of their mother's room. Like witches, they can use their power to act in an antisocial manner and to cause serious illness in other family members.[28]

The picture provided is of twins as unpredictable and disruptive tricksters, privileged with non-human powers that let them overcome infant vulnerabilities to dominate and subjugate adults. As in Yorùbán traditions, Mawri twins also pose a threat to the health of their families. Elaborate rites of appeasement are employed to alleviate rivalries and keep twins content. The suspension of authority that adults ordinarily exercise over children, the transformation and reversal of relations of care between parent and child, bring a different set of expectations regarding filial vulnerability, responsibility and duty into stark relief.

How African communities speak about twins had a lasting effect on missionaries, scientists and other settlers, who were variously intrigued, perplexed, troubled and horrified. As the critic of African art and culture Imani Roach has written, 'a major part of the extra-human mystique surrounding twins derives from their connection to the animal world.'[29] This mystique also extends to their connection with European and North American social scientists; it is they who find these cultures alien to their own. And twins do not so much connect with the animal world – rather, twins emerge from, converge with and are often indistinguishable from animal life. This is the source of their danger and delight. Yorùbá hunting and divination verses are particularly effective for demonstrating this convergence between the human and non-human. Twins are compared to monkeys in these verses. Unlike what Jane Belo observed in Indonesia, this is seen as a positive comparison, one that does not carry the compromising proximity of multiple birth and animal behaviour found elsewhere in parts of Africa and Asia. These monkeys also carry their offspring both on their front and on their backs, as many Yorùbá tend to do. Here the relationship between animal and human is one of similarity or simple anthropomorphism; the colobus monkeys are multiples, too. However, other praise songs stress a more complex connection that fully merges human and animal kinds:

> Éjiré, natives of Ísokún
> Relatives of the Colobus Monkey,
> Colobus Monkey of the treetop
> Who rises early in the morning to meet the sweeper.
> The hard-hearted one cannot give birth to twins.
> Only the good-hearted one will give birth to the Colobus Monkey,
> Who jumps with both feet in the house of the ragged person
> And thereby turn that ragged person into somebody with a rich wardrobe.[30]

The common nickname for twins in the region – *Edunjobí* – simply means 'relatives of colobus monkeys'. This makes for playful confusion about who or what is the subject of this song; there exists a stronger suggestion that twins and monkeys are interchangeable. Metamorphosis and transformation are spiritual for some Yorùbá, who believe that twins may reincarnate as monkeys. These twins are thought to be uniquely animal at birth. As one Yorùbá man reported: 'twins who come down again and go up again. They keep being reborn and dying again'.[31] The Belgian anthropologist and curator Jan-Lodewijk Grootaers summarizes that 'twins are given a unique classification among humans',[32] but this sense of singularity should, paradoxically, dispense with the idea that humans are a discrete class of organism. Contact with and permeation of twins by non-human forces – spirits, objects or animals – raises questions about who, or what, 'gives' twins this unique classification among humans. Grootaers's own work among the Ubangian-speaking people of the Republic of Congo and the Central African Republic shows how the Ngbandi and other groups have associated twins with snakes. Missionaries travelling to the Congo in the 1920s found Ngbandi people simply saying, 'twins are snakes', or *ayafo te angbo*, 'children of snakes'.[33] Still the Ngbandi word for 'twin', *ngbo*, designates 'snake'. Twins of the Kedjom (or Kejom) in the Cameroon grasslands are also familiar with snakes, rats, praying mantises, chameleons and caterpillars. As the anthropologist Susan Diduk shows in her study of *fentah* (shape-shifting),

> If mothers confront such animals while working in
> their households or on their farms, they are careful
> not to disturb them, lest the animal familiars become
> irritated and harm the twin children.[34]

The anomalous, hybrid mix of human, spirit, inanimate thing and animal has captured the imaginations of (predominately) white, European and North American sociologists and anthropologists. Much of what we know about twins in West Africa, for example, has been filtered through anthropologists and their systems of data collection and analysis. In many senses they do not describe 'relationships' between humans and animals so much as intergenerational, ecological and interspecies identifications. That twins can be viewed as simultaneously animal and human, for example, has provided a licence to those wishing to collate and tabulate various oral, written, material records of custom and belief in order to understand what motivates local practice. Twins, like the spirits that are said to possess them, are understood to be the visible, manifest content of deeper, more latent structures of cultural meaning and social reproduction. The logic is that, were it possible to find a prior cause for the classificatory anomalies that twins are understood to represent, then wider patterns and rationales of social organization may become clearer.

It is possible to trace a history of European academic responses to twins and then map some of the more significant debates about anthropology and anthropological method. In the 1930s E. E. Evans-Pritchard (1902–1973) reported that, much like the spiritual simian flight of the Yorùbá or the snake-born twins of the Ubangi region, the Nuer of South Sudan viewed their twins as sacred children of God. With striking parallels in terms of birth and marriage rites, the sacred aspect of Nuer twins was expressed to Evans-Pritchard in a way that also drew attention to their animality. In a statement that has now become a formative one in the history of anthropology, the Nuer told Evans-Pritchard that 'a twin is not a person, he is a bird'.[35] This statement about twins and birds came to dominate debates in social anthropology: was it a metaphor or a literal description? A poetic engagement with the environment or an example of how the Nuer think and feel?

There were racist and colonial anthropologies, advocated by Lucien Lévy-Bruhl (1857–1939) and others, that dismissed the Nuer for their 'primitive mentality' and their allegedly pre-conscious incapacity to resolve what Europeans viewed as rational contradictions. Compared to 'modern' people, 'primitive minds' thought twins were birds and were unable to examine why. Keen to develop a more symbolically sensitive approach to human rite and ritual, Evans-Pritchard argued that the Nuer were pragmatists. Twins, in this view, are malleable people who are brought into the dynamics of cultural need. Rather than there being one single way to value a person or object, there could be many different ways according to different times and different interests.[36] Saying that twins are birds is not so dissimilar to saying that anyone is a species of animal: it is not a matter of fact but a sign of common access to God and spirit. Later, in his book *Nuer Religion* (1956), Evans-Pritchard argued that birds are 'a suitable symbol in which to express the special relationship in which a twin stands to God'.[37] He argued that the spiritual and animal qualities of twinship for the Nuer were not to be taken at face value:

> an imaginative level of thought where the mind moves in figures, symbols, metaphors, and analogies, and many an elaboration of poetic fancy and language; another reason why there has been misunderstanding is that the poetic sense of primitive peoples has not been sufficiently allowed for, so that it has not been appreciated that what they say is often to be understood in that sense and not in any ordinary sense.[38]

The distinction between poetry and its hidden meaning is one that wholly supports the role of a reader, mediator, analyst or interpreter. In short, it is the business of the trained anthropologist to bring meaning to the poetry of others. Modern British anthropologist Wendy James has claimed that all human actions, even plain and mundane happenings, are ambiguous and require interpretation. They 'tend to carry something of the ambivalent about them, to refer implicitly to other actions and actors off-stage, and thus to resist reduction to plain singular meaning'.[39] Anthropological practitioners can acknowledge their partiality and their descriptive compulsion as part of a common metaphysical problem; twins are not unique and alone in attracting the expert intervention of anthropologists to be made meaningful, but their presence – observed, reported or discussed across anthropological history and theory – leaves the many different things they could mean uncertain. Again, it is not that anthropologists dispute that twins exist and that they form a category of their own. The problem is that their meaning is multiple, their ambivalence part of what anthropologists describe.

At the heart of what revolves around the meaning of twins and twinship, and especially the generative and creative role they have played for social scientists, is the degree to which anthropologists wish to pursue a scientific, empirical and universal understanding of social life. The French anthropologist Claude Lévi-Strauss (1908–2009) intervened, arguing that the cause of totemism should shift from subjective utility to objective analogy, from 'external analogy to internal homology'.[40] In other words, links between spirits, animals and human groups like twins should not be based on self-interested comparison of similar characteristics, but on universal and objective conditions that give common structures. Lévi-Strauss argued that the meaning the Nuer ascribe to twins and birds reflects 'a series of logical connections uniting mental relations'.[41] He, like Evans-Pritchard, was not interested in saying that the Nuer lacked modern logic. Instead, Lévi-Strauss sought a structure of analogy that placed twins above other humans in a way that birds are to other animals. Therefore, what is being expressed by the statement 'a twin is not a person, he is a bird' is a form of relational thinking. What is distinctive to anthropological thought and the way it uses twins is that it takes a geographically and culturally isolated belief, where twins are birds, and finds room for further elevation. Lévi-Strauss gives them universal significance: 'this kind of inference is applicable not only to the particular relationship which the Nuer establish between twins and birds . . . but to every relationship postulated between human groups and animal species.'[42] It is within this context – in a discussion regarding the quasi-animality of twins – that Lévi-Strauss first declares his now famous *bon mot*: 'natural species are chosen not because they are "good to eat" but because they are "good to think [with]".'[43] This widely quoted and influential statement – which starts with Nuer twins and comes to define a way of thinking about cultural practice in general – encapsulates a way of seeing and interpreting the cultural beliefs of others. It recognizes how material objects, animals and other totems do not exist in order to serve straightforward utilitarian purposes. Rather, these are things by which the world comes to be identified and understood, objects of thought whose symbolic substance reflects the ways in which humans construct and assign meaning.

What is especially complex is that the equivalence made between animals and twins, in whatever context, is understood as an instrument for modelling social relations while, of course, being a social relation in their own right. Their lack of unitary exclusivity, as mobile and symbolic intermediaries, makes twins thinking, feeling things; they do work for both the subjects of study (for example the Nuer) and for the practising anthropologist, who seeks to refine a descriptive expertise and, like Lévi-Strauss, may use twins to provide the evidence for a foundational and widely observed definition of human cognition. It must be emphasized, therefore, that twins in these anthropological texts are objects with which to establish, test and debate not only 'nature' but the nature of anthropology's power and authority.

In the second half of the twentieth century, the structuralist anthropology of Lévi-Strauss competed with symbolist approaches, where theories prioritized higher-order unity over contradictory, messy or contingent realities. Victor Turner (1920–1983) studied twins among the Ndembu in Zambia and developed the idea of 'hybridity' in anthropological thought, providing a means to account for the diverse responses to twin births and higher-order multiples in African societies. Summarizing his influence, Misty Bastian claims that Turner's study 'helped to frame most anthropological debates about multiple birth', especially for those who seek to foreground tension, conflict and discomfort as an explanation for ritual process as well as tacit evidence for social development.[44] It is telling that Turner's analysis is one that keenly focuses on category distinctions and their transgression – defining cultural hybridity according to how twin births cause members of Ndembu society 'classificatory embarrassment'.[45] The birth of twins is simultaneously 'a blessing and a misfortune' because in terms of kinship, corporate relations and social status, twins do not fit into single-born norms, such as the norm of bearing one child at a time. Nor do they conform to the birth orders ordinarily used as a way to share out resources among families. Hence Turner argues that what he calls the 'hybridity' of twinning is expressed in these socially embedded terms: 'what is physically double is structurally single and what is mystically one is empirically two.'[46] Such a formulation works to locate hybrid identities both internally, as part of the twin relation, and externally, in terms of cultural organization and social practice. On account of being so riddled with yet further paradox, Turner argues that twins gain an explanatory capacity:

> In many societies, twins have this mediating function between animality and deity: They are at once more than human and less than human. Almost everywhere in tribal society they are hard to fit into the ideal model of the social structure, but one of the paradoxes of twinship is that it sometimes becomes associated with rituals that exhibit the fundamental principles of that structure; twinship takes on a contrastive character analogous to the relationship between figure and ground in Gestalt psychology.[47]

To the trained observer, twins are an enlightening paradox that illuminates and provides a measuring stick for social order and ritual necessity. The ritual treatment of twins is, therefore, an expression of collective desire to restore an ideal order. Though twins are disruptive and liminal figures, attempts to incorporate and manage difficulties associated with twins can help to clarify the ideals and the ground that are commonly hidden.

Regardless of what a given community understands the birth of twins to mean, specialists in the study of culture and society have recognized these events as positive and constructive in terms of enlightening outsiders about society at large. Philip M. Peek writes that 'from cosmologies to daily behaviour, twins are marked off, and something, be it good or bad, is made of them . . . they are not simply abnormalities to be eliminated or elevated – they participate in larger paradigms.'[48] In statements such as these we see how twins are not just a particular group of people but persons with which to think and work. The extent to which twins have agency and the extent to which their experiences, intentions and desires inform how they 'participate in larger paradigms' are an important but unpredictable aspect of how social scientists think about twins. Under their watch, twins are said to traffic knowledge between particular places and across particular times, where their meaning originates in 'local understandings' to form a kind of apparatus that 'illuminat[es] broader cultural concerns reflecting changes, such as in technology and work, that have occurred universally but in many different ways in different locales'.[49] The range of sacred rites, religious beliefs and social and economic expectations that twin lives make visible – the many norms felt to be identified, measured and tested by twinship – extend their exemplary capacity and make them illuminating beings, telling objects of calculation, and forms of living evidence.

Bombshells of agitation are useful; concern can be consumed. Caught between the structuralism of Lévi-Strauss and the interpretative anthropology of Victor Turner are different uses of twins: the former seeks to resolve the disharmony within a larger structure of reference and analogy, while the latter harnesses the ambiguity of twinship as stranger-outsiders. Whatever magic, mystery or malevolence might be attached to them, twin identities are measured by their participation in an exercise of anthropological power – the power to describe human life. Some, like anthropologist Susan Diduk, place the telling capacity of twins in the hands of twins themselves:

> By doubling personhood, by appearing to be so extraordinary, twins allow exploring the ordinary qualities of the person in Kedjom and Grassfields society. They help to construct a language of difference that ironically is contingent upon and reveals the mundane. Put another way, twins are both extraordinary and ordinary; both their similarities to and differences from other people help to understand the nature of personhood.[50]

Twins 'appear', 'allow' and 'help' to elicit the broader nature of what it means to be a 'person' among the Kedjom of Cameroon – twins are both active and inactive in these verbs. In a quite simple sense, twins do all these things by doing nothing at all. This is, I think, more than a rhetorical formulation but subtle proof that twins are used as evidence of a society trying to organize itself and to effect distinctions between the extraordinary and the everyday. They are neither asked to assist, nor allowed to object to the inferences made in their name. Whether or not recuperation into a norm is possible or even desirable, anthropology has sought to safeguard twins as a tool of cultural analysis because they appear to be beyond the manipulation of dispassionate observers. As a consequence, it is important to observe how 'classificatory embarrassment' felt by the communities discussed is in sharp contrast to the professional confidence that supports descriptions of that ambiguity. 'Twins are never children, never adults,' writes Walter E. A. van Beek in connection to the twins of the Kapsiki/Higi of north Cameroon and northeastern Nigeria, 'but forever liminals: they are born initiates, they remain so during their whole lives, forever in-between, powerful but fragile, a dangerous blessing'.[51] Thanks to twins, anthropologists have said they can get a better view of the political, gendered and generational tensions that have shaped the course of the social sciences in recent decades, using twins to bring clarity to the kind of societal change that anthropologists are so invested in tracking.[52] Born and made into monitoring instruments, the ambivalent status that is repeatedly given to (and frequently reserved for) twins gives insight to anthropologists at home and overseas. Resonant with earlier instrumental treatments of twins and with the biomedical practices that will be examined in the next chapters, the practice of anthropology has also been formed through its willingness to see twins as a kind of 'natural experiment' whose empirical outcomes – the lives of twins – are recruited as evidence of cultural and societal change.

6

TWINS ARE EXPERIMENTS

I sit in a large London hospital opposite the Houses of Parliament, hungry and unwashed, wearing nothing but a thin gown. In one corner of the room my brother lies on a bed while a plastic bar hums over his body. Since he is taller than the bed, he has to turn his toes towards each other, and so the scans appear to capture a moment of musculoskeletal embarrassment. As twins we are not at all rare in this laboratory for twin research. But we happen to be monozygotic ('identical') men under the age of thirty; we are twins whom scientists say share almost all their DNA. Other twin volunteers who come to the laboratory tend to be women (over 80 per cent) with a mean average of 55 years of age.[1] Despite this difference we are just two more people among thousands whose health information is used by this group of researchers. Our bodies are being measured against standards, our data made to fit: collected and computed in ways that match thousands of others.

Our tests continue. The group collects biometric information, measuring our height, weight and blood pressure, also the strength of our grip and the capacity of our lungs. We give hair, spit and blood samples, from which DNA, RNA, metabolites and numerous other molecules can be extracted. Our faces are unwashed because they are swabbed in different places to test our sensitivity to different chemicals. We chat and laugh through these tests, not only because they are many, unexpected, with a touch of the unreal, but because we so rarely spend time together in ways that actively or explicitly draw attention to us being twins. Our pictures are taken as if we are crime suspects, first from the front and then from the side, and a smirk creeps into the corner of his mouth that I know he reserves for when he can't say the funny thing he wants to say. This is hilarious; who are these people? Why do they care? It is a weird recreation, having our bodies handled, measured, poked and prodded by people whom we may never meet again; being quizzed in familiar ways about ourselves, while we can quiz them about what it is like to meet hundreds of twins. Our handlers are professional, of course, blending the care of a nurse and the conscientiousness of a driving-test examiner – lift that up, then do this, and keep going until I stay stop. Stop. It would be too easy to act up, to see where the limits are, but we follow protocol. All is recorded. We are incorporated.

The machine whirs to a rest and the curtains are drawn while I get out of my gown and into my regular clothes, taking a moment to prop myself up and look out of the window across the silk-silvered Thames to the Houses of Parliament beyond. I imagine the tone of voice used by my 82-year-old grandmother for dispensing facts. From here the palace does look serious and venerable. The Gothic style gives it some baronial rust. But beneath the towers and arches is a neoclassical frame, Palladian in proportion, an odd compromise between Gothic revival and imperial pastiche. Back to the trials and the tests, the battery of questions, the litany of answers, the self-evident idea that twins should be useful to scientists – this, too, looks as if it has always been so. While this book has shown that the relationship between twins and knowledge is long and complicated, and far older than some imagine, the invention of modern science and the incorporation of twins into biomedical research was being formulated as the last stones of the Palace of Westminster were put in place. The history of using twins in biomedical science, like the parallel history of researching twins in foreign lands by anthropologists, has been driven by ordinary self-evident truths, plain-speaking doctrine and violent self-interest. I would not be in this hospital were it not for this history, but opportunities to learn about twin research are few.

Even when a partial history of twin research is known to those that conduct and design twin studies, that history is often a matter of little consequence or great embarrassment. And yet the reason my brother and I attend this well-funded and well-equipped laboratory, nestled within a research-intensive hospital named after

St Thomas the Apostle, the 'Twin of Christ', here in one of the wealthiest cities in the world, is because science relies on historical, political and economic developments that affect every practice, method, technique, research group and style of thought. So my brother and I participate in histories that extend beyond the formal questions and tests, the letters of engagement and consent to which we agree. We participate in the longer and historically incomplete work whereby twins have given, or been coerced into giving, their bodies to science – a complicated, bitter, confusing and unresolved history.

* *

FRANCIS GALTON (1822–1911) was an English scientist best known for his focus on eugenics, the study of intelligence, racial types and 'degeneration', and the biological inheritance of mental and physical characteristics. For him, eugenics was based on the science of 'quantitative results. It is not contented with vague words such as "much" or "little" but endeavours to determine "how much" or "how little" in precise and trustworthy figures'.[2] He was also the first scientist to use twins in the formal, qualitative and quantitative biometric study of human development, ageing and disease.[3] One of the most enduring features of his work on twins was his claim that they could help unravel the two powers that gave shape to human life – 'nature' and 'nurture' – and it is largely thanks to Galton that this bipolar understanding of human behaviour entered into scientific and popular imaginations.[4] In his article 'The History of Twins, as a Criterion of the Relative Powers of Nature and Nurture' (1875), Galton responded to his critics. They had argued that fortune or misfortune could influence the character and behaviour of individuals: poor health, a large inheritance or a miscarriage of justice could affect a person's life chances. So Galton looked to twins for a 'new method by which it would be possible to weigh in just scales the effects of Nature and Nurture, and to ascertain their respective shares in framing the disposition and intellectual ability of men. The life-history of twins supplies what I wanted.'[5] He compiled biographical information for 94 sets of twins via postal correspondence.[6] The narrative details of twin lives became the experimental means to an experimental end – a means to measure the relative influence of biology and society, nature and nurture.

The wider aims of Galton's early use of twins also shaped the research objectives of subsequent studies using twin people. In a time before genetic or embryological categorization, Galton grouped the twins according to three types – 'strongly alike', 'moderately alike' and 'extremely dissimilar' – and asked these related questions: were twins thought to be strongly alike at birth able to develop physical and behavioural differences in later life? Were twins considered moderately or extremely dissimilar able to grow more alike in later life? Galton concluded that twins 'either grow unlike through the development of natural characteristics which had lain dormant at first, or else they continue their lives, keeping time like two watches, hardly to be thrown out of accord except for some physical jar'.[7] Though Galton lacked an embryological or genetic understanding of twin difference, since categories such as monozygotic (identical) or dizygotic (fraternal or non-identical) twins would not become firmly established and incorporated into experimental designs until the 1910s and '20s, he followed the conviction that twins of varying types made legible something hidden, a 'mechanism' that is immune and indifferent to external interference.

The involvement of twins in scientific research is now an international enterprise. In the last fifty years, approximately 17,800 traits have been assessed using data drawn from more than 14.5 million twin pairs across 39 countries.[8] The registry of which I am a member has over 14,000 participants, and some registries have as many as 200,000 twins.[9] Despite developments in technical sophistication and increases in scale, two particular aspects of the scientific research of twins have not changed since Galton's first experiments. One concerns the exclusivity and significance placed on twins to achieve 'objective' kinds of scientific observation. The other concerns how that exclusivity and significance extends throughout what he called their 'life-histories'. For Galton, scientific objectivity could be found in every detail of twin life, and this meant no aspect of what twins said or did was too small, inconsequential or personal.

Every phenotype or trait led back, or could lead back, to a common wellspring of genetic or environmental cause. Cases of mistaken identity, attempted or achieved suicides, toothaches, malformed fingers, even a person's slow movement down a flight of stairs were noted down by Galton and connected to the rhythms of 'inner clockwork'.[10] The twin body had become a newly abundant source of scientific interest, a place where traits could be calculated and placed within a scale of difference; not only were twins now a testing ground for new hypotheses about what or who shapes human life, but they were themselves transfigured into the living, embodied and unmediated site of experimental observation. The emergence of twins in scientific biomedical research arose through the explicit identification of the notion that they are rich in evidence that is otherwise secret and hidden, and that they offer experimental opportunities whose meaning – and reality – exceed those afforded by a scientist's laboratory. Such a transformation is historical in formation and has political consequences, as twins are led into scientific research around the world.

There are now many ways of using twins in research, and methods have developed to suit the needs of researchers working in the life and human sciences. I will outline the historical sources and uses of the most influential research designs. Each design approaches the 'nature and nurture' divide that Galton said twins equipped him to describe. Each accepts that a division between the two is either actual or necessary to impose by statistical design.[11] The principal use of twins in biomedical research in the twentieth century was to calculate heritability scores, a statistical measure of variance in a given trait that can be attributed either to genetics or to the environment. Essentially, these are measures of how 'genetic' or 'environmental' a trait is in a particular population. Heritability scores require a clear understanding of genetic relatedness. One lasting effect of research that uses twins has been to institutionalize the categorization of twins according to genetic type – monozygotic or dizygotic. These categories have become standard international classifications because research science needs such distinctions as a basis for its work. The earliest twin studies depended on a series of tests of likeness because genetic difference was largely imagined and the structure of DNA was not yet established. Ever since, twins have become the living torchbearers of genetic difference. In the late nineteenth and early twentieth centuries, their biological cause had yet to be known but their contribution to the science of racial difference became paramount to governments in Europe and North America.

In the 1920s a German dermatologist called Hermann Werner Siemens (1891–1969) developed a way of using twins to study what types of people have moles on their skin and why. In the process, Siemens invented the so-called 'classical twin method' or study, used to calculate the trait resemblance between reared-together monozygotic and same-sex dizygotic twins.[12] The method assumes that monozygotic twins share almost all their genes, while dizygotic twins are said to share on average 50 per cent of their genes. The variation between the two groups can be used to calculate the genetic and environmental basis of any given trait, the heritability score.[13] In the classical twin study, each individual in a zygotic group is measured for a trait. Then, a numeric index of heritability ranging from 0.0 (no genetic contribution) to 1.0 (complete heritability) is generated, expressing a ratio of between-pair variation to total variation, known as an intraclass correlation.[14] In a world of research where human behaviour is divisible into different traits, researchers of the twentieth and twenty-first centuries have used twins to study diverse and complex behaviours ranging from mobile telephone use to nail-biting, sexual dysfunction, happiness, loneliness and intelligence,[15] calculating their heritability in the fields of human genetics, behavioural genetics, psychology and psychiatry. The work of Siemens was influential in Europe because it provided a mobile template, a way of reaping the rewards that twin research promised to Galton and others. Twins could be used to study *any* phenotype; any trait can be measured to assess the relationship between 'nature' and 'nurture', heredity and environmental influence.

For approximately 145 years, twin research has been criticized for producing results that are deterministic, reductive, based on the simplified genetic comparison between mono- and dizygotic twins, and producing confusion about what a 'non-shared' environment means for individuals and populations. Critics have expressed their concern at a number of related flaws in twin research: the false and equivalent treatment of complex, time-specific behaviours such as 'criminality' or 'fingernail-biting' as quantitative traits reduced to numbers, which are then projected beyond discrete populations to create universal heritability statistics; the use of twins as a kind of predictive data; or by ignoring the ways twins of different zygosities share environments differently (the so-called 'equal-environments assumption').[16] It is becoming increasingly clear that no two people can ever 'share' a genome,[17] and the universal descriptions of human health and behaviour that twin researchers present have attracted vociferous criticism. Critics of twin research try to reveal the flaws in those universal descriptions, with some wanting twin research to be discarded alongside other 'pseudosciences of bygone eras, such as phrenology, alchemy and craniometry'.[18] Some twin researchers have themselves abandoned the idea that exploring nature versus nurture is helpful, moving to the fields of epigenetics, metabolomics (the study of metabolites), neuroscience and microbial research, fields distinguished by their uses of big data used to collapse the categories used by 'interaction science' – genes and environments – for more complex systems-based approaches. But twin research, like any scientific subdiscipline, is not simply the application of discrete methods but an organizational and rhetorical process. It involves ways of categorizing, monitoring and tracking groups of humans and ways of valuing human life, two human lives, and a group of people who have twinship in common in different ways. Bitter arguments about whether or not designs achieve stated results can often overlook a simpler problem: why should scientists and twins continue to invest money, time, energy, emotions and bodily matter in the advancement of a publicly contested science? The history of twin research indicates some answers, not just for how twin research tends to think of twin lives as data and twin lives as tools for validating twin studies but also for how twin research became embedded in the great political struggles of the twentieth century.

Earlier German researchers considered twin research to be fundamental to the improvement of the human race. Siemens did not work alone, collaborating closely with another researcher, Heinrich Wilhelm Poll (1877–1939), who developed another hugely influential twin-research design that is still in use today. From 1914 onwards, Poll used monozygotic twins who differed from one another by a particular trait or disease – for example one sister being taller than the other; one brother developing a speech impediment and the other not. This design also assumed that monozygotic twins 'share' almost all their genes. The observed differences reveal the presence or absence of a genetic or environmental cause. Poll thought that using genetically identical twins who are discordant for the same trait would become 'an essential first step in all human genetics investigations'.[19] By 1922 he had become Germany's first professor of human heredity and influenced the careers of a younger generation of researchers, like Siemens. His work was distinguished by his twin research into the hereditary qualities of light refraction in the human eye.[20] Over the next decades, twin research was

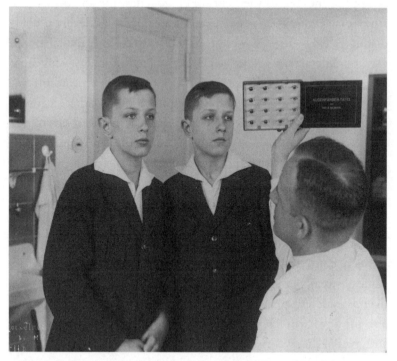

7 Otmar Freiherr von Verschuer, a leading twin researcher in Nazi Germany, examining the eye colour of twin boys.

incorporated into the National Socialist pursuit of racial purity and *Rassenhygiene* (racial hygiene). Poll and Siemens were nominated for a Nobel Prize in 1933 for their work's 'fundamental significance for general hygiene, for eugenics and consequently for the future of humanity'.[21] Race science was essential to the ideal of a Nazi health system and twin research foundational to its public health policy.

Contemporary twin researchers owe the scale, intensity and infrastructure of current research, particularly the creation of large-scale data registries and the careful management of detailed, complex data sets, to mid-century European eugenic race science. Germany's other leading twin researcher, Otmar Freiherr von Verschuer (1896–1969), was appointed director of the Institute for Genetics and Racial Hygiene at the University of Frankfurt in 1935. His first priority was to establish a genetic register for all twins and families in the greater Frankfurt region. He successfully recorded all 'significant' physical and mental character traits of a population of more than 500,000.[22] By 1938 the German Institute for Psychiatric Research in Munich (later renamed the Max Planck Institute of Psychiatry) employed eleven researchers working on material on over 9,000 identical and fraternal twins. And, shortly before the Second World War was declared, Verschuer addressed the Royal Society in London to tell his audience about 'twins camps'. Until 1944, twins in Berlin and nearby regions were offered six-week summer vacations during which Verschuer's team would monitor their behaviour to learn 'from early morning until bedtime, the daily rhythm of life, the succession of moods, the reaction to difficulties, to successful and unsuccessful experiences and to conflicts'.[23] This kind of observation was supplemented by experimental psychological tests introduced into daily life. 'These investigations', concluded Verschuer for this British audience, 'have led to essentially new conclusions about the hereditary nature and development of normal psychological tendencies.'[24] The resources and rigour of German twin science were envied by colleagues and rivals, their methods and workflows admired and mimicked. Horatio Newman (1875–1957), a biologist in Chicago whose own research in the 1930s became influential to subsequent generations of North American twin researchers, described Poll's work as 'the first systematic study of the degrees of resemblance and difference present within identical twin pairs'.[25] It became acceptable and common to speak of twins as 'material' for scientific discovery.[26] Such research treated twins as a kind of scientific resource and formed a protocol for thinking about particular groups of people as material *for* research rather than the subject *of* research: a means to an end.

The purpose of twin-research groups in cities such as Frankfurt, Munich and Berlin during the 1930s was to provide the evidence for the heritable nature of pathological mental and physical traits, in order to assist the Reich's programme of forced sterilization and racial purity.[27] Verschuer's institute was responsible for equipping a new workforce for genetic assessments, counselling, examinations associated with sterilization, and the complex issue of certifying the 'race' of people with uncertain or disputed ethnic or genealogical backgrounds – creating *Rassegutachten*, or racial certificates – to separate Germans from others considered 'racial aliens'. It was twin research and twin researchers that provided the basic biological research and developed the evidence base for the heritability of pathological traits, while also carrying out the administrative tasks associated with *Rassegutachten*. It was here that Hans Grebe (1913– 1999) and Josef Mengele (1911–1979) were employed in this capacity by Verschuer, with Mengele taking his PhD in medicine under Verschuer's supervision. Later, when Verschuer returned to the Kaiser Wilhelm Institute for Anthropology, Human Heredity and Eugenics in Berlin as director, and Mengele transferred to become the SS chief physician at Auschwitz-Birkenau in 1943, the two seized an opportunity to fast-track the research that they had been conducting for many years. They wanted a biological marker to identify Jews.[28] With no regard for the health or emotional well-being of twins, Mengele forced amputations, deadly infections and twin-to-twin transfusions, and when one twin died, the other might be killed for post-mortem comparison.[29] The experimentation on twin children at Auschwitz-Birkenau is often described to illustrate the history of Nazi race science – brutal, maniacal, inhumane and systematically murderous. And yet Mengele's relationship with Verschuer is not always foregrounded. Their collaboration in twin studies is frequently forgotten, and the international context of their work overlooked. The Auschwitz-Birkenau experiments get separated from the many other sites where intensive experimentation on twins was normal practice. The participation of twins in research in the cities of Frankfurt, Munich and Berlin could be obligatory or voluntary and was frequently a mixture of both – incentivized, nationalist coercion. Though methods of recruitment and consent now follow the Declaration of Helsinki, developed by the World Medical Association in 1964, which governs and safeguards the uses and participation of human subjects in research, the idea that twins are an extension of laboratory apparatus, a tool or instrument of science, has never gone away.

* *

IN 1979 TWO men in Dayton, Ohio, discovered they had been leading a life in parallel. The 'Jim Twins', as they became known, had been separated at birth. When reunited, it became clear they shared some striking similarities. Both suffered from heart problems, were compulsive nail-biters and struggled with insomnia. They had both married women named Linda, divorced, and subsequently married women named Betty. One had named his son James Alan, the other James Allen. Both called their dogs Toy. They had worked as deputy sheriffs and petrol station attendants and at McDonald's, taken their holidays on the same Florida beach, smoked the same brand of cigarette and drank the same brand of beer.[30] The Jim Twins became celebrities, thrust before American audiences, who were wowed by the idea of improbable lives lived beyond statistical reason. What are the chances? Accordingly, the Jim Twins became foundational to a far-reaching, influential and controversial research study called the Minnesota Study for Twins Reared Apart (MISTRA) – an investigation into the social and genetic determinants of life. MISTRA was a study not content with vague explanations. It aimed to give precise and trustworthy figures for 'how much' or 'how little' the lives of twins like the Jims were led by fate or accident. Twin research, and some of the genetic thinking that it tended to inspire, was about to be reunited with its pre-war past.

In the spirit of American showmanship, the Jim Twins became celebrities for a time, before being outdone by an act that was bigger and more shocking. When a nineteen-year-old man called Bobby walked onto a college campus for the first time, his nerves gave way to confusion. He was greeted as if he was already well known – strangers wrapped their arms about his broad shoulders, asked him why he'd come back. Bobby, confused and amused, tried to explain that he wasn't this 'Eddy' everyone seemed to take him to be. Before long he was introduced to this Eddy whom everyone said he looked just like, another nineteen-year-old. Their physical resemblance was mirrored by their shared birthdays, as well as their place of adoption. They were twins, separated soon after they were born and now miraculously reunited. Like latter-day Shakespearean heroes, they were celebrated by the local news media. What were the chances that this sea, as cruel as it is kind, should have brought these ships together, a full nineteen years after they passed in the night? And then they received a call from David: the third in their flotilla; their triplet brother. Local news interest erupted into nationwide sensation. These three cheerful young men were cast into stardom, appearing on national radio and prime-time talk shows, in advertisements and Hollywood films.

Like the Jim Twins, the triplets entered MISTRA, which used the twins to develop what is called the 'twins-reared-apart' model. The method compares twins of both zygosities who have been separated through adoption or by other means, at or near the time of their birth, studying them in later life to model how their shared genes but different environments have affected them. Early pioneers of this method include Horatio Newman, Frank Freeman and Karl Holzinger in Chicago (1937), and their European counterparts the British psychologist James Shields (1962) and Danish psychiatrist Niels Juel-Nielsen (1965). However, none of their studies compares in scale (137 reared-apart pairs), longevity (20 years) or number of published outputs (more than 150 papers and chapters) to MISTRA.[31] As a logistically complicated and expensive form of twin research,

MISTRA's influence flourished thanks, in part, to the wondrous and culturally long-standing narrative genre of twins reunited. The study profited from pre-existing fantasies reserved for twins in general, and the idea that twins may be lost and found in particular. Television and print media helped the study to recruit other pairs, so that through their appearance in the media, twins became an influential part of the study's methods of research dissemination.[32]

Working in union with classical twin-study methods using reared-together twin data, the MISTRA group argued that their data showed how reared-apart twins were viewed as broadly sharing intraclass correlations with reared-together twins for a range of personality traits, including measures of general 'intelligence'.[33] They took this as proof of the marginal influence of non-shared environmental effects compared to genetics, and used their twin data to conclude: 'about 70% of the variance in IQ was found to be associated with genetic variation.'[34] While certainly not the sole finding from the 15,000 questions asked of each twin pair during a week-long assessment process, MISTRA's emphasis on the genetic component of complex traits left many questioning the study's methods and political intent – from the relatively small sample size to the amount of time twins may have had together either before or after their separation; to the way in which confidential protocols made data inaccessible to other researchers; to concerns about how stressing 'genetic' influence over, say, intelligence implies the actual or potential irrelevance of policies aiming to improve educational attainment and, by proxy, to alleviate the social, economic and health inequalities that continue to run deep in American society.[35]

High-profile studies like MISTRA marked a resurgent interest in twin research during the 1980s and '90s, with important new registries set up, such as the Vietnam Era Twin Registry (1987), TwinsUK (1993) and Twins Early Development Study (1994), building cohorts of thousands of twins who are tested and retested at intervals, expanding from the statistical measure of genetics to include the next-generation sequencing technologies that have revolutionized the speed, cost and detail of human genomics. Unlike many twins or higher-order multiples, who had a lifetime to get used to their siblings before entering into a study, triplets Eddy, David and Bobby were different. First, they needed to reckon with each other as brothers they both have and should have had. They came to wonder and worry about who their biological parents were, why they lost a childhood together and why their adopted parents were never told they were born a trio. As the successful documentary film *Three Identical Strangers* (dir. Tim Wardle, 2018) shows, MISTRA was the first study they had entered into knowingly, with their consent. But it was not the first programme of twin research that had used their life histories as 'material' for understanding the causes of human character, behaviour and physical traits. They soon learned that their lives had been hijacked by twin research.

The brothers discovered that the adoption agency had placed each brother with a different family in New York state and enrolled them, without telling them or their parents, into a secret study conducted by an eminent psychologist, psychoanalyst and twin researcher, Peter Neubauer (1913–2008). Neubauer was born to an Austrian Jewish family, trained in Vienna and Bern, and emigrated to New York in 1941. He was a student of Anna Freud, daughter of Sigmund, who like Neubauer was another Austrian Jew in exile and a leading paediatric psychoanalyst. The Freud family moved to London in 1940 in the company of a wealthy New York heiress, Dorothy Burlingham (1891–1979). As the sister of twins, Burlingham had a particular passion for twin children. And, while working with Anna Freud, she opened one of the first psychoanalytic clinics for twin children in the world, where she developed an influential set of ideas about the development of twins and twin psychopathology.

By engineering a twins-reared-apart model, Neubauer was able to separate twins and conduct tests that measured the heritability of traits – every part of their childhood development was observed and scrutinized, as well as the longitudinal effects of their parent's relationship to the children.[36] In this case, the justification for separating the twins was both scientific and therapeutic. In the theoretical and historical context of mid-century psychoanalysis, however, the decision to separate identical twin children into different homes could be justified: psychoanalytic theory at the time believed twin children

8 Dorothy Burlingham (left) and her twin sisters, 1898.

were better off that way, avoiding the troubling things that Burlingham saw in her clinic.

The twin children Burlingham worked with displayed problems that she identified as being connected to having a twin sibling, problems that she thought sprang from being a twin. If a problem of identification, attachment, neurotic dependency or anxiety was observed in these children, twinning was to blame.[37] Her work was celebrated by leading psychologists of the time as groundbreaking and conclusive; Donald Winnicott (1896–1971) declared it 'probably the most comprehensive work of its kind in existence'.[38] From this clinical psychoanalytic point of view, twins and higher-order multiples such as triplets or quads are better off going it alone. The experimental design of Neubauer's research cannot be separated from the assumption that the single-born psychological development of an 'individual' was taken as the standard and norm by which twins and triplets were judged.

Little thought seems to have gone into the long-term psychological effects of separating twins and keeping their status as research subjects a secret. Unpublished, the Neubauer study archive was bequeathed to Yale University when Neubauer died in 2008 and was embargoed until 2066. Bobby and David fear they will never know the truth about what happened to them. Eddy never will: his brothers link his suicide in 1995 to his inability to cope with a past whose unification was impossible, insurmountable. The history of twin studies is rarely written by those who take part in them as witnesses and primary data sources. Such histories, if they could be written, would act as a reminder that the history of science is never complete but is continuously reinscribed into different pasts and possible futures. Like other twin stories saturated in sensation, celebration and discovery, touched by weird narrations of magic and coercion, the story of these brothers puts more than Peter Neubauer's twin study in the open. Since the release of *Three Identical Strangers*, campaign groups and legal cases have been awakened; people have discovered they have siblings and have been reunited with one another. Many audiences have confronted the history of post-war human experimentation and its lasting effects on people's lives.

It is important to shun the simplistic idea that eugenics, race science and other kinds of violence, linked to science conducted with human twins, came to an end in 1945. Likewise, it is important to scrutinize the companion assumption that unethical research is unique to fascist politics. One legacy of the Nuremberg trials has been to put Nazi race science in a past tense. And contemporary twin researchers themselves are eager to put distance between their work and the most unethical practices associated with their research methods.[39] And yet the influence of Nazi-era research is still felt in a number of academic disciplines, not only in the techniques and comparative principles used but in the ways findings are gathered, disseminated and discussed. Verschuer, Grebe and Mengele escaped prosecution.

Verschuer was given safe haven to launder his reputation in the city of twins, Rome, by collaborating with the Italian physician, politician and eugenicist Luigi Gedda (1902–2000).[40] Rome's Institute of Medical Genetics and Twin Research provided Verschuer a frequent venue for discussing his post-war twin research, and Gedda, with financial assistance from the Italian government and the Catholic Church, founded *Acta Geneticae Medicae et Gemellologica* (now the flagship Cambridge University Press journal *Twin Research and Human Genetics*) and the International Society for Twin Studies. Both remain central to the professional concerns of contemporary researchers as, respectively, the pre-eminent journal in which to publish new twin research and the most important international network through which to disseminate study findings. Scientific legacies can come in many different forms. Some are methodological or organizational, while others refer to the status and reputation of individuals or communities. It is a belief that has travelled so evenly from Galton to the present: twins are a vital group for experimentation, which justifies a scientific way of seeing, isolating and using a group of humans. Recruiting them into research science is defended based on their comparative rarity, since every aspect of their lives is seen to be enriched with scientific potential.

* *

MANY CONTEMPORARY TWIN researchers celebrate their research subjects, research methods and the findings of their studies as grounded in 'natural' phenomena. Their study subjects are a 'naturally occurring experiment' and an 'experiment of nature'.[41] Despite the investments made in laboratory resources, statistical designs, educational and data infrastructures, and organizational and political labour, and despite the history of scientific racism and prejudice outlined above, there remains a pervasive language of human utility attached to twins participating in biomedical research, whether using classical, discordant, reared-apart or combined methods. Twin research is seen as more 'natural' than other kinds of investigation. Twins are humans – not Petri dish cultures, cell lines or laboratory animals – and so there is no need to 'translate' findings from laboratory bench to hospital bedside. Thomas J. Bouchard Jr, leader of MISTRA, whose extensive, costly, politically contested studies into human intelligence I described above, claims that 'molecular genetics looks at genes, not whole, live human beings' and that twins studies 'add a very necessary human element to genetics'.[42] Similarly, for Nancy Segal, an evolutionary psychologist and twin researcher who began her career with Bouchard's MISTRA group, 'twins are an experiment of nature' and a powerful investigatory community capable of generating 'unique insights . . . simply by acting naturally'.[43] The presence of twins continues to provide a powerful experimental licence.

It is because twin bodies are treated as a method, a global population of research subjects and a gateway to a standardized order of scientific utility that twin researchers such as Tim Spector at TwinsUK claim that they have '11 million natural identical-twins experiments to choose from'.[44] Elsewhere, in a statement odd enough to raise the eyebrows of both animal rights activists and the twin-research participants in his care, Spector has said that his twin studies are 'the closest we can get to doing animal experiments on humans'.[45] Taken together, these statements might appear to present contradictory fantasies of experimental availability, intervention and manipulation. But twins offer all the power of animal research without the confinement of a laboratory setting. The sense of experimental abundance and opportunity that comes unburdened by the need to translate model to target organism.

In the pursuit of modern rationality, human manipulation, emotion, volunteerism and coercion are habitually written out of scientific and popular accounts of twin research, which stress the spontaneous power of twin people to generate evidence. One overall effect has been for twin studies to find new power, beyond that power identified by Belgian philosopher Isabelle Stengers as characterizing modern scientific objectivity: 'the invention of the power to confer on things the power of conferring on the experimenter the power to speak in their name'.[46] Twin studies do not only confer power to speak on behalf of mute phenomena. They also render twin bodies experimental and explanatory vectors for scientific truth. Twins promise that each and every life event, every trait, habit or decision can be resonant with universal information. This promise, as we have seen, grew from small beginnings but galvanized an international scientific platform for eugenics and race science. As we shall see in the next chapter, it continues to energize experiments in embryology and genomics, shaping how twins are valued and how twins are made.

7

TWINS ARE MADE

We crashed about its wood and corrugated iron frame, wobbling across the uneven concrete floor on our bikes and skates. Empty for most of the year, the sheep shed was our playground among shit-stinking playgrounds, a hall of echoes, empty for most of the year. The shed had an added attraction: John's cabin. This little house was wedged into the apex of the roof and only accessible by a long ladder. The cabin was a thing of exquisite intrigue, off-limits, perilously high and full of deadly chemicals. It had a magical effect on us. So we reasoned a glimpse couldn't hurt and we'd venture up the ladder to stare at all the things a shepherd needs: a bed of no obvious comfort, a bare table, two little windows adorned with single-sheet curtains like you find in old caravans, and, to our great fascination, a television linked to a CCTV network.

Overexcited and knowing better, our conspiracies cast John as an unlikely undercover policeman or Soviet agent, but tall tales unravelled when the season's work arrived baa-ing in fear and anticipation. The little cabin became John's makeshift home for a few weeks each year during the lambing season. Our playground became a place of blood and toil. The cause of his nightly vigil, the events captured in the low flicker of CCTV footage, became clear to me years later. John's sheep were twin machines. The cabin was a watchtower over a reproductive and economic experiment, built to look over multiple gain and compound loss – twin life that was both many and multiple.

We were not the only twins being raised on the farm: Dad had his cows, Mum had us, and John took care of the sheep. It was John who decided to rear a breed that became ubiquitous in British fields by the 1990s, the British Milksheep. A composite breed that crossed familiar British breeds like the East Friesian, Bluefaced Leicester, Polled Dorset, Lleyn and perhaps others, the British Milksheep was established in the late 1970s and introduced to the UK livestock markets around the time John expanded his flock. Hornless, white-faced and of medium build, they arrived with plenty to offer. Their titular advantage was in the large quantities of milk they can produce – up to 900 litres per 300-day lactation. The other strength, from a farmer's point of view, was the prolific number of lambs that these ewes can bear. British Milksheep are an industrial breed, multiples their productive norm. Average litters produce two lambs; mature ewes frequently bear triplets or more.

With hundreds of ewes having two or more lambs, John walked about the lambing shed as if he were carrying an invisible sack of rocks, so weary for work. He would deliver lambs knowing that the breed's strength was also its weakness – multiple births meant more born small or premature. More work, more decisions, more interventions to make, more restless shifts giving way to nights spent in the makeshift cabin, more hours on the lookout for ewes needing his help.

John showed us remarkable patience when we trooped in to see what was happening. We'd clamber into the pens with the smallest babies, which were separated from the others because their mother was unable to support them. Too small and abundant, too many and too multiple. Wanting to help, we would play with these orphans in the lamplit beds we called the Orphanage, the heat lamps casting an unreal glow over the straw. If we got our timing right, John would give us a bottle to feed these jubilant survivors. But getting into the Orphanage meant we had to pass the Blue Bin, a thing so awful I had to peer inside to see what the night had made. There I would find an eye looking up at me from the bloodied body of a lamb, stillborn or too weak to survive, rejected or suffocated by its exhausted mother. The British Milksheep: engineered to be born two by two, prolific at life made multiple, plentiful in the death that is bred in multiple life. The Orphanage and the Blue Bin were the twin stations in a high-stakes breeding programme: object lessons in the perils encountered by those born in twos, threes, or more.

The mean economy of small-scale sheep farming in the 1980s and '90s made the problems associated with British Milksheep a risk worth taking; those abundant gains outweighed their associated costs. The early development of the breed ran in parallel with a change in the way humans started to reproduce themselves. During the 1980s and '90s, a set of technologies emerged that would transform how and in what number humans are born, changing the way that human society creates life.

* *

IN 1978 LOUISE Brown was born in Oldham, England. She was the world's first human baby born using *in vitro* fertilization (IVF). The technique, first pioneered in animals, allowed Louise's parents to conceive using extracted eggs and sperm, combined in a laboratory environment and returned as a fertilized embryo to the womb of Louise's mother, Lesley. Since 1978 approximately 5 million babies have been born worldwide using *in vitro* techniques and related technologies. Though Louise Brown's birth gave many people hope, it also brought reasons to be anxious – would this lead to consumer-led eugenics and genetic modification, market exploitation, or the legal separation of people and their reproductive matter? IVF and other techniques are now routine, accounting for as much as 5 per cent of the birth rate in some countries.[1] Assisted reproduction has also transformed the way that people can give birth to and become twins.

The first IVF twins were born to a 31-year-old woman called Radmila Mays, in Melbourne, Australia, on 6 June 1981. Stephen and Amanda Mays were the seventh and eighth babies to be born using *in vitro* techniques. Born with them was a new kind of twin identity, an identity that stalks conceptions of what is normal or natural. It concerns not just where or with whom twin people are born, but how – by what technological means, at what expense and with what risks. And so, instead of simply being a wondrous product of nature and of blind love or cruel chance, twins now border new ways of living and unexpected ways of being. Now mothers of twin babies can be asked if their children are born or made: are they natural?

Fertility treatment makes possible new differences between twins, new values and hierarchies that track how human life can be entangled with, and enhanced by, technology.

The Mays twins were the first of many thousands of multiples to be born using new reproductive technologies. Born a month premature and by Caesarean section, Stephen Mays was significantly smaller than his sister. Being premature gave him severe bowel inflammation, and this, along with a congenital heart defect, meant he required immediate surgery.[2] These early warning signs from the beginning of the IVF era were not heeded. The first IVF twin birth came with severe complications. The first reported IVF death involved twin pregnancy.[3] It would take years before anyone would challenge the idea that two is better than none.

The birth of twins can now begin with a cycle of IVF. Eggs are fertilized in a laboratory and then placed in a woman's uterus to develop as embryos. Though IVF is often spoken of as if it is a single procedure, it is actually a series of linked processes. For this and many other reasons, studies show that people tend to overestimate

9 Louise Brown with thirteen-month-old IVF twins, Antonia and Henry Veary, 2003.

the effectiveness of IVF. For example, a woman in her twenties – considered to be in the most fertile period of her life – has only a 28 per cent chance of conceiving using IVF.[4] For her to become pregnant a course of drugs and hormones is used. She may take these drugs initially to prevent ovulation and then to stimulate the ovaries to produce multiple eggs – a process known as superovulation. The hormones used at this stage form a fundamental phase in how IVF has succeeded as a reproductive technology, and as a twin-producing phenomenon, one that tries to regulate and augment the human body's capacities. Clinicians see the use of these hormones as a way to maximize the number of eggs that can be fertilized. The eggs are then monitored using ultrasound and blood analysis. Then they are not simply extracted: they are 'harvested' (a reminder of how this process originates from animal research and agriculture), and the clinical team inserts a fine needle into the vagina and then into the ovaries, to remove many eggs at once. As the patient continues a course of drugs to prepare for pregnancy, the eggs are mixed with the sperm of a partner or donor. In a sterile laboratory, the embryos are allowed to mature to the blastocyst stage of development (approximately 5 days after fertilization). Their progress is carefully monitored. At this point the embryos can also be 'graded' for their potential to develop into foetuses. What happens next is crucial in deciding whether single or multiple birth is likely: one, two or more embryos are inserted into the woman's uterus using a thin catheter, and after two weeks a pregnancy test reveals whether the whole process has been successful.[5] Twin births have increased because hormone stimulants promote the production of many eggs, and this can lead to twin pregnancies even before IVF has taken place. Multiple embryo transfer – or transferring two or more embryos back into the uterus – significantly increases the chances of conceiving twins.

Twin birth rates have rocketed over the last forty years, in large part due to drug therapies, IVF treatments and other forms of assisted reproductive technology (ART). The growth in birth rates has been particularly rapid in the U.S., accelerated by a multibillion-dollar fertility industry. In 1980 almost 19 in every 1,000 babies born in the U.S. was a twin. By 2018 this had risen to more than 33 in every 1,000.[6]

Twin birth rates in England and Wales have followed a similar pattern of growth: approximately 18.5 in every 1,000 births in 1980 was a twin, climbing to almost 33 per 1,000 by 2014.[7] This means that populations in the u.s., England and Wales have experienced a 40–45 per cent increase in twin births in the last three decades. Although estimates vary, some studies suggest that two-thirds of the increase in the u.s. twin birth rate is likely to be associated with fertility treatment.[8] One study has put the rate of twinning among people undergoing fertility treatments at 22 times higher than in the general u.s. population.[9] This helps to explain why almost half (44 per cent) of all the babies born using IVF in the u.s. in 2012 were twins or higher-order multiples.[10] As far as we know, there has never been such a rapid acceleration in twin birth rates. A consequence of this acceleration has been a transformation in the way that twins are seen and valued.

The extraordinary pact between biology and technology achieved by IVF treatments has been aided and abetted by deepening administrative and economic powers. Recording twin births and distinguishing between different kinds of twin has widened in scope and accuracy. We can now recognize variations within the recent rise in twin births. One important insight gathered from population data has identified how fertility treatments affect a certain kind of twin: dizygotic, or fraternal. This is because monozygotic or identical twinning is a relatively constant biological phenomenon: monozygotic twins comprise approximately 3.5–4 births per 1,000. By contrast, the rate of dizygotic twinning varies.[11] That is not to say that the rate of monozygotic twinning is unaffected by fertility treatment – some have noted an increase in rates of monozygotic twinning, too, pointing to how ovulation induction, micromanipulation of the embryo and the extended exposure of embryos in Petri cultures can cause an embryo to split in two.[12] But, for the most part, IVF is boosting dizygotic twin birth rates in ways that only add to an already complex distribution of twin birth rates worldwide.

Biology, technology and administrative powers have fused with a transformation in the way we work and reproduce. Louise Brown's birth occurred in the same year that a columnist writing for the

Washington Post coined an expression that sealed reproductive time within women's bodies: the 'biological clock'.[13] Increases in twin birth rates are intimately linked to who is able to access expensive fertility treatments in private and state health systems and how reproductive choice is framed by the restrictions of wage labour. One of the striking findings to emerge from population data collected in recent decades has been to show how birth rates break down by maternal age. Between 1980 and 2009 the rate of twin births in the U.S. rose by 76 per cent among women aged 30–34, by almost 100 per cent among women aged 35–9, and more than 200 per cent in women aged 40 and over. By 2018, as in 2014, twinning rates increased with advancing maternal age. For both years, mothers aged 30–39 were more than twice as likely, and mothers aged 40 and over were three times as likely, to have a twin birth compared with their counterparts under age 20.[14] One theory is that dizygotic twinning occurs when more than one dominant ovarian follicle has matured during the menstrual cycle – a process regulated by a hormone called follicle-stimulating hormone (FSH). Different people produce different quantities of FSH. And this variation depends on geographical location, season, maternal ethnicity, height, weight, age and (of course) access to fertility treatments.[15] FSH levels also increase in women approaching the end of their so-called 'reproductive lives'. Studies of fertility and reproduction show that the propensity to multiovulate – to produce many eggs in a menstrual cycle – tends to increase until women reach the age of about 38, and then the rate sharply declines.[16] Approximately two-thirds of the increase in twins born in the U.S. is the result of fertility treatments. But pregnancies among women in their late thirties and early forties account for what remains.[17] The end of the twentieth century brought a transformation in human and non-human reproduction, from lambing sheds to hospital delivery rooms, stirred by economic gain and technological change and rising physical and financial costs.

Twins born using IVF technologies are bought at a price. Depending on medical insurance cover, a single cycle of IVF can cost approximately $12,000 in the U.S., $7,500 in the UK and $3,500 in India.[18] These costs increase if donor sperm, donor eggs or surrogate services are also involved. Countries with state welfare systems may offer a limited number of IVF cycles for 'free' through taxation. For example, the UK's National Health Service (NHS) rations cycles of IVF to women under 40. These are limited to those who have been unable to conceive through sexual intercourse or artificial insemination.[19] Given the relatively low success rate of IVF treatments, patients can undergo many cycles. Critics campaign for clinical providers to be regulated, since people who want fertility services may be desperate to have children and be prepared to make huge financial sacrifices to undergo treatment. As the health economist Deborah Spar has said, 'demand is too high and desire too deep to be stopped.'[20] As an industry geared towards fulfilling enduring hopes, the baby business is a trade with enormous potential to generate profit.

Researchers and clinicians are concerned about the large sums of money involved in fertility treatment and the conflicts of interest this might produce, describing fertility treatment as a part of a growing 'bioeconomy' – an economy where biology, technology and capitalism meet.[21] The bioeconomy is different to other kinds of markets where commodities are bought and sold because the fertility market is ultimately known, felt and lived through the bodies of human beings. The product in this market is life itself. There are a lot of 'players' in the fertility market – public and private fertility clinics, producers of synthetic hormones, brokers of gestational surrogates and donor gametes (eggs and sperm). These players come together in a market where demand is high and risk-taking behaviours are encouraged.

Since human life has entered the marketplace, product development has advanced rapidly to meet a demand that is both deep and various. Depending on national regulations, clinics can be powerful brokers. Fertility clinics in California provide safety and quality by maintaining personalized breeding programmes. They trade only in donor sperm and eggs from those bearing certain physical characteristics, health histories and genetic backgrounds – people educated to graduate level at the most prestigious universities.[22] It might be useful to liken these fertility clinics and services to other luxury traders – they develop brands to compete on service and quality but also build prestige and exclusivity.[23] One company, California Cryobank, has a 65 per cent market share of a u.s. sperm trade estimated to be worth $100 million annually.[24] California Cryobank is proud to accept fewer than 1 per cent of applicants who want to become sperm donors, and all those accepted are well educated, highly paid and genetically screened.[25] By screening their donors, vendors seek to eradicate 'undesirable' physical traits and develop niche markets that cater for would-be parents who may, for example, select their preferred racial or ethnic background, level of educational achievement, and sexual or political orientation. The genetic science for such traits is contested and the clinical services being offered by these companies are criticized for profiting from market-led eugenics. But the logic of customer choice passes ethical responsibilities to consumers, who are imagined to be free and sufficiently informed to choose what is best for themselves and their unborn children. Companies can complement sperm and egg donation with gestational surrogacy services, where a woman is paid to carry a foetus to term but has no genetic or legal relation to the child born.[26] This is reflected in the legal language used – a surrogate 'carries' a foetus.[27] Before they know it, IVF twins can be part of a biological, legal and commercial transaction on which their lives depend.

It is now possible to choose twins in ways that were impossible prior to the invention of IVF and other reproductive techniques. Advances in reproductive medicine as well as changes in labour markets and policy make new kinds of human relationship possible. Long-standing prejudices connected to female sexuality and twin births have become reformulated in fertility markets. The development of twins can be induced, managed and monitored by clinicians who have been trained to optimize Petri and laboratory environments for their creation. Children may never come to know the identities of their biological parents; in other cases, IVF babies can create new kinds of family.

* *

10 Il Sodoma (attrib.), copy after Leonardo da Vinci, *Leda and the Swan*, *c.* 1510–15, oil on panel.

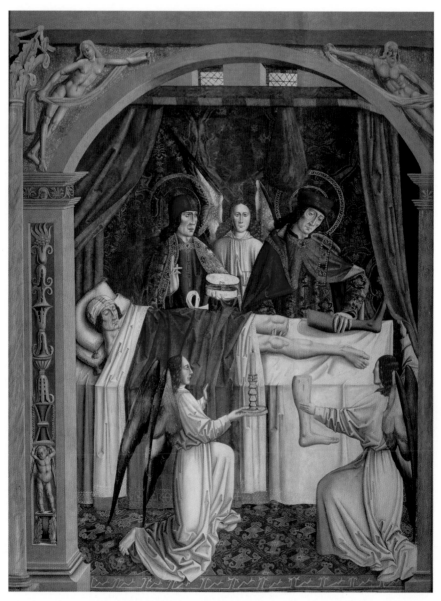

11 Master of Los Balbases, after Alonso de Sedano, *A Verger's Dream: Saints Cosmas and Damian Performing a Miraculous Cure by Transplantation of a Leg*, *c*. 1495, oil on panel.

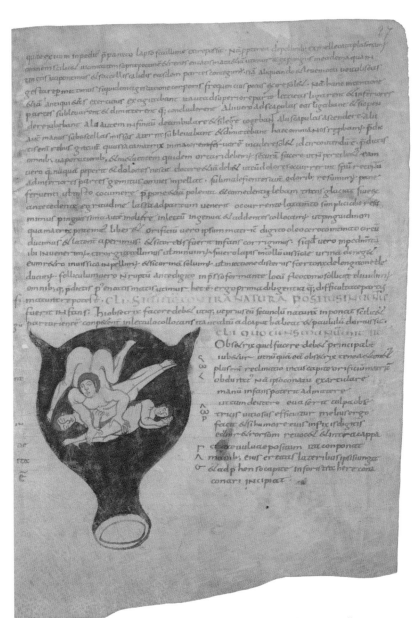

12 Muscio's *Gynaecia*: 10th-century illustration of a 6th-century text.

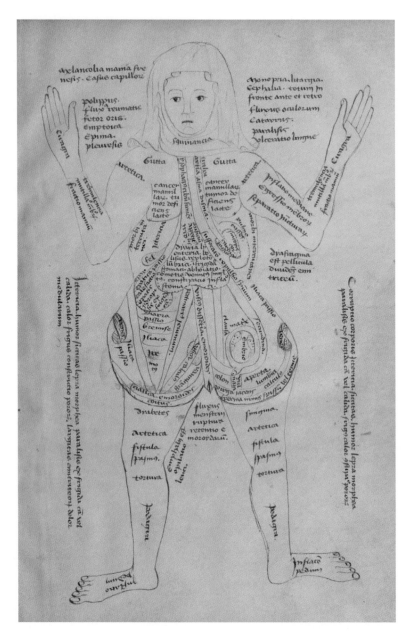

13 Figura infirmitatum, from *Petits Traités d'hygiène et de médecine*
(Ms. Lat. 11229, fol. 31r), *c.* 1400–1425.

14 Albertus Magnus, *De animalibus*, 13th century, folio 134r.

15 Twin memorial figures (*ère ìbejì*), Yorùbá peoples, Nigeria.

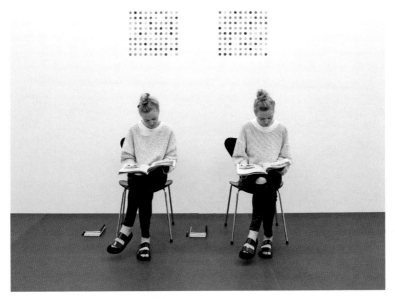

16 Damien Hirst, *Melanie, Stephanie*, 1992, documentation of performance at *14 Rooms* (2014), Art Basel, Basel, Switzerland.

17 The Twin Days Double Take Parade at the Twin Days Festival in Twinsburg, Ohio, 2017.

18 Brian and Eric Deacon as the Deuce twins in *A Zed and Two Noughts* (dir. Peter Greenaway, 1985).

19 Lisa and Louise Burns as the Grady daughters in *The Shining* (dir. Stanley Kubrick, 1980).

THE BRITISH COUPLE Barrie and Tony Drewitt-Barlow have created multiple firsts. They were the first gay couple to have a child through IVF surrogacy, and, thanks to multiple-embryo transfer, they are the first gay couple to have a second IVF baby born by surrogacy. Aspen and Saffron Drewitt-Barlow were born in December 1999. Barrie and Tony made a choice to have twins instead of a single child. And they also chose to adapt the genetic parentage of their twins. Aspen is the biological son of Tony; Saffron is the biological daughter of Barrie. They were born in Modesto, California, with U.S. citizenship, and the Drewitt-Barlows paid $322,000 for Aspen and Saffron to be born to the same gestational surrogate, Rosalind Bellamy, and with this specific parentage. Both were conceived using the donor eggs of a married California woman, Tracie McCune – completing what one journalist called 'a sexless ménage à quatre'.[28] The twins are genetic half-siblings, born in a single gestation to different biological fathers, with a 'biological mother' and a 'gestational mother'. Politically and biologically, their relationship to their parents and to each other has been uniquely queered.[29] The unusual status of their family relationships had legal repercussions. First, the California Supreme Court ruled that the children had no legal mother but after a short legal dispute Barrie and Tony became listed as 'Parent 1' and 'Parent 2' on Aspen's and Saffron's birth certificates. Second, the twins were also the first people in the UK to be registered with two fathers and no mother.

Though it is tempting to see the birth of Aspen and Saffron Drewitt-Barlow as emblematic of our newfound reproductive powers, their case contains an unusual combination of clinical and extra-clinical powers, and a proliferation of twin identities. Aspen and Saffron are neither monozygotic nor dizygotic twins. They fall between the polarizing distinctions that have dominated modern conceptions of twinning, and their sibling relationship suggests that a singular sense of being an 'IVF twin' is an inconsistent identity. Aspen, moreover, is an IVF twin twice. He is a gestational IVF twin to his sister Saffron and a monozygotic, non-gestational IVF twin to his brother Orlando. Orlando is four years his junior.

When Tracie McCune donated her eggs to the Drewitt-Barlows, clinicians also cryogenically froze some of the remaining embryos.

20 Aspen and Orlando
Drewitt-Barlow, 2010.

At least one of these had split from Aspen's embryo – as noted above, it is possible for embryos to split at various points during *in vitro* fertilization. From one of these cryogenically frozen embryos, using a different gestational surrogate, a third baby was born, Orlando. In an embryological and genetic sense, Orlando is a monozygotic twin. But he was born four years after his monozygotic brother, Aspen. The most obvious effect of this is to partially unravel the relationship that twins have to ageing, genetics and generation, three commonly shared experiences that come as part and parcel of twinship. Indeed, being the same age; sharing a genome; experiencing a similar exposure to diets, education and cultural phenomena; and forming common memories are often how people define what makes being a twin different to being born alone. These are developmental and genetic sources of identity shared among twins: the basis for treating them as 'two peas in a pod'.[30] Aspen and Orlando may share a human genome, but they do not coincide with Nancy Segal's criteria for being a twin: 'simultaneous conception, shared prenatal environments, and common birth'.[31] In an era of time-lapsed IVF twinning, the peas-in-the-pod metaphor is literally and figuratively out of time. The different ways by which twins can now be born transform how we might imagine twins as people in a chronological relationship, people who exist according to a shared set of biographical origins. While biology and technology may become more intricately enmeshed in IVF births, the pact between biology and biography can be put out of joint or become untwined.

The case of the Drewitt-Barlow twins is not only an extraordinary tale of technical and social engineering. It is also an extraordinary story of intersectional privilege, specific to the ethical and legal jurisdictions in which the twins' birth took place. Their births would not have been possible in Islamic or Catholic countries where the use of donor eggs and sperm is considered tantamount to adultery (the children seen as 'biotechnological bastards'[32]). This is an extraordinary and culturally specific tale of two white, gay men from northern Europe with the wealth to travel to California and employ the clinical labour of less wealthy, heterosexual women. Following decades of anti-discrimination activism by LGBT communities, the Drewitt-Barlows successfully challenged Supreme Court rulings in the U.S. so that they would be recognized as parents. The UK Home Secretary had to intervene so they could return home as the legal parents of their twins. These IVF babies did far more than challenge what it means to be an IVF baby.

In the era of assisted reproduction, human twinning cannot be viewed as a biological anomaly. Twins can help highlight and change norms, values and behaviours. Almost twenty years after Aspen and

Saffron were born, a survey conducted by Twins Trust, a UK charity that supports the parents of twins, found that 80 per cent of same-sex couples who became parents to twins had used reproductive services.[33] This is one way in which technologies form a kind of reproductive platform, a catalyst for social change. The medical anthropologist Sarah Franklin has noted that surrogacy and IVF have created new kinds of kinship, new kinds of 'biological relative' – making traditional kinship structures different from those that can be created in laboratories.[34] Twins no longer need to be conceived *in vivo* and so they no longer need reproduce the heterosexual models of kinship that tend to form those conceptions.

The possibility of freezing genetically 'identical' embryos and bringing identical foetuses to term at different times sparks fears for those invested in the family as a moral and economic structure, and stirs further anxieties about the future of human cloning and genetic engineering. Colloquially, monozygotic twins are called 'nature's clones', but twins have also been used to define what people imagine clones to be. Conservative definitions of clones usually argue that clones and twins are different because twins share the same experiences. One twin's life does not determine the unwritten future of the other. A clone, according to one report by the U.S. President's Council on Bioethics, is 'a genetic near-copy of a person who is already living or has already lived. This might constrain the clone's sense of self in ways that differ in kind from the experience of identical twins'.[35] Some twins might have very similar genes, but they are not clones in this technical sense, since they develop without a prior knowledge of their biological potential. IVF twins like Orlando Drewitt-Barlow cut a wedge between these neat definitions – he is neither a twin in the conventional sense, living his life in parallel, nor is he a human clone in the sense described above. When you are born an only twin in a society that values being treated as an individual, as a one-off, what happens to the idea that life should be authentic, significant and genuine? In what part of your biology, biography or wider social background do you make a home?

As Orlando grows older he may – or may not – view his brother as a kind of precedential figure, holding before him a sense of possibility, as guide or premonition. Aspen's biography may include the technological novelty of a twin life that begins *in vitro* but that runs askew and diverts from the sequential rhythms of reproductive time that are the pulse of reproductive individualism, generation after generation. IVF twin identities make for increasingly plural relationships and enlarge the ways that people can feel twinned with others and untwined from their closest kin.

* *

I HAVE GIVEN a lot of time to thinking about the lives of these two gay men and their twins, in an effort to show just some of the possibilities afforded by reproductive technologies. And yet the chief cause for people seeking expensive and painful reproductive treatment is infertility. In recent decades, having children in European and North American democracies has been described as a choice, or freedom. Any obstacle to that choice or freedom is to be measured, modified and treated as if it is a biological fact separate from other human values or decisions.[36] One effect of fertility treatment in wealthy societies has been to make involuntary childlessness a condition to be treated, a kind of illness that afflicts individuals and deserves medical treatment. If fertility can now be added to other relatively modern measures of health, such as blood pressure or body weight, then some might describe current levels of infertility as an epidemic or a public-health emergency. This is because modern estimates suggest that infertility affects millions worldwide: roughly 10 to 15 per cent of all adults experience infertility in some form.[37] Yet the question remains: what kind of health ideal is being promoted when we label infertility a kind of illness? And what kind of birth outcome is a true expression of fertility health?

Health specialists usually divide infertility into two kinds: primary infertility affects those who have never had a child, and secondary infertility affects people who have had a child but struggle to conceive again. It is secondary infertility that is particularly prone to regional differences, with access to healthcare and the depth of global wealth inequalities determining how different women access treatment for post-partum sepsis or various kinds of sterilizing infection, for example.[38] In one survey conducted across fourteen sub-Saharan nations, the percentage of women with secondary infertility surpassed 25 per cent.[39] The relative scarcity of IVF clinics in the global South means that new reproductive technologies can be beyond the reach of those populations who are most affected. Twins born through fertility treatment are concentrated among populations that can afford them, and they indicate the concentration of clinical technologies in certain parts of the world. IVF twins may represent human ingenuity incarnate, a triumph of 'man over nature', but they are also a further expression of the gratuitous disparities between rich and poor, those that have access to technologies linked to new expressions of health and those that don't.

One major benefit of multiple embryo transfer is to increase the chances of pregnancy among those who most desperately seek it.[40] Multiple embryo transfer can save time and money, and it gives individuals who have wrestled with their fertility a chance to conceive two babies. It can also be used as a means to increase the rates of conception within clinics that are under pressure to prove that their methods are effective, meaning that twin births are a special kind of marketing tool for the private sector.[41] When twins are viewed as a desirable and elected birth outcome, they are thought to be a 'luxury good'. But to read the growth in twin births as a convenient remedy or a symptom of free-market fertility treatment is overly simplistic. Some see twin pregnancies as dangerous and best avoided at all costs. The promise of IVF twinning for those seeking treatment can stand in sharp contrast to the ways that many medical, legal and state representatives view twin pregnancies. The era of IVF twinning has met with considerable opposition.

Ever since assisted reproduction provoked a rise in twin births, many health professionals and policymakers have reported IVF twin birth rates using the language of contagious disease. For these professionals, infertility is not a public-health concern – it is IVF twinning rates that are the true 'epidemic'.[42] Hence for two leading clinicians, twins constitute 'the biggest challenge facing assisted reproductive technology (ART) specialists in the United States'.[43] The Human Fertilisation and Embryology Authority (HFEA), the UK regulatory organization set up in the wake of Louise Brown's birth, also came to view multiple pregnancy as 'the single biggest risk to the health and welfare of children born after IVF'.[44] When in the early 2000s twin births in the UK were at an all-time high, with one in four IVF cycles resulting in the birth of twins, an HFEA report showed that, in 2001, at least 220 deaths were attributable to the excess risk of multiple births after assisted conception.[45] 'If this number of new-borns died from hospital-acquired infection,' stated the author of this report, 'this would be treated as a major medical scandal.'[46] Too abundant, too many and too multiple. By the early 2000s, evidence pointed to the catastrophic effects of twin birth rates and the burdens they placed on families and on health systems. The fertility industry was revealed to be a big business, a big business with a big Blue Bin. The HFEA tightened its regulatory powers over state-run and pri-vately owned clinics as it linked twin births to higher infant mortality, increased rates of prematurity and lower gestational weight.[47] It is easy to focus on the joys of newborn babies that come in pairs. Some parents, clinicians, regulators and politicians would rather avoid looking into the multiple problems that can beset multiple pregnan-cies. Yacoub Khalaf, a leading fertility specialist, states that 'every maternal risk and stress is exaggerated during twin birth.'[48] Rates of pre-eclampsia, developmental delay, preterm delivery and dou-bled rates of physical and cognitive disabilities all increase in twin pregnancies.[49] Other studies put the chances of a twin being born with cerebral palsy to be at least six times higher than for singleton babies.[50] These are the health risks that affect twin foetuses and babies. Twins, of course, can also increase and intensify medical, financial and parenting stress.[51] The delicate consequences of fash-ioning infertility as a condition or illness, for which treatment is a cure, has led some clinicians to view some forms of treatment to be more harmful than the problem it seeks to address.

Clinicians, public-health policymakers and advisers and fertility experts point to the cumulative effects that twin birth rates have on individuals or healthcare systems. It is not simply that twin pregnan-cies are beset by potential problems but, as was the case for Stephen Mays, these problems can be multiple and compound, and may lead to devastating cases such as mothers who are expecting IVF twins experiencing numerous complications during the same pregnancy. In one report, a 29-year-old mother who had received a double embryo transfer experienced bleeding intermittently during her pregnancy; her twins' growth was restricted, they required regular monitoring, and they were born premature, underweight and by Caesarean section. After two weeks of inpatient hospital care for mother and children, one twin was confirmed to have cerebral palsy.[52] Such case studies seek to inform national policies and restrict the future availability of multiple embryo transfers. All clinicians, stress the authors of one letter, 'must consider singletons the ideal outcome of treatment. If pregnancy rates were equal, it would surely become unethical, in most cases, to perform multiple rather than single embryo transfer.'[53] IVF twins not only constitute the confluence of biology and technology when crafted as a desired gestational ideal, but they also place complex demands on clinicians, who find themselves ethically responsible for higher-risk pregnancies. When regulated according to such public health imperatives, IVF twins are viewed as a negative externality, an industrial problem, an example of market failure.

The HFEA decided to limit the number of multiple-embryo transfers provided by UK clinics. It is not the first time that twin births have been regulated. Ever since the authority was established to guide public and private fertility care in the UK, the issue of multiple-embryo transfer has been a concern. In the Warnock report, published in 1984, the number of embryos transferred in a cycle of IVF treatment was considered to be a matter of clinical judgement:

> We have considered arguments that a limit should be imposed on the total number of embryos that should be transferred on each occasion, but we believe that in each individual case the number of embryos to be transferred must be a matter of clinical judgment on the part of the practitioner responsible for the woman's care.[54]

Since the growth in twin births in the UK, the responsibility for regulating and governing the technological possibility of twins has rapidly shifted away from the 'clinical judgement' of an individual practitioner towards the oversight of the regulative body, the HFEA, which the Warnock report sought to establish and empower. Having monitored the growth of IVF twin conceptions and by documenting the adverse outcomes for mother and child, the HFEA now openly campaigns against IVF twin conceptions with its 'one-at-a-time' policies.[55] These measures include setting national targets for IVF multiples and demanding that all providers have a multiple-birth minimization strategy. The HFEA also demands that all providers audit their strategies to ensure compliance, and report their data to the HFEA.[56] This brings UK legislation closer to other European countries such as Belgium, which makes single-embryo transfer mandatory for first cycles among younger patients, or Sweden, where multiple IVF pregnancies have been reduced to less than 5 five per cent through a similarly strict single-embryo transfer policy.[57] The HFEA claims that an upsurge in single-embryo transfer from 5 per cent to 29 per cent between 2008 and 2014 has caused an overall reduction in the twin birth rate, while recent figures suggest that since 2008 the overall multiple pregnancy rate fell from 27 per cent to 16 per cent by the first half of 2014.[58] Such measures show preventive public health policy restraining complex, commercially oriented treatments, in a market where twin births can be a highly prized outcome. Marcia C. Inhorn's research into IVF clinics in the Middle East identifies the tragic tension between 'women's desperate desires to become pregnant, especially with twins', and the ethical and religious prohibitions surrounding abortion procedures that may be life-preserving.[59] Many will travel thousands of miles to conceive in countries with more relaxed legal codes for fertility treatment, only to discover that their twin babies are seriously unwell and demand a quality of care the new parents struggle to afford.

The complications encountered by twin pregnancies may require choices that are morally and emotionally tortuous. When a twin pregnancy is judged to be dangerous, patients who may have struggled for years to conceive can be asked to decide whether to abort one or both of the foetuses. Foetal reduction is just one such measure, whereby a potassium chloride solution is injected into the heart of one or more of the foetuses.[60] The tangled emotional, financial and vital economies of fertility treatment are dramatically exposed in these decisions, where a life that has been carefully planned and engineered must be aborted.

Reproductive treatments have resulted in the birth of unprecedented numbers of human twins. They have also created moral and ethical decisions, multiple and many, that surround the desirability of those lives. Fertility treatments such as ovulation induction and multiple-embryo transfer create difficult decisions – to bring life to an only twin or no life at all. These technologies manufacture and transform twinning and will challenge the biological basis that has been used to define twins for generations. Sexualized and ableist associations connecting the dangers of twin pregnancy and their need for regulation have returned to twin cultures with renewed intensity. What is striking about the ways in which twin lives matter through the modification of reproductive substances is that twins are no longer 'natural' in the ways once imagined. Each and every twin whose being owes its germinal condition to assisted reproductive treatments is a life that has been managed and co-created by machines.

Twinning is no longer dependent on two people who are conceived, gestated and born together. They are what can be mixed, human and non-human, synthetic and organic, at different times. This brings twins into a world that hosts more twins than ever, in a greater variety than ever. And while many IVF twins may enter the world safely, some will be orphans and others will be lost. With new powers over the creation of life comes greater responsibility for the death that life creates.

8

TWINS ARE PERFORMERS

For more than 25 years the British artist Damien Hirst has invited twins to accompany his prints, displaying them in galleries around the world since 1992. In 2009–10, as part of the exhibition 'Pop Life: Art in a Material World at Tate Modern', Miranda and Felicity Thompson were exhibited with Hirst's dot paintings. Miranda gives her perspective:

> Questions about the painting. Questions about being a twin. Questions about Damien Hirst. Yes, it's pretty. Yes, I like being a twin. Yes, we're getting paid. No, not enough. No, we haven't met Damien. It's over two hours in and the chairs are getting hard. I cross my legs from left to right and poke Felicity to do the same. We have to sit identically too.[1]

Why are twins being put on display at one of the largest museums of modern art in the world? If this episode in Miranda's life was an artistic performance, then it is an episode that was gradually modified, corrected and adjusted for the satisfaction of others. On the one hand, she had little to do, little to say. The work of art incorporates her. A set of rules and assumptions frames her experience:

> I talk to a woman for ten minutes. It's the fourth time she's been to this exhibition. We're her 'favourite set of twins'. I wonder if she says that to all the twins who sit here. I speak to some French people. I delight in their shock, art springing to life and speaking their language. I remember Felicity doesn't speak French. I'm breaking the rules.[2]

Hirst first used twins at the Unfair art fair in Cologne in 1992. The works were named after the participants: *Ingo, Torsten* and *Marianne, Hildegard*. Later, he extended this work at the Tate Modern exhibition, in which the Thompson twins featured. In this version, forty sets of twins were used. In 2010 seventy pairs appeared when the exhibition toured to the National Gallery in Ottawa.[3] The installation is serialized, generic and oddly personalized. Each iteration is unique and the form stays the same. The overall series is named after the first pair to sit for Hirst in 1992: *Ingo, Torsten*. But the title of each performance changes with each set, its name changing with the particular twins sitting in the gallery; changing and remaining the same.

Since 'Pop Life', putting twins in front of paintings has seen further returns for Hirst, at the Ruhr Triennale in 2012, as part of 13 Rooms in Sydney in 2013, and again at Art Basel in 2014. Painting, wall, chairs and twins may be common features of the series, but each performance, and each set of twins, are not and cannot be 'identical' to another. Twins and dot paintings are simultaneously unique and 'identical', diverse yet equal.

Twins are not simply being exhibited or becoming art objects by entering the space of the gallery. For Hirst, twins are already aesthetically charged, with a pre-existing power to capture the attention and imagination of viewers; he uses them to assess and contemplate the relationship between the ordinary and the extraordinary:

> identical twins are like a crazy aberration; they make you look again . . . What I need the identical twins to do [in this performance] is sit in front of two spot paintings, which are two random arrangements of the same coloured dots. Whatever colours you use, the same random arrangement of dots from a certain distance will sort of look the same. They are uniquely different and in a unique arrangement but they look the same.[4]

Hirst has said that twins are compromising, they arrest what we think of as being unique, they are iterative without a sense of repetition: 'Twins don't make logical sense to me. It's like saying something and then saying it again in a different way, but the same way.'[5] As they express this tension between repetition and difference, as pairs and as a population of pairs, Hirst treats them as accomplices in a kind of contemporary art that embraces art's commodity status and the value of art workers, random and alike. So in a call for participants that was widely disseminated before the Tate exhibition, twins were invited to 'sit, stand, talk, read, or do anything else'.[6] They were free to be twins in the ways that suited them, to behave in the exhibition as they chose. But Hirst hired only identical twins, and he insisted on them wearing matching clothes and duplicate accessories, and 'whatever they do they have to do the same thing'.[7] So for Hirst, twins are a crazy aberration provided they act the part, perform, stick to the task of being alike. By knowing the desires of the wonderstruck, twins are used to beguile onlookers. They are both born and paid to be wonderful.

Where there is art there is an opportunity to learn what connects mundane events of education and work, rite and ritual, to other spectacles – exhibitions, displays. In the English language the word 'performance' can evoke a theatrical, musical or sporting event, such as a play, concert or match, as well as the 'accomplishment or carrying out of something commanded or undertaken; the doing of an action or operation'.[8] The word is highly powered and nimble – accomplished – since it names an act and an activity, as well as the business of attributing value to that activity: 'the competence or effectiveness of a person or thing in performing an action; *spec.* the capabilities, productivity, or success of a machine, product, or person when measured against a standard'.[9] The word 'performance' is both the action and the quality of that action, the object and the process, the executed thing and the competence of its executor. And so individuals and groups can be said to carry out many kinds of task or activity, and 'perform' behaviours and identities in the course of being and living.[10] Human life, when viewed through this prism of performance, makes twins 'actors', people who manipulate their presentation of self and selves before 'audiences'.

Previous chapters considered how scientists have used twins to develop ideas about how the world works, biologically and socially, emotionally and historically. Not only do twins perform within these experiments, but scientists train twins to make their ideas spring to life. To enter this performance, twins may consent to be experimented with, worked upon; or they may be coaxed or coerced into participating in the categories that Europeans and North Americans live by, categories that form performance criteria: 'nature' and 'nurture', 'biology' and 'society'. These criteria allow human life to be measured and quantified, optimized and enhanced. As we have seen, twins have played the monster and muse, the marvel or tool, as a shadow or foil by which human and non-human life can be judged. Twins, as the performers that evidence other people's categories, have had limited involvement in designing these experiments or the ideas they validate.

The sociologist and psychologist Erving Goffman (1922–1982) used theatrical concepts to explain how people interact and make sense of how others see them. In Europe and North America, Goffman popularized the idea that interpersonal interactions are always in some way theatrical: social encounters involve 'actors' who play before 'audiences', according to specific scripts and conventions of performance in 'situated activity systems'.[11] Individuals 'pass' in these systems depending on whether they manage audience expectations and whether or not they conceal the backstage activities that make their onstage presentations appear authentic.[12] For a sociologist like Goffman, the dichotomy between authentic and inauthentic performances, as well as the margins that separate success and failure, reveals the norms and rules that govern social life. It is by analysing 'performance' from this perspective that we can see why different individuals or communities are celebrated and adored or punished and shamed.

To return to Miranda Thompson and her kin: she and other twins who work for Damien Hirst confront an audience, 'a crowd around us',[13] for whom an authentic encounter with twins is sought. The instructions given by Hirst, to 'do the same thing', as well as mimic each other's movements and speech, forces Miranda and her sister to enter a kind of performance that was explicitly scripted. The performances are more dynamic than this script, however. Impossible to follow, Hirst's rules are easily forgotten and the people Miranda interacts with have their own ideas about what makes a 'good' twin. She can neither anticipate these nor be sure that each audience member will agree. Visitors compared the Thompsons' performance ('we're her "favourite set of twins"') and reveal the oblique and partially improvised standards that ruled her contribution. She can shock in the moment, but her twin relationship, their performance as twins, has a prior life. Cultures and histories of being twins shape the way Miranda can act, 'pass' or break the rules.

* *

ONLINE GAMING AND social-media identities, wrestling matches and funerals, chess playing, beauty pageants, arable farming, commodity trading – all these activities and the events they stage require different kinds of practical, physical and verbal behaviour, formed by acceptable and unacceptable outcomes in any given situation. Some academic researchers discuss twins and twinning using these ideas, showing how twins perform their twin relationship at particular times, for particular people and in particular places. Contemporary art installations that feature twins are relatively extreme or unusual places to find twins 'performing' twin identities. But here, as in other aspects of twin lives, being a twin is partly guided by codes of value that circulate beyond the gallery's walls.

The British sociologist Elizabeth Stewart has applied some of the central ideas of interactionist sociology to explain how twins manage their public appearances. Stewart calls this the 'drama of twinship', in which 'the relevant actors are twins who, according to the model, may perform in face-to-face interaction, create impressions, manipulate perceptions and seek to control their audience.'[14] Being a twin is not simply a situation you are born into but is a relationship that requires practice – it is developed, negotiated, and worked through and individuated, rather than passively adopted. The American anthropologist Dona Lee Davis also explains that, for her, twins and twinning are a kind of performance: 'the lifelong negotiation of same and different, both within the twin dyad and as twins in a singleton-dominated world'.[15] Twins fashion how they present their twin selves in order to 'actively construct and negotiate their own twinscapes'.[16] Being a twin is not simply a fact of birth or a part of someone's past but an ongoing and creative process that takes place on a stage built by a predominately single-born audience. From this point of view, the idea that twins must negotiate their way in the world is more than a metaphor. It is the tactic used by them to determine what they know and how they feel, and to build an escape route from fatalistic, often biological, accounts of twin identity: 'it is the visible surfaces of our bodies, not genotypes or hidden codes,' writes Davis, 'that shape our senses of I and we.'[17] This sense of twin identity – fed through the idea that being a twin is a performance – makes being a twin a thing that is fluid and contingent, involving countless acts of self-presentation, collaboration, description, critical refusal and resistance.

Twins caught up in the performance of being twins may split and divide their different interests and find their companies, troupes and groups, combining pronouns between me and you, him, her and they, them and we. Negotiation and interaction, framed in a lattice of competing ideals, may bring together the active or passive, free or restrained, novel or repeated; one-off shows or serial acts. Though Stewart is interested in how deliberate interactions between twins and others are constitutive rather than merely expressive of twinship, she is keen to show the ways that audience expectations constrain dramatic possibility. Twins are not free to do whatever they please. If they do, they risk losing their twin status in the eyes of others. In Stewart's understanding, twins only play before audiences according to culturally specific and already available ideas, 'dominant in their cultural milieu'.[18] And so, when social scientists have asked European and North American twins about their twin relationships, they have found three ideals that press upon twins more than others: sameness, togetherness and closeness.[19] Twins are expected to be the same, they are best known and viewed together, and they are expected to be emotional and psychological intimates.

* *

THE MIDWEST AMERICAN town of Millsville, Ohio, was settled in 1817 having been speculated by the Connecticut Land Company.

Twin brothers Moses and Aaron Wilcox arrived two years later. As entrepreneurs they took their twin relationship as seriously as the growth of their real-estate portfolio. Popular American histories like to emphasize that they were physically identical, held their assets in common, married sisters and were close friends. They bought thousands of acres of land and resold parcels to other settlers at discounted rates. They gifted land for the town square and a school on the condition that the town's name should be changed to 'Twinsburg' in their honour.

Since the 1970s the city of Twinsburg, Ohio, has held 'Twins Days'. The annual Twins Days Festival now attracts thousands of twins and is the largest of its kind in the world. Many twins take it as an opportunity to perform, celebrate and participate in what Davis characterizes as 'the twin game' – the earnest and earnestly satirical theatre of twin life. Twins visiting the festival can take part in a Double Take Parade and process through the city in costume, either dressing alike or in elaborate fancy dress outfits (see illus. 17). Entrants are judged each year in the curious spirit of American promenades and carnivals, with the coronation of kings, queens, princes and princesses. Meanwhile, twins socialize, prank and play, shop, eat, enter competitions and interact with a huge number of researchers massed in tents, eager for twins to complete their tests. Davis says twins 'perform or enact the cultural persona of twinship or society's stereotypical caricature of them' because in North American society, 'looking as alike as possible is the performance goal of most twin pairs.'[20] Although not limited to festival events, this annual event for performing stereotypes and enacting *the* cultural and scientific persona typifies something particular to American culture, its science and media, and the way both are communicated around the world to influence how twins are understood.

If I happen to be asked about my family and I mention that I have a twin brother, the first questions tend to concern our physical and behavioural similarities. I have noticed that people are charmed when I say I'm an 'identical' twin or tell them that my brother and I are alike. I have satisfied something that can run deep, a curiosity powered by a preference that twins should look a certain way and be more alike than dissimilar. I have met mixed-sex twins who have simply told me that they are not *real* twins and mothers who say their mixed-sex twins are 'fake twins'. If you aren't alike then you don't pass, and passing as twins in the eyes of others is what is perceived to matter. To extend a commercial metaphor: though twins may be active in these negotiations, they have a limited capacity to attain a satisfactory deal with others. After all, these trading standards are coded by non-twin contemporaries.

European and American ideals of twins and twinning tend to lead to the celebration of visual and behavioural similarities, at the cost of other kinds of likeness or difference between twin siblings and between pairs. Those similarities and differences are structured by those cultures at large, which, as we have seen, have been shaped by the dynamic and uneven interplay and exchange with, and colonization of, other cultures. And twin ideals express wider historical, technological and geographical changes that affect how some twins are valued more than others. The paradox is that while the ideals that are displayed and valued with such enthusiasm at Twinsburg Twins Days – sameness, togetherness and closeness – may be the dominant ideas about twins in some contemporary societies, most twins do not or cannot choose to look or live alike, since human bodies are not easily accommodated to a visual hierarchy of likeness. Now, in an era of IVF and other fertility technologies, there are many more dizygotic twins born each year compared to monozygotic twins, and so there is an ever-greater proportion of twin people slipping away from cultural ideals that demand that twins be similar, proximate and intimate.

In 1993 Wilma Stuart from the Netherlands learned she was pregnant with twins after IVF treatment. When her sons, Koen and Tuen, were born they had different skin tones and different colour eyes. Genetic tests revealed that Koen was the Stuarts' baby but Tuen was not biologically related to Willem, Wilma's partner. Tuen is the biological son of an anonymous donor from the Dutch Antilles whose donated sperm had been mixed up in the IVF clinic. This sperm donor did not want to be recognized as Tuen's biological father. Legally, the Stuart twins share a parent, a gestational and biological mother, but they are also modern-day examples of superfecundated twins who do not share paternity, like the Greek legends, medieval folk tales or theologies encountered in previous chapters.[21] Wilma was rumoured to have had an affair and stood accused, like a medieval noblewoman. The Stuarts describe their experience of ART as violent and disabling, suggesting that ART moves along vertical axes of care and enablement: 'When I finally learned the truth I felt as if I had been raped,' Wilma told one British tabloid newspaper; 'we love our twins equally, but when you discover one of your twins had another father, someone you never saw or knew anything about, then the shock is unbelievable.'[22] The perception of racial disparity between the twins was then singled out as a source of estrangement: 'He [Tuen] really did not like his curls. And his color, he wanted to be white.'[23] In the context of reproductive whiteness, the cultural ideal of sameness and homogeneity reinforces and is reinforced by racialized concepts of belonging and authenticity. Being perceived as 'mixed' – fraternal, dizygotic, superfecundated, black and white – was viewed as a failure that jeopardized Koen and Tuen's twinship, and compromised their ability to attain their 'own content'.

At the age of just nine years old, Koen and Tuen were refused entry to the annual Twins Day Festival because they didn't conform to the so-called 'stereotypical caricature' of twinning, as Davis describes them, and, more importantly, the racialized foundations inherent in the festival's system of valuing and validating twins. As their mother explains:

> I was very disappointed. But I was also a bit angry. I told them that you need to ask yourselves, 'What makes a twin? Is it a biological fact? Or is it the fact that you grow in the same womb, being born on the same day, growing up together? I think these things make a twin.'[24]

Wilma highlights the ways that competing biological understandings of twinning can permeate and inform the ways that twin communities patrol access to who or what gets called a twin. Although the Stuart twins were admitted to the festival in later years, and won a competition awarded to the twins considered 'least alike', their exclusion reveals the subtle, unpredictable ways that their genotypes as well as the surface effects have brought them to judgement. Twins may be able to subvert twin norms and expectations that are managed by single-born society, but North American twins are not neutral players of the game, and nor are they above defending twin caricatures or excluding those that do not fit in.

Twinship is not only a natural or biological attribute of a person, and it is not a wholly constructed social or linguistic category. The uses of twins have had an important influence on how culture and biology have been separated, blended and reconnected. At different times, in different places, the ways twins have been valued have not produced coherent consensus. The practices that make twins useful and that produce old and new scripts for twins to follow, augment or ignore, happen over time, and often involve what Judith Butler has called 'the reiterative and citational practice by which discourse produces the effects that it names'.[25] This circular truism is described by the cultural historian and critic Steven Connor: performance 'presumes what it produces, as it produces what it presumes'.[26] All performances involve the co-option of the performed by performance, and vice versa. Each performance, like a prediction, includes another, folded in its wing as a turbulent or 'flustered' temporal logic. Each performance includes a second – 'the drama of the relation, of compliance and betrayal, between the performing and its performand'.[27] The twin 'performand', to use Connor's term for whatever the performance is trying to perform, serves as a point of departure, a point of reference, and the link between the two that summons expectations. But the formation of 'us', 'we' or 'them' has biographical as well as historical indexes, citations or performands, referring to many rather than one point of departure.

How much control do twins have to act, and to act independently of their siblings and others? Many twins go off script, improvise or refuse 'the twin game' all together, forging relationships beyond traditional family structures. Twins can and do seek ways to 'untwin' themselves, to break up and to spurn stereotypes and expectations.[28] Viewed both historically and globally, twins are a heterogeneous and constantly changing collective, profoundly different in combinations of gender, sexual orientation, race, access to technology, economic power and bodily capacity. If they share anything in common – and this, too, is open to refusal – then it may be the twofold task of reconciling their twin relationship with non-twin individuals, as well as to the historical category of 'twin' with all its local, regional and global variation. Those that veer from, queer or even disavow the status of being a twin may not be threatened by sanction or violence in European or North American cultures, but they may endure foreclosure of the kind experienced by Koen and Tuen Stuart.[29] Adding the practice of citation to the grail quest of twin authenticity may seem convoluted, but it has the benefit of looking both ways: it affords twins who are differently bodied or who undergo physical and psychological transformation to adapt without being cast as failures according to a set of static standards. It ensures that, over time and across different times, the 'right' way of being together can change. Being a twin, with its enduring transformations and separations, the suspended minutes, weeks, years between performances, provides a way of seeing through the dominant norms or expectations of sameness to recognize how twins are profoundly different from one another and with one another.

The cultural historian Hillel Schwartz has observed how eerie likenesses and duplications riddle modern American life. Despite its apparent individualism and appetite for celebrity, North American culture is also a culture of routine replicas and repetitious 'cultures of the copy' that have frequently turned twins and twinning into an affidavit of the real.[30] As in other industrialized countries, the companies that export American products and services, such as the media companies that broadcast American twins across the globe, seek to guarantee or even monopolize standards and control the means of reproduction. One reason to challenge the expectation that twins should be the same, together and intimate, is that it puts them onstage alone rather than showing how powerful and power-laden industries profit from sameness, togetherness and intimacy. Sameness, togetherness and intimacy are key ingredients of advanced capitalism. Twins embody a quality of capitalist power – to make and remake the same.

One way to illustrate the links between how twins appear to others and the economics of those appearances is through modern social media. In recent years there has been a boom in the number of twins using social media to entertain other social-media users. These so-called 'Twinfluencers' monetize their relationships on YouTube, Instagram, TikTok, Twitter and other Silicon Valley platforms.[31] Pairs such as Ethan and Grayson Dolan (the Dolan Twins) or Teagan and Sam Rybka (the Rybka Twins) reach millions of subscribers with dance routines, hoaxes, interviews and memes. Made by and for Internet users in their teens and twenties, their vaudeville routines gather and circulate twins within media that is repetitive and easily shared, made for technical mastery and mimicry, and made global in ways that perforate national and linguistic boundaries that once helped to define what sociologists called a 'milieu'. Just as the Rybkas' acrobatic mix of gymnastics and dance incorporates short-form media and lip-sync mime, the twinship performed by these young online stars is invariably synchronized, identically dressed, energetically cybergenic and carefully edited. Fighting for a favourable current in a social media algorithm means their version of twinship is deeply enmeshed in the digital technologies that are designed to carry their brands around the world. High-profile and increasingly visible versions of twinning play up to, and monetize, already well-established fantasies about having, being or wanting a twin sibling. But they do not only represent a certain kind of twin relationship. They help to shape media that is adapted to and adapting with twin performers, in the production and consumption of audiovisual content.

Through the statues of Rome, the texts written in medieval Europe, and the religious songs, objects and rites that were practised in nineteenth- and twentieth-century West Africa, twins have had 'influence' in multiple ways. Prior to the age of social media, the entertainment industry brought twins to public attention in popular cinema and network programming. In the history of popular drama, the fine line between making twins and enacting twin roles has rarely been straightforward. As it is with contemporary stars of social media, the feedback loop between stereotype and inversion, repetition and riot, crackles in cinema, and the contained sense that twins perform dominant codes or scripts for non-twins shapes as well as reflects twin stereotypes. After all, twins are not singular performers – they come in multiple pairs, in many variations. When twins play twin characters they are performing twinship twice over, with an instantaneous synergy between the body playing and the body being played. Noted examples of twins on-screen include Lisa and Louise Burns as the Grady sisters in *The Shining* (dir. Stanley Kubrick, 1980), actors Brian and Eric Deacon as zoologists Oswald and Oliver Deuce in *A Zed and Two Noughts* (dir. Peter Greenaway, 1985), Michael and Mark Polish's performance as conjoined twins Blake and Francis Falls in *Twin Falls Idaho* (dir. Michael Polish, 1999), or James and Oliver Phelps as Fred and George Weasley in the Harry Potter films (dir. various, 2001–11). While the Burns, Deacon, Polish and Phelps twins play very different characters in those films, their joint performances are underpinned by prior sibling relationships. While on-screen twins may appear to be straightforward performances, what they perform is based on a relationship beyond the world of the film and the secondary drama of a fiction and its reality.

In the surreal *A Zed and Two Noughts*, brothers Oswald and Oliver Deuce change and develop throughout the film, and so does their performance as twins. After the deaths of their wives in the same fatal car crash, the Deuce brothers become increasingly absorbed in their twin relationship. At the film's beginning it is not clear that they are twin brothers. As the film develops, however, they begin to dress alike and even start wearing a specially constructed suit that makes them appear conjoined. The brothers then become the fathers to twins. Their lover Alba – named after the city on which Romulus and Remus founded Rome – renames herself 'Leda' when the infant twins are born and suggests naming the babies Castor and Polydeuces. It is unclear if one or both are fathers and they embrace the children together (see illus. 18). A web of citations extends to Graeco-Roman mythology and its superfecundated twin children. The brothers make and lead a double life, heaping performances upon performances. The meaning of being twins changes over time, both in the film's narrative and in the way that it pulls on the grey area where fictional characters are played by twin siblings and on-screen performances contrast with the biographies of entwined life that make it possible.

There may not be a more famous filmic use of twins as engines of horror than Stanley Kubrick's Grady twins in *The Shining*. In some ways the performand is clear: to be absolutely indistinguishable is a picture of horror. The twin girls appear on-screen together, they are silent or they speak in unison. They are seen in identical dress, standing side by side, clasping one another's hands (see illus. 19). Only when they are shown violently mutilated does their eerie simultaneity appear broken. But if the fictional Gradys have catalysed or facilitated an expectation that twins could or should look and act alike – a claim that would place a heavy burden of responsibility on the fictions of the Hollywood film industry – then their creation was born from a meticulous and unreal sense of duplication.

The Gradys are apparitions or ghosts, who haunt Danny and show his hallucinatory connection to the past and the future. Kubrick's inspiration and model for the twins was a celebrated photograph by Diane Arbus, *Identical Twins, Roselle, New Jersey, 1967* (1967).[32] The monozygotic twin sisters captured by Arbus were photographed at a Christmas party held for twins and triplets, an occasion intended to isolate and observe twinship as a kind of performed identity, and a forerunner to the Twins Day Festival at Twinsburg.[33] While the Gradys in Kubrick's film appear as almost faultless copies, surreal and quasi-supernatural duplicates in dress and behaviour, the 'identical' twins in Arbus's image reflect subtle differences in facial expression, hairstyle and accessories, the fall of their clothes and even the slight wrinkles of their knees. The image is one that sees medium and content permeated by flaws that run against the ideal of visual reproduction. Their image, with its interior series of permutations, also saw serial adaptation in cinema. Performance is not limited to what twins do: the adaptive qualities of visual media multiply twin performands. The invitation that the Grady sisters offer to viewers of *The Shining*, to play 'forever and ever and ever', articulates the iterative repetition of images and visual ideals.

Some of the most commercially successful films featuring twin characters have involved actors who were born as singletons but are transformed on-screen into twin siblings. Mark Hamill's and Carrie Fisher's appearances as Luke Skywalker and Princess Leia in *Star Wars* (dir. George Lucas, 1977), *The Empire Strikes Back* (1980), *Return of the Jedi* (1983) and, more recently, *The Force Awakens* (dir. J. J. Abrams, 2015) and *The Last Jedi* (dir. Rian Johnson, 2017), tell the epic tale of actors playing twins, and twin people emerging to take an epic part in late twentieth-century popular culture. As the *Star Wars* series dramatized the troubled love of twins in one galaxy, in another, the outlandish comedy *Twins* (dir. Ivan Reitman, 1988) featured the unlikely pairing of Arnold Schwarzenegger and Danny DeVito as a pair of highly discordant, dizygotic, superfecundated twins called Julius and Vincent Benedict. As the science of twins reared apart was having its moment in the limelight, Hollywood responded. In this sense, *Twins* is a satire of twentieth-century twin research. The Benedicts are conceived during a bungled eugenic science programme, with Julius Benedict (Schwarzenegger) accruing the Aryan physique of a champion bodybuilder, contrasted to Vincent, played by DeVito, who is affected by a rare genetic disorder that restricts growth (multiple epiphyseal dysplasia, or Fairbank's disease). The film is a synthesis of twin research and its critique, and dramatizes the legacies of state-funded eugenics through the Californian biotechnology industry.

The dramatic and comedic content of twin films is frequently driven by characters either unable or unwilling to recognize themselves as twins, leading for example to the incestuous kiss shared between Luke and Leia in *The Empire Strikes Back* or the moment when Julius first meets Vincent in *Twins*: 'Oh, obviously!' responds the incredulous Vincent, 'the moment I sat down I thought I was looking into a mirror.' Films like these acknowledge that twinning is an act or a play of circumstances, but reserve laughter for those who don't yet realize this. Twinning is presented as a natural form of sameness but one open to differences and confusions, laughs, where the ideals pinned to twins are made amusingly fragile.

Another way of screening twins is to have one actor play a double role, performing both characters single-handedly.[34] There are many examples, but perhaps one of the more influential is David

Cronenberg's psychological thriller *Dead Ringers* (1988). The film illustrates the different structures of recognition and comparison, tension and adoration availed to cinema's twins.[35] In the film, Jeremy Irons stars as two celebrated New York gynaecologists, Beverly and Elliot Mantle. But the film also enacts a number of other real and imagined twin lives. Cronenberg's screenplay is based on a book by Bari Wood and Jack Geasland, *Twins: A Novel* (1977), a fiction-alized retelling of the real-life story of Stewart and Cyril Marcus, identical twin physicians who lived and worked together in New York before withdrawing into drug-addicted isolation and death.[36]

Though the Mantles' clinic is furnished in glass and steel, and appears to employ the most technologically sophisticated instru-ments, the titles that begin the film represent foetuses either in the globular pockets that pre-date early modern writings or within the self-revealing wombs common to early modern anatomic texts.[37] The first title shows twins *in utero*. The film establishes this tension between the history of gynaecology's violent misogyny and the oblique dimensions of human psychology and relationships, with images from sixteenth-century obstetric texts contrasting with the sleek modernity of the Mantles' clinic. Irony builds as Beverly, a char-acter played by a man playing two men, declares that 'there should be beauty contests for the insides of bodies.' The bodily environ-ments imagined by the titles contrast not simply with modern scientific reason but with the visual and rational tools used to judge twins and their performances of twinship.

Early modern theories of fertility and twin birth also affect how Claire Niveau (played by Geneviève Bujold) experiences her body and understands her infertility. When she is told by Elliot Mantle that she has a 'fabulously rare' trifurcate uterus, she asks whether this will make her more likely to conceive multiples: 'could I have triplets, do you think? One in each compartment?' She is made to speak with historically redundant obstetric knowledge, which once thought of twins and higher-order multiples as a consequence of female anatomy and sexual desire. The film's reluctance to present biomedical knowledge as simply progressive, modern, rational or consistent means that the Mantles' psychological dissonance and their emotional co-dependence, drug-induced psychosis and death are hard to disentangle. But if confusion and uncertainty are one of the overwhelming outcomes of this film, then the fact that Jeremy Irons plays both twins in the pair is central. Far from 'the visible surfaces of our bodies' serving as the place where twin identities are being negotiated, twin exteriors are disavowed as the privileged locus or guarantor of human identity, and viewers are made aware that the same body occupies two separate positions in space and time.

Dead Ringers was one of the first films to depict an actor playing twins without the constant use of a body double. Ron Sanders, the editor of *Dead Ringers*, said the cinematic aim was to keep technical secrets off-screen: 'the major thing we want to do was not draw attention to them as twinning effects. We wanted the coverage to be absolutely normal, the way it would be if they were two actors.'[38] Through a combination of screen doubles, split-screen effects and motion-control camerawork – innovative when the film was made – Irons performed both adult twins and appeared on-screen as two separate people. The surreal was made real. These visual illusions 'naturalize' the marvellous effect of a twinship based on visual and bodily replication: Irons appears as two separate beings on the same screen. The biological relationship that twin actors share in *The Shining* or the Harry Potter films makes twinship a rival to cinema's technological power and control. When twinship is fabricated by special effects, it becomes another expression of cinematic control. For Cronenberg the idea of twinning passed into a state of unreality: 'I invented my twins as impossible creatures.'[39] The overall effect is not to confirm the stereotype that twins should look alike but to show one way in which this stereotype is nothing but an illusion, a trick.

In times when twins are routinely chosen and made, assisted reproduction means that twins are no longer the natural counterparts to technology's powers to create duplicates. Films like *Dead Ringers* use technology to make twins perform. Their performance does not reach us through a shared stage; we cannot value their meaning as simply 'authentic' or 'false', 'embodied' or 'artificial'. Twins on these big screens as well as on social-media apps such as YouTube, Instagram and Twitter are people immersed and enmeshed in media. With new technological prototypes come creative engagements with twin people, their shared and discrete histories, and a reorganization of the content, form and geographical spread of type and stereotype.

The uses, expectations and narratives that involve twins can travel and migrate through visualizing them in different media, old and new and mixed. Twins enter technical and popular products and become media objects, distributed into a huge number of national and international contexts. This is not simply a symptom or expression of what twinning is in any given moment in time, nor the satisfying sum of their different discursive representations, but the process by which an ever-changing blend of different ideas, beliefs, customs and practices is materialized. European and North American sociologies of twinning often focus on twins for their data – in this they find categories of twinship, which look a lot like the sociological categories created by those same cultures' academic fields and practices. The risk is that we may overlook the ways that twins change in media produced in their lifetimes, and how the media of both past and future change to accommodate the reproductive variety of multiple people.

Twins have their bodies swept into currents of history whose direction and velocity depend on innumerable practices, crossing and intersecting one another with dizzying complexity. As they perform 'twinning' in and for different communities, they negotiate powers both human and non-human. The idea that twins are beholden to a limited and limiting set of norms, stereotypes or personas overlooks both dynamic twin kinds and the types that go unrecorded by social-science methods, as well as the media technologies that provide new ways of creating and being twins, together or apart.

9

TWINS ARE WORDS

The modern British poet and philosopher Denise Riley begins her book *Impersonal Passion: Language as Affect* (2005) with this observation: 'language is impersonal: its working through and across us is indifferent to us, yet in the same blow it constitutes the fiber of the personal.'[1] Words are obedient to form and are form-giving, taking licence from us to have their way. They affect who we take ourselves to be in flows that may be stilled, tripped, while common formulae persist. Words illuminate us with a strength that gives a shape without shadow, bestowing that fibrous sense of me and mine, you and yours.

As I write these words, my son is powering through his ninth month. Among many other things he has learned lately, a single sound has been forming him, a sound with which he is monumentally pleased: *Da*. Since he has so few other sounds that work for him, *da* is the multi-purpose sound he uses to give comment on more or less everything that happens around him. So you walk into the room – *da!* – quite hungry? *Da!* – really tired? *Da, da, da*. I find it almost impossible not to *da-da* with him to see a smile spread across his inflated cheeks. We have little else to pass between us besides *da*, and because the last eight months have been a bath of noise, *da* feels like it brings all kinds of possibilities. Not least the sense that he may learn other sounds, the first words that will help him share more of his world.

It is common to hear that people learn languages and even that they own them, like possessions, but it might be more accurate to say that languages and the voice are used to make people visible to one another. Languages are a kind of landing light, and stigma is attached to whoever is without language or those by whom language is used in non-normative ways. The voice animates me for you and animates the world in us.[2] The fantasy of words is that they enhance and extend our selves in time and space, so to be called a competent speaker of many languages is to become superhuman, a 'polyglot' (from the ancient Greek *poluglottos*, 'many-tongued'). You 'bite your tongue' to avoid giving offence; find yourself 'tongue-tied' when lost for words. Normative ideals of order, structure, part and whole are in turn understood in such anthropomorphic terms. We prize some writing according to its supposed 'weight' and 'form', its 'strength' and 'energy', or, more negatively, for being 'lacklustre', 'limp', 'weak', 'inelegant', 'ungainly', 'ham-fisted' and so on – as if writing were a sentient and lively organism. And woe betide that writer who returns to feast on an older 'body of work' and is accused of 'self-cannibalizing'. These are not just indications of language's particularly bodily terms of reference, or the able and active kind of body we idealize as language's accomplice; these metaphors of the body embed language in kinship systems that encourage and punish, correct and cajole language learners.

If I labour on about language – to use another corporeal metaphor – it is only because my parents and their friends still recall how my brother and I sat side by side in the kitchen with our faces covered in food, enjoying our post-supper speeches from our high-chair perches. I don't remember giving those speeches, but in every telling they were a part of us, a trick we shared over which we had no control. Speech bubbled from our young mouths and disappeared without trace. We deliberated about I don't know what with babbling sound, in a grammar without sense, roaring together with laughter. In this we were each other's captive audience, a private view of great lolling fabulations spun in *aagahhhs* and *oaaaaaauohhs* and other stuttered sounds, birring and winding up to a pause, a glance, a look, followed with more gleeful laughter. Not knowing how to share the joke with us, the adults would laugh at us – those funny twins, so different to the rest.

Next to the performance anxieties they may have about having twins, the parents of twins may worry that language does not always reach their children in the same way as it does single-born others. As René Zazzo (1910–1995) was keen to investigate clinically, twins have been observed to develop their own languages that others cannot understand. If my son had a twin to *da* with then they might *da-da-da* together to their hearts' content. It is appropriate, then, that these languages that can get shared among twins do not have one name but many. Singletons cannot seem to decide what to call them: secret or autonomous languages, twin-speak, idioglossia or cryptophasia. Languages are spoken by children in ways that appear indifferent to their primary carers, bypassing the common hierarchies that stratify families into linguistic haves and have-nots. Expected, feared, revered and celebrated, twin languages confirm that twin experience takes a different developmental course than that of individual people.

For a time in the 1970s, one of France's most distinguished modern novelists, Michel Tournier (1924–2016), collaborated with Zazzo, France's leading child psychologist of twins. The pair entered an exchange of theories and ideas, stories and fantasies about twins and twin relationships.[3] Zazzo was one of the first child psychologists of language to study twins closely. Tournier's novel *Les Météores* (1975; translated in English as *Gemini*, 1981), contains commentaries on many of Zazzo's clinical insights. Some years after the novel's publication, Tournier returned the favour and contributed to Zazzo's popular work *Le Paradoxe des jumeaux* (The Paradox of Twins, 1984).[4] The dialogue between psychology and fiction is tested throughout *Gemini* as it uses myths, types and archetypes to contextualize the biography of a pair of identical twins.

In contrast to professional observations made by non-twins working in psychological and psychotherapeutic disciplines, the drama of *Gemini* is told from the perspective of twins themselves, Jean and Paul.[5] Tournier uses a series of first-person accounts whose sequence begins with the twins' early life together in Brittany. The twins are the narrators and co-authors of their story. Then, enacting the disintegration of their relationship, Paul becomes the novel's sole narrator. Paul describes Jean's disappearance, a disappearance of dialogue that ends in Jean's silence. The despairing and dis-paired sense of twin estrangement is startling in itself, especially in contrast to descriptions of their shared childhood.

A key insight from Zazzo's clinic was that the language development of twins might be different to that of non-twins. And so physically, psychologically and textually, Jean and Paul are imagined to be a single being named 'Jean-Paul'. The twins are also a play of words, and really nothing more: an effect of language. Their names are not their own, invoking Jean-Paul Sartre, the philosopher of French twentieth-century existentialism, and Jean Paul, the eighteenth-century writer who first coined the German term *Doppelgänger* ('the double'; literally 'double-walker').[6] Together entwined in love and language, in the philosophy of European pairs, Jean-Paul defy the routine alienation that Sartre claimed was integral for the formation of social being.[7] The sleeping twins

> reverted to their most private selves – reduced to what is deepest and most unchanging in them – reduced to their *common denominator* – they are indistinguishable. It is the same body entwined with its double, the same visage with the same lowered eyelids presenting at once its full face and its right profile, the one chubby and tranquil, the other pure and clear-cut, and both entrenched in a mutual rejection of everything outside the other.[8]

When writing *Gemini*, Tournier found that there was little point in telling others about his interests in twins. 'People knew them already, *and recited them to me in advance*. I congratulated myself: it was proof that my subject was of a mythological nature.'[9] Jean-Paul as a Janus-faced composite have their personal pronouns merged – they are known by the plural 'they' or impersonal 'it'. In language and body they are one and two: 'the same body entwined with its double' and 'the geminate cell'.[10] The scene above is also typical of the novel's absorption in a canon of twin stories, the book's engagement with twin myths a way of rethinking what writers are doing when they engage with a subject which their readers seem to know and recite in advance. Relinquishing the power to transform the meaning of twins because these are 'as changeless as the constellations',[11] Tournier's framing of twins makes them and him a node, channel or vector within a network of significance that is novel, his novel, fictional but also already familiar.

The performance of twins is a linguistic accomplishment. Jean-Paul perform the non-linguistic basis of their communication:

> With their mouths full, the twins embark on one of their long, mysterious confabulations in the secret language known in the family as Aeolian . . . now they are re-creating their geminate intimacy by adjusting the direction of their thoughts and feelings and by this exchange of caressing sounds which can be heard as words, wails, laughter or simply signals, whichever you like.[12]

Zazzo's clinical work revealed possible delays in language acquisition among twins. The private language spoken by Jean-Paul in *Gemini* is described as a 'language of the wind' or 'Aeolian' – a fictionalized instance of what Zazzo called 'cryptophasia'.[13] By definition, a cryptophasic language is shared between specific twin pairs. *Gemini* draws oblique parallels between the exclusive acoustic range of non-verbal sounds specific to these twins, and the legibility of oral and written stories transmitted across time, such as the tradition of historical-novel writing in which *Gemini* participates. Like laughter, twin languages extend across the specific and mythological, breaking partitions between the personal and impersonal, the communicable and non-communicable. But Tournier leaves readers in no doubt about how twin language emerges from 'the silence of visceral communion and rises to the verge of speech used by society, but without ever reaching it . . . It is a dialogue of silences, not of words.'[14] Paul says that in Aeolian, '*the words are incidental, silence is the essence. This is what makes geminate language a phenomenon absolutely incomparable to any other linguistic form.*'[15] With Jean-Paul communicating either through cryptophasic means or by silent gesture, Tournier imagines a twin relation that is the basis for a kind of communication so personal it is impersonal.

* *

FRENZIED MEETINGS OF modern media technology, science and mass consumerism have led to the celebration of twinning in the late twentieth and early twenty-first centuries. High levels of public exposure have changed how Europeans and North Americans feel twins could and should behave, bringing to the boil a set of anxious and delightful stories about how twins communicate. Grace and Virginia Kennedy were two unsuspecting stars of this period. Born in 1970 in Columbus, Georgia, to a German mother and American father, they later moved to the suburbs of San Diego, California. By the age of six they came under the scrutiny of paediatric doctors, speech therapists and psychiatrists for their inability – or refusal – to speak a language that others understood. Poto and Cabengo, as they called themselves, were born economically poor, to parents in low-paid jobs. They were left at home in the care of their German-speaking grandmother. With money short and their parents frequently out of the house, they were isolated from other children. Their father complained that he couldn't understand them and they were referred to a local hospital, where medics and speech therapists assessed them. They couldn't understand them either. By the age of seven their reputation had spread to media headlines ('TWIN GIRLS INVENT OWN LANGUAGE') and to the pages of *Time* magazine, which declared them 'the world's most celebrated twins'.[16]

Poto and Cabengo caught the attention of French avant-garde director Jean-Pierre Gorin, who in 1980 made a documentary about them, *Poto and Cabengo*. In an interview Gorin explained why he wanted to make the film: not because he was wowed by the Kennedys' savant insularity or linguistic creativity but because it was clear to him that their social isolation, their parents' rapid Southern American English, spliced with the German of their monoglot grandmother, allowed them to cultivate a tongue of their own. And very happy they were, at least according to Gorin's film, as they can be seen energetically, playfully, riotously haring through libraries, hauling the books from their shelves. Their rehabilitation started as the key to their secret unravelled: *pinit, putahtraletungay* ('finish, potato salad hungry'); *nis, Poto?* ('this, Poto?'); *liba Cabingoat, it* ('dear Cabengo, eat'); *la moa, Poto?* ('here more, Poto?'). It was not the twins who were the real oddities for Gorin but the norms and expectations that they made strange, turning the world of words upside down and making collective rites and norms appear abnormal: 'the singsong of the twins', he said, 'reveals the shaky grounds of institutional power.'[17] The structures of family, media and science were incapable, for a time, of putting the twins in their place, but they did eventually. And so, for Gorin, the twins and their language 'offered a marker for the way people around them used language and were used by it, and were spoken through it'.[18] Like so many others who have encountered twins before him, Gorin saw them as a kind of optical device through which he could see (and reconceive) the world and its politics. While the film begins with the question 'what are they saying?' it comes to answer a quite different one, closer in kind to this: 'why should their language be such a threat?'

On the other side of the Atlantic were two other twin sisters, June and Jennifer Gibbons. Their parents were first-generation migrants from Barbados and the twins were born on a Royal Air Force (RAF) base in colonial Yemen in 1963. Their father was employed by the RAF and they spent their early life moving about England, to one rural RAF base and then another. Teased, bullied and racially abused in these provincial English places, the twins became increasingly intro- verted at school and at home. They stopped talking to everyone but each other, including their parents, and were heard conversing in a language others couldn't decode, a twin creole of their own. They moved again in the early 1970s to Pembrokeshire, in west Wales, where, mute and often physically motionless when under the scrutiny of others, they encountered more racism. They took refuge in each other. Social services, teachers, therapists and psychiatrists all tried to inter- vene, to perforate the silence, yet the girls appeared to resist attempts to draw them into a wider shared world and instead, as teenagers no longer at school, they devoted their energies to unsuccessful attempts to write novels and form romantic relationships with local white boys, who invariably took advantage of them. Still electing not to speak, and thrilled by a string of minor crimes, their lives then turned upside down. They were arrested, detained and put on trial. The justice system dealt with them as outsiders in multiple and compound ways. Their twin relationship and their refusal to communicate was too personal, too exclusive, and their behaviour judged a threat to society. The

21 June and Jennifer Gibbons.

courts heard medical opinions that recommended a psychiatric diagnosis. In the early 1980s, juvenile offenders in the UK served a maximum of two years. June and Jennifer Gibbons were sent to Broadmoor Hospital, a high-security psychiatric institution, for eleven years.

During their imprisonment, the Gibbons sisters continued to live in silent isolation, both together and apart. They were often separated, as they fought. Their relationship was far from harmonious. Finding them heavily supervised and frequently sedated, mental-health activist and journalist Marjorie Wallace got to know them and brought their case to national attention, first in the news media and then later in her book *The Silent Twins* (1986). Jennifer died in 1993 and, as part of a pact the sisters made before her death, June agreed to break her silence and gave interviews to magazines and newspapers about her sadness but also her sense of newfound freedom.

The development and use of language has played an important role in how people organize themselves and other members of the natural world into hierarchies of intelligence. The power of verbal communication has been central to the history of European philosophy and politics, where the greatest intelligence and agency have been attributed to those who speak, and can control others with language. But this is part of a wider system of thought that has stratified life according to notions of 'animacy' – the perceived sentience and liveliness of person, animal or thing.[19] Twins who develop private speech or are happy in silence may face sanction in such a world, since verbal communication (and the mastery of verbal communication) has been used as a way to differentiate humans from and elevate them above other kinds of living and non-living being. The Kennedy and Gibbons twins created a verbal envelope, an enclosure that was seen as exclusionary. Deviant uses of language by twins threaten something fundamental to the authoritarian power of family, state or market, since these languages appear rich in tone, timing, feeling and rhythm, having all the texture and humour and variation of common speech, but make outsiders feel superfluous. And so twin language is considered a threat or risk, subverting the assumption that language makes us equally social. When held against singleton peers, this is perceived by parents, as well as by the speech and language therapists who advise parents, as yet another hazard, risk, problem or deficit that faces their twin charges. Twin languages are another reason to worry about the behaviour of twins rather than resist the standards by which they are judged. And while the Kennedys and Gibbonses are female, it is male twins who are thought to have a higher risk of developing language delay as young children.[20] For some developmental psychologists, it is not delay that is a concern but the way that the uses of language between twins may mask or interact with long-term language development.[21] But the long-term consequences are not well understood, and rarely is the communication of twins wrested from the normative ideals of child development. Twins, as they grow older, continue to develop their communications or, in some cases, learn to keep their silence.

* *

THERE ARE BIOGRAPHIES and autobiographies about the vagaries and idiosyncrasies of personal experience. These are stories that detail the uniqueness of a life. Then there are those narratives that describe a world, an existence in that world, and what it means to live as a social and cultural subject.[22] These are stories that detail life's common ground. Biography and autobiography can be divisive genres, since they make us choose between describing the lives of individual people, their achievements and times, and illuminating subjects formed in a world of others. The literary scholar Caitríona Ní Dhúill argues that contemporary life writing has taken an individualistic turn: 'we go to biography asking, "what was she like?" rather than "who else was she like?"'[23] When twins write accounts of their lives, these questions blur into one another. Twin narratives are always double-voiced, as autobiographies *and* biographies, as stories written by two people and stories told by one about the other, and vice versa. The implications are complex. When lives are written and narrated by twins as co-authors, some of the distinctions between individuals and 'subjects', the personal and the 'cultural', come to fray. Co-authored twin narratives assume a structure of likeness between their narrators and their narrated subjects, a likeness that shifts between an authorial 'I' and its shadow 'we', a likeness and descriptive agency shared by two people.

Identical twin sisters, Pamela and Carolyn Spiro are the subject of their book *Divided Minds: Twin Sisters and Their Journey through Schizophrenia* (2005). It tells the tense, tender and occasionally tempestuous story of a sibling relationship and a shared 'journey' into an emotional and psychopathological terrain. Though the title may suggest that both sisters are similarly afflicted by ill health, Pamela's psychotic experiences, hospitalizations and medical treatment contrast with the experience of her sister, Carolyn, who trains as a psychiatrist and journeys 'through schizophrenia' in relation to her sister. It is not a story of triumph, overcoming or 'recovery', since Pamela's suffering is not redemptive. That these dual narratives are interwoven – the story of being twins on the one hand and the story of one twin's experience of schizophrenia on the other – is one of the dispersing effects of writing and communicating as twins, as well as a reminder that the purpose of twin life is not simply to be chosen from a list of available cultural performances or storytelling devices. Co-authorship, to these twins, means that the subject of the work is also its constituting premise and the grounds for creativity.

The Spiros approach their autobiographical texts as diarists. Each sister writes her account in the first person singular, with a heavy use of the present continuous tense. These passages vary in authorship and episodic duration: some episodes describe events that last minutes or hours, others cover months or years. The gaps, variations and shifts in perspective reveal the different kinds of editorial decision-making that come with writing together. European and North American readers are habituated to assume a single author, where authorship and authority are legally and creatively geared towards an individual with a proper name. Only with explicit guidance does a text get read differently.[24] The persistent challenge when reading *Divided Lives* involves negotiating what kind of life emerges through the cumulative effect of its episodes, and what kind of regulative effect the authors' twinship has on their experiences and their interpretation. Usually, when we read an autobiography, we separate the 'I' that appears on the page from the person we must imagine has written it: 'the I which writes the text' and the 'paper-I'.[25] But in twin narratives the 'I' that writes and the 'I' that is written responds to the possibility and actuality of a 'we', and a sense of 'we' that reads, narrates and is described.

The Spiro sisters both divide up their text into separate, interwoven passages, and use a 'we' that is presented as prior to, rather than simply occurring through, the process of writing. Carolyn describes her early life as one characterized by 'mutual dependence', and explains that in their first year of college, 'we divide our world into hers and mine: Pammy writes, I dance; I sing, she paints; and so on. As long as the competition is eliminated, we can enjoy a degree of mutual dependence'.[26] So long as their perspectives are differentiated, a single world written apart, their interlaced lives can be understood as 'mutual' rather than indistinguishable. Efforts to manage difference and sameness take an unexpected structuring role: not as unachievable fantasies but as compromised or shunned realities. Carolyn describes their childhood in terms of authorial agency and its relationship to their shared language and cognition:

we can finish the other's sentences, sense each other's thoughts, and tune out the rest of the world. Pammy understands me completely; she is my best friend. Through high school I am addicted to this ease, but inside I sense it isn't good for me and I'm lonely.[27]

From this moment, Carolyn decides to 'start thinking of myself as *I*, not as *we*'.[28] It is this moment of pronominal distinction and writerly difference that is given retrospective value later in the work when Carolyn reflects upon the different courses of their lives: 'she's lived her life and I've lived mine ever since high school. I don't know where she's been, let alone what she's done'.[29] The suggestion, of course, is that twins in general, and these twins in particular, can – indeed did – live each other's lives; they did once know where and what the other had done. In the shadow of convergent, authorial identities – those who finish another's sentences – the co-authored twin narrative can take shape. In the rustle of sounds and experiences, felt to be prior to the linear progress of singular identity, something like an agency of twin narrators emerges, one whose generative, dynamic, material conditions may produce stories like *Divided Minds*.

The process of composition is not without difficulty. Editorial decisions and disagreements are foregrounded. Seemingly innocuous events are given lifelong significance. One explicit staging of composition occurs when the sisters meet to write together, a writing session that results in an explosive argument about who is the 'main subject' of their book and who is 'only a supporting actor'.[30] Concerning an event from their childhood, the twins revive a bitter memory of jealousy and resentment. The argument is one that has been purposively woven into an earlier part of their book and revisited. The 'scene of writing' is not solitary, and the narratives generated there do not produce agreement. Foregrounding the compromises, jealousies and restrictions of a twin upbringing and extending the consequences into adulthood produces the feeling that the content of their disagreements is less significant than their textual presentation. When Carolyn is accepted to study medicine at Harvard, she risks throwing their different situations into sharp relief. Carolyn recalls:

I call Pammy the next day. She's still at Brown. After a few minutes of chitchat, I tell her.

'Harvard? Oh, wow. Really?' Deep breath. 'Congratulations!'

'You don't hate me?'

'Why should I?' She sounds genuine. 'Lynnie, I couldn't do what you're doing. Your going takes the burden off me.'

Burden? What does she mean?

We talk and it feel [*sic*] like old times. Things are getting better, she assures me. She'll graduate soon too. Not so sure what she'll do after that. Maybe for once she'll follow in *my* footsteps. We laugh. That would be reversing roles but good.[31]

Immediately following this, on the next two pages, we read of Pamela's account of this conversation:

Then she says she's gotten in.

'Congratulations,' I manage, feeling a band tighten around my chest. 'That's really cool. So, where?'

For the briefest of moments, she pauses. 'Please don't be upset. Pammy –'

'Where?' The band clinches two notches tighter. I know her answer. *Of course. Where else?*

'Harvard.'

I swallow. *Harvard.* For the first time in years, I feel the weight of what has happened to me. I am not supposed to cry. I am not supposed to care. But I am supposed to say something, brave and gracious.

'*Harv–* Harvard?' I croak at last. 'Well, I couldn't do it.' And I couldn't. That hurts like hell. We talk about a lot of little things, I tell her everything is fine, that I'm happy for her. I *am* happy for her. But when we hang up, I burst into tears.[32]

What was said during this conversation? Recorded dialogue, dispersed by interior monologue, proves the signature style of both accounts. And yet in tension with this stylistic homogeneity are clear discrepancies, not just on the level of interpretation but also on the level of factual content. Was it the news that Carolyn has been admitted to medical school or the fact that she has been admitted to Harvard that prompted Pamela's congratulations? Is Pamela surprised or not by her sister's choice of school? Does Carolyn fear Pamela's reaction? Does Pamela express relief or defeat at her sister's news? With these questions unanswered we are invited to see the text in a state of dissonance. The discrepancies between accounts mean we must also acknowledge how these particular speakers are simultaneously co-authors and co-readers, autobiographers and the subjects of biography; models, collaborators, protagonists and antagonists all at once.

Schizophrenia is an illness that is often characterized as having an effect on language. Its symptoms may include a disturbance of linguistic functioning.[33] It can disrupt how someone describes what is happening to them and what has happened to them in the past, clouding how events are understood and are meaningfully shared.[34] Despite shared concerns about living 'mutually', the transformative effect of Pamela's illness is repeatedly seen as a threat to a 'we' of resemblances that *Divided Lives* utilizes as a kind of guarantor. 'This person', writes the estranged and incredulous Carolyn about her sister's catatonic states, 'can't be my twin'.[35] Carolyn finds it impossible to reconcile her memories of her 'with the person schizophrenia has so wrecked'.[36] When Carolyn visits her sister in hospital she fails to recognize Pamela, finding a 'strange, bedraggled person' in her place; the extremes of twin sameness and difference are seen as a personal threat: 'To the rest of the world she isn't my twin; to the rest of the world she is nobody – she is an eccentric, fat, crazy, lumpy-purse-waving beggar.'[37] Carolyn's shock is animated by specific behavioural, bodily and socio-economic prejudices, reflecting the change that she sees in her sister but also the change she sees in her sister compared to herself – the person Pamela has become is no longer the person that was so similar to Carolyn.

Rather than isolating and atomizing her illness, Pamela's health is already social, and her twinship is a measure of social and individual change. It is not an essential or 'inner' aspect of their selves but an enduring relation. 'If Pammy's life is at stake,' writes Carolyn, 'so is mine.'[38] 'You can't kill yourself,' Carolyn tells the suicidal Pamela, 'because you'd murder me too.'[39] It is not easy to read Pamela's illness without the structuring presence of her twin, without the implicitly 'healthy' Carolyn as an alternative or model, without the pre-existing condition of belonging to or being bound to one another. This is of particular relevance to those definitions of schizophrenia that focus on 'failure[s] of narrative competency'.[40] Pamela's retrospective descriptions of her drug-induced catatonia and psychotic experiences stress social and cognitive forms of disconnection or miscommunication – failures to speak, understand or be understood. Her delusions, paranoia and auditory-verbal hallucinations leave her without a clear distinction between inner and outer spheres: 'I have no privacy at all, not even in my own head.'[41] These experiences are, however, lucidly described: 'I am connected to nothing, able to hear without responding, to think without pursuing any train of thought.'[42] The ability to describe what has happened is achievement shared. They offer one another a kind of narrative anchor, a position from which to work through an improved set of circumstances that is not absolutely dominated by mental ill health. Co-authorship transforms how Pamela experiences and reflects upon the changes in her life and the effects of her illness:

> As I read Lynnie's [Carolyn's] description of my hospitalizations in the fall of 2003, which ECT [electroconvulsive therapy] has largely erased from my memory, I am by turns horrified and ashamed . . . I've been living inside the nightmarish fragments of a time and country beyond understanding, an everlasting present that has no connection to anything anymore. I've been literally in a world of my own. Small, terrifying, and constricted as this is, it's all I know.[43]

Passages like these challenge the individuation that accompanies ideas of writing, as it does the desire to self-create or even regenerate during or after illness. Pamela does not and cannot make sense of her hospitalizations – 'I acted solely upon impulse, delusion, and hallucination. That was my reality'– and her sense of loss is not straightforwardly recovered with her sister.[44]

Before it became a successful Netflix documentary film directed by Ed Perkins, Alex and Marcus Lewis published their twin biography, *Tell Me Who I Am* (2013), to give a measure of life and health through their twin relationship. Both brothers find writing difficult because of their dyslexia, and the book was written with the assistance of Joanna Hodgkin. She gives an external viewpoint that a twin biography like *Divided Minds* forecloses. By introducing this example, I want to find another vantage point on how being a twin is communicated.

The book begins in 1982 as Alex is involved in a motorcycle accident at the age of eighteen. His brain injuries leave him without his childhood and teenage memories: all the memories from before his accident. He never recovers them. Instead, on waking from a coma, he recognizes only his twin brother, Marcus, and is reintroduced to the world with the help of his twin. As an aide, supplement and cognitive prosthesis, his brother Marcus is able to explain why and how things are as they are: '"What Marcus did for me in those early days [after the crash] was to fill in the gaps," says Alex. "I always say to people, 'I remember this,' but I'm only remembering what Marcus has told me. So I've basically got his memories in my mind."'[45] While Alex claims to have his brother's memories, these are revealed to be a flawed and incomplete archive. Alex's memory deficit is also a structuring device in the biography.

Throughout their late teens and early twenties, 'Alex had become totally dependent on his twin. Even when they were apart that sense of dependency never went away.'[46] Their lives are described as being 'enmeshed'; they live 'as if they were one person, as if Marcus was [Alex's] feelings and his story'.[47] Yet, in the circular fashion that may be a recurring hallmark of co-authored twin stories in which acquired medical conditions are structured by prior twin interactions and intimacies, the developmental conditions of twinship are presented as a precondition for making the story of acute amnesia inseparable from what the twins were, are and can be. When referring to the time before the motorcycle accident, before Alex's dependence on Marcus for a childhood he could no longer remember, their relationship is described as an enduring, exclusive and enveloping 'twin world', one that 'no one else could understand'.[48] The meaning and significance of their subsequent discordance in childhood memory cannot be disentangled from the meaning and significance given to this quality of being born and remaining together. With echoes of the Spiro sisters' co-dependence, their childhood is described in the following way:

> They had something that no one could take away: they had each other.
>
> No matter what was going on around them, they existed in their own private twin world. They did everything together. At almost every moment of their childhood, whether they were being bullied at school, being terrorised by Jack or carted around by their mother, getting up early to clean the shoes and clear away the dishes from the night before or retreating to their icy-cold room from the rest of the family, their fellow twin was a constant presence, a companion and a refuge, a cheerful reflection and a source of complete acceptance and approval.
>
> In some essential way, everything that happened outside their private bond was an irrelevance. 'When we were little, no one could touch us,' Marcus told Alex. 'We were in our own little bubble world. Always together.'[49]

For Alex, the imperative to 'tell me who I am' is enclosed by a greater demand that is abundantly present in passages such as this: to 'tell me who we were'. The primary response to the latter is to characterize their relationship as being immune from and almost indifferent to motorcycle accidents, sexual abuse and memoir writing: 'everything that happened outside their private bond was an irrelevance.' This is an overpowering claim to a twinship that transcends physical and emotional damage – they were, are and will always be twins. Their relationship challenges the personalized and privatized understandings of selfhood that assume the easy translation of experience into writing. Sidonie Smith and Julia Watson write that 'it is easy to think that autobiographical subjectivity and autobiographical texts have little to do with the material body. But the body is a site of autobiographical knowledge, as well as a textual surface upon which a person's life is inscribed.'[50] Though this might provide a sense of authenticity to some, the individualism, unitary exclusivity and possessive singularity implied by 'the body' and 'a person's life' fail to accommodate the conceptions of twin subjectivity provided by texts like *Divided Lives* or *Tell Me Who I Am*. The authors do not fully overcome illness or abusive pasts through singular stories; they cannot claim executive power; and their stories maintain forms of dissonance and fragmentation that demonstrate productive kinds of disparity felt between each contributor. These stories make more sense in terms of two lives whose significance is distributed across differently experienced and experiencing bodies.

As in *Divided Minds*, *Tell Me Who I Am* stages scenes of composition to provide opportunities to understand the shift between the entanglement of twin lives and an emergent status of inscription. When an offer to produce a book is suggested to Alex and Marcus they see it as an opportunity to translate a clear sense of experiential enclosure into an object, a text, a story that tells of their unusual sibling relationship, but also how the process of narrative entwinement informs the presentation of that relationship. This process takes unique experiences and understands them through distributed, communal narratives of lived multiplicity: 'their journeys had been so intertwined there was no way one could be described without the other. It would be a chance, once and for all, to sift through all the conflicting narratives and create a solid story'.[51] Dialogical, psychological discordance and authorial determination are pursued in the midst of lived multiplicity; they take place and make sense against a prior notion of being somehow en-bubbled, inseparable, untouched.

Our access as readers to their past also depends on what Marcus can (or is prepared to) remember. It is gradually revealed that their childhood was marked by abuse at the hands of their mother, stepfather and their friends – years of sexual exploitation, servitude and psychological degradation. At the age of eighteen, at the time of the accident, Marcus had begun to repress his memories of their abuse. Rather than confront these painful experiences, he chose not to tell Alex about them. Through the course of the book, Alex forces Marcus to excavate his distorted and conflicted memories of what happened to both of them.

The night of Alex's motorcycle accident is recounted on three separate occasions. The first two descriptions tell how Marcus was away in Scotland at the time of Alex's accident. Marcus had a premonition that something was wrong and travelled through the night to be at his brother's bedside. On the third telling, where both twins are present with Hodgkin, direct dialogue carries the content of their past and the event of its active recovery. In this third iteration, a quite different sequence of events is produced. Marcus, rather than being in Scotland during his brother's accident, is back in the family house. With this revelation comes other memories associated with their childhood. He recalls how their mother abused them, how he repressed these memories and how their recovery is figured as constituting not only 'a' story about their childhood but 'the' story:

'I haven't thought about it for years. She used to make us touch each other in that bed, Alex.' He broke down completely. 'I remember! I just remembered that. She really was a horrible woman!'
'I didn't know that,' said Alex quietly.
    'That's why I don't remember anything. Because I don't want to remember anything! Much nicer that I was in Scotland.'
    'Once remembered,' said Alex, 'it can be let go. I'm a great believer in that. I think you did really well, Marcus.'
    'No!' insisted Marcus. 'For me it's never about getting rid of it. It's about telling the story.'[52]

The activation, recovery and validation of their autobiographical memories depends on thinking together. Although Alex is told what happened to him as a child, he can neither claim to be the creator of these memories nor possess them as his own.

What philosophers of cognition have called the 'extended mind' may help to make sense of these shared autobiographical narratives. Philosophers Andy Clark and David Chalmers have argued that all human cognition is achieved through acts of cognitive coupling and extension:

the human organism is linked with an external entity in a two-way interaction, creating a coupled system that can be seen as a cognitive system in its own right. All the components in the system play an active causal role, and they jointly govern behaviour in the same sort of way that cognition usually does.[53]

Clark and Chalmers imagine a man called Otto who suffers from a mild form of Alzheimer's and carries a notebook. The notebook is not simply an object like any other; it is instrumental to Otto's ability to solve everyday problems, create knowledge and act on his beliefs. They concede that for 'an unusually interdependent couple, it is entirely possible that one partner's beliefs will play the same sort of role for the other as the notebook plays for Otto'.[54] That is to say, twins may share cognitive systems to usurp the 'hegemony of skin and skull' dominant in cognitive science. Alex and Marcus certainly demonstrate how minds extend and how 'information lies beyond the skin.'[55] The environment they have shared and the environment they co-produce, as well as the memory deficit that exists for one and not the other, has led information to exist between their skins. Stories like these show that being born with another can afford alternative ways of describing, sharing and managing change throughout the course of entwined lives.

Commenting on the linguistic co-dependence of twins, Dona Lee Davis has observed that 'if there is one thing twins know how to do, it is to interchangeably lead and lean while sharing the stage.'[56] Davis bases this observation on the interviews she has done with identical twins at large American twin festivals. Turn-taking, leading and being led may be skills developed by twins interviewed at these kinds of events. But twins can pass lives in the absence of their twin sibling. Many twins cannot share a stage. They and their siblings are unable or unwilling to be together. It is so much more difficult to acknowledge and document the lives of twins when they are spent in silence, in isolation, when the ties of twin communication have been lost. One rare example of this kind of writing is given by British journalist and writer Jeremy Seabrook: 'My brother and I were separated at birth,' he explains in a short biographical piece published in 2006, 'even though we lived in the same house with the same mother, for the first eighteen years of our lives.' He continues: 'all we had in common was a shared introversion, and this made communication between us even more difficult.'[57] Their mother jealously guarded and divided their affections and encouraged the twins, who were different in physical appearance, to cultivate their differences. They also lived through a moment in British history when the class system 'emphasized competitiveness, disunity and division; the dislocations of kinship were aggravated by social circumstances'.[58] Rather than enjoy the 'sweetness of uninhibited companionship',[59] they were emotionally, educationally and vocationally streamlined into irreconcilable situations, encouraged to take their separate lanes.

Jeremy was educated at an independent school and then studied at the University of Cambridge. He became a successful journalist and writer. His brother studied at a state school and joined the army rather than going to a university to study. Afterwards, he worked in the construction industry, an occupation that fatally exposed him to asbestos. Their separate paths through life rarely crossed. When they did, as they did at their mother's funeral, conversation between them had become impossible. At the funeral, Jeremy's brother could say simply, 'I'll shake your hand and that's it.' After that, years passed until the news of his brother's death reached Jeremy 'like confirmation that the body of a missing person had been found after a long search'.[60] In the absence of communication comes the drama of its lost potential, the terrible conclusion that even this, an intimate imaginary, can no longer be realized.

The lives of the Spiro, Lewis and Seabrook twins, like the fictional Jean and Paul, depart from the performance ideal made familiar to us in the previous chapter. Although absolute identicalness plays a part in some of their stories, it is an experience that is recalled as an intimacy that has long past, and, if it has been possible for them, then it can be the reason they became separated. Twins are rarely alike, together or intimate – their sameness is often made impossible. Being alike is remembered in these stories as an image and an achievement of language, an experience that the process of writing negotiates but can never fully recover or perfect.

Writing together may build and develop a relationship, but it cannot dissolve its co-authors into a single authorial being, and there are important reasons why this is neither possible nor desirable for twins. Narrative follows words, and, like all words, the word 'twin' is not really one but a congregation of many. English words are silted with the contours of related others as riverbanks are to the ancient braids of previous flow – Middle English (*twinne, twynne*) and Old English (*ġetwin, ġetwinn*) each derived from a previous Proto-Germanic twoness (*twinjaz, twinaz*) that may have sprung from a Proto-Indo-European current, *dwino-* (twin) and *dwóh* (two). Prior forms and sources can be hypothesized, subsequent uses irrigated. For now the noun 'twin' still denotes two, a couple or pair, and, for English-speakers, the specific phenomenon of people born together; people, towns, towers, brought together in significance or form. This word, like all words, is associated with what it means, a link between written marks or acoustic signifiers with their signified meanings. But the signified thing or concept can be many and contradictory, personal and impersonal. Consider all the different meanings of twinning as they adapt to the many different uses of twin people – spiritual, religious, political, scientific or artistic; visual, logical or conceptual. More than a word, then, twins are a part of language that allows us to name the significance of simultaneous conception, gestation, birth and all that may follow. The verb 'to twin' is used to match and bring together these pairs, to twine and make two one. But no language speaks into the univocal present alone. Prior uses of the verb 'to twin' meant 'to part, sever, sunder'[61] – two once connected things torn apart. Recent history has tended to prefer the idea that language binds twins together; there is no reason to believe the history of twins will remain the same.

Postscript

A NOTE TOWARDS
A COLLECTIVE HISTORY

The history of twins has been a history of testing – testing limits, thresholds, taboos, borders, technologies, identities and ideas. From the entry of gods into human affairs to being socialized into novel technical and technologically blended identities, twins have provided the vital material for evaluating and even creating different conceptions of what 'the human' means and how it is experienced. It is not simply the case that twins provide a figure of ambiguity in an otherwise black-and-white world; they have been used as instruments to calibrate what is black, what is white, and the shades of grey that lie between. To recognize that twins provide non-twins a testing figure is to recognize that twins may have a past and, despite all their differences, their past can be shared, protected or rewritten. From there, we may build more opportunities to construct a vocabulary with which to process and address what twins have in common with other twins that does not reduce them to limited set of essential qualities or characteristics – biological, emotional, psychological or geographical – but that acknowledges a history formed through common knowledge and understanding. While this is something these pages have attempted to bring together, it can only be part of a broader process, one that other twins may want to contribute to. If this book has catalogued twin uses and their attendant impacts – intellectual and philosophical, religious and scientific, political and artistic – then it does so with a long and incomplete index. The superstitions and fears, myths and fantasies attached to twins, the spiritual and geopolitical horrors born with and attached to them, and the scientific utility and opportunism that drives knowledge beside itself to the edges of reason, are episodes built into this book.

The examples are not exhaustive. Twins afford writers, artists and film-makers opportunities to explore the possibilities and limitations of how lives are mediated by people and technology. The ways that the concept and experience of 'twinning' appear as a performance, in films or on television, radio or contemporary social-media platforms, mean twins absorb and are available to be absorbed by wider prac-tices of human experimentation, self-measurement and self-regard, confusion, curiosity and knowledge creation. At each occasion, the twin body is used as a figure of potential. This says as much about the metamorphic potential of 'twins' as a category of people as it does about the way those practices are moulded and are affected by the twins that they use. The question remains for twins to respond to in ways they feel are just: for whose future are you being used?

REFERENCES

INTRODUCTION

1 For example, John Hall, 'Identical Twins Die after Seeking Euthanasia When They Discovered They Would Go Blind and Never See Each Other Again', www.independent.co.uk, 14 January 2013; Meredith Bennett-Smith, 'Twins Born 87 Days Apart Could Break Guinness World Record for Interval between Births', www.huffingtonpost.com, 30 April 2013; Tanyel Gumushan, 'Twins at Uni: We Look Alike, but We're Very Different People', www.guardian.com, 13 November 2015; Susan Dominus, 'The Mixed Up Brothers of Bogotá', www.nytimes.com, 9 July 2015.

2 Kenneth Gross, 'Ordinary Twinship', *Raritan*, XXII/4 (2003), pp. 20–39.

3 There is a small industry dedicated to giving out such advice; see, for example, Carol Cooper, *Twins and Multiple Births: The Essential Parenting Guide from Pregnancy to Adulthood*, 2nd edn (London, 2004); Natalie Diaz, *What to Do When You're Having Two: The Twins Survival Guide from Pregnancy through the First Year* (New York, 2014); Barbara Klein, *Twin Dilemmas: Changing Relationships throughout the Life Span* (London, 2017); Joan A. Friedman, *Twins in Session: Case Histories in Treating Twinship Issues* (Los Angeles, CA, 2018).

4 See Chantal Hoekstra, Zhen Zhen Zhao, Cornelius B. Lambalk, Gonneke Willemsen, Nicholas G. Martin, Dorret I. Boomsma and Grant W. Montgomery, 'Dizygotic Twinning', *Human Reproduction Update*, XV/1 (2008), pp. 37–47.

5 Niklas Luhmann, *Social Systems* (Stanford, CA, 1995), p. xxxiv; see also Paul Rabinow, *Marking Time: On the Anthropology of the Contemporary* (Princeton, NJ, 2008), pp. 64–65.

6 Here and throughout this book I frequently play on the double meaning of the word 'matter' to signify both material substance and value. In this I follow Mel Chen, who writes that language is enmeshed in animacy hierarchies that 'manipulate, affirm, and shift the ontologies that matter the world'; see Mel Y. Chen, *Animacies: Biopolitics, Racial Mattering, and Queer Affect* (Durham, NC, 2012), p. 42.

7 Ian Hacking, *Historical Ontology* (Cambridge, MA, 2004), p. 106.

8 This has been my experience at Durham University, particularly at the Centre for Medical Humanities, where I was Research Fellow 2012–16. The fruits of the centre's interdisciplinary practice may be seen in

Wellcome Trust-funded projects such as Hearing the Voice and Life of Breath. The former has created a series of guides to interdisciplinary practice called Working Knowledge, a free collection of practical resources available to those embarking on or funding interdisciplinary research: www.workingknowledgeps.com.

9 Hans-Jörg Reinberger, *Toward a History of Epistemic Things* (Palo Alto, CA, 1997).

10 See Barbara Herrnstein Smith, 'Scientizing the Humanities: Shifts, Collisions, Negotiations', *Common Knowledge*, XXII/3 (2016), pp. 353–72.

11 Rita Felski, *Doing Time: Feminist Theory and Postmodern Culture* (New York, 2000), p. 3.

12 See also Paul Ricoeur, *Time and Narrative*, trans. Kathleen Blamey and David Pellauer, 3 vols [1988] (Chicago, IL, 1990). For a useful overview of time in cultural and critical theory, see Joel Burgess and Amy J. Elias, eds, *Time: A Vocabulary of the Present* (New York, 2016).

13 Michel Serres, 'Science and the Humanities: The Case of Turner', *SubStance*, XXVI/2 (1997), p. 15.

14 Similarly, Steven Connor has preferred to see 'culture as a meteorological phenomenon. Almost immeasurably complex interactions of a small number of determinate variables – wind-speed and direction, pressure, temperature – produce determinate weather effects. There is no difficulty in establishing whether it is or is not, at any particular place and time, raining. But what is the "it" that is raining, and that, so to speak, wills or weathers the weather?' Steven Connor, 'What Can Cultural Studies Do?', in *Interrogating Cultural Studies: Interviews in Cultural Theory, Practice and Politics*, ed. Paul Bowman (London, 2003), p. 214.

1 TWINS ARE MYTHS

1 Homer, *The Odyssey*, trans. Robert Eagles (London, 1996), II.342.

2 Pindar, 'Nemean x.v', in *The Odes of Pindar*, trans. C. M. Bowra (London, 1969), ll. 85–91.

3 See J. Rendell Harris, *The Cult of the Heavenly Twins* (Cambridge, 1906).

4 Apollodorus, *The Library of Greek Mythology*, trans. Robin Hard (Oxford, 2007), 3.10.4. And compare the description of Apollo in Callimachus' hymn: 'Lightly would the herd of cattle wax larger, nor would the she-goats of the flock lack young, whereon as they feed Apollo casts his eye; nor without milk would the ewes be nor barren, but all would have lambs at foot; and she that bear one would soon be the mother of twins.' Callimachus, *Hymns and Epigrams. Lycophron: Alexandra. Aratus: Phaenomena*, trans. A. W. Mair and G. R. Mair (Cambridge, MA, 1921), p. 53.

5 Véronique Dasen, *Jumeaux, jumelles dans l'antiquité grecque et romaine* (Zurich, 2005), p. 284.

6 Mischa Meier, Barbara Patzek and Hans Beck, 'Procles', in *Brill's New Pauly*, antiquity volumes, ed. Hubert Cancik and Helmuth Schneider, Brill Online, 2015, http://referenceworks.brillonline.com, accessed 26 May 2015.

7 For example at the riding academy in Saint Petersburg, Russia.

8 Pier Luigi Tucci, *The Temple of Peace in Rome* (Cambridge, 2018).

9 Jacobus de Voragine, *The Golden Legend: Readings on the Saints*, trans. William Granger Ryan (Princeton, NJ, 2012), pp. 582–4.

10 Though Cosimo de' Medici was born on 10 April 1389, he celebrated his birthday on 27 September, the feast day of St Cosmas in the same year.

11 Jacalyn Duffin, *Medical Saints: Cosmas and Damian in a Postmodern World* (Oxford, 2013), p. 154.

12 Livy, *The Early History of Rome: Books I–V*, trans. Aubrey De Selincourt (London, 2002); Livy, *The Rise of Rome, Books 1–5,* trans. T. J. Luce (Oxford, 2009); Ovid, *Times and Reasons: A New Translation of Fasti,* trans. Anne and Peter Wiseman (Oxford, 2011); Plutarch, *Lives*, trans. Bernadotte Perrin (Cambridge, MA, 1914).

13 For a history of Rome's relationship with wolves, the she-wolf and iconographic history, see Cristina Mazzoni, *She-Wolf: The Story of a Roman Icon* (Cambridge, 2010).

14 See T. P. Wiseman, *Remus: A Roman Myth* (Cambridge, 1995), and *The Myths of Rome* (Liverpool, 2008).

15 Quoted in Silvia Barisione, *The Birth of Rome: Five Visions for the Eternal City*, ed. Matthew Abess (Miami, FL, 2013), italics in original.

16 Penelope Farmer, *Two, or The Book of Twins and Doubles: An Autobiographical Anthology* (London, 1996), pp. 331–2.

17 Dona Lee Davis, *Twins Talk: What Twins Tell Us about Person, Self, and Society* (Athens, OH, 2014), p. 177.

2 TWINS ARE MONSTERS

1 V. Bazaliiskiy and N. Savelyev, 'The Wolf of Baikal: The "Lokomotiv" Early Neolithic Cemetery in Siberia (Russia)', *Antiquity*, LXXVII/295 (2003), pp. 20–30.

2 The twin remains of Lokomotiv are summarized in Angela R. Lieverse, Vladimir Ivanovich Bazaliiskii and Andrzej W. Weber, 'Death by Twins: A Remarkable Case of Dystocic Childbirth in Early Neolithic Siberia', *Antiquity*, LXXXIX/343 (2015), pp. 23–38. I am grateful to Barbara Graziosi for bringing this article to my attention.

3 Ibid., p. 35.

4 See L. Crespo, M. E. Subirà and J. Ruiz, 'Twins in Prehistory: The Case from Olèrdola (Barcelona, Spain; s. IV II BC)', *International Journal of Osteoarchaeology*, XXVI/6 (2011), pp. 751–6; Siân Halcrow, Nancy Tayles, Raelene Inglis and Charles Higham, 'Newborn

Twins from Prehistoric Mainland Southeast Asia: Birth, Death and Personhood', *Antiquity*, LXXXVI/333 (2012), pp. 838–52.

5 Plato, *Republic: Books 6–10*, vol. II, ed. and trans. Chris Emlyn-Jones and William Preddy (Cambridge, MA, 2013), 377a.

6 Penelope Murray, 'What Is a *Muthos* for Plato?', in *From Myth to Reason? Studies in the Development of Greek Thought*, ed. Richard Buxton (Oxford, 1999), p. 253.

7 Although it sounds like these terms and processes are being applied anachronistically, as modern ideas projected onto a past, they are explored extensively in Aristotle's *History of Animals* (though he uses the term 'superfetation' to describe both). See Aristotle, 'History of Animals', in *The Complete Works of Aristotle: The Revised Oxford Translation*, ed. Jonathan Bates (Princeton, NJ, 1991), 7.585a1–24. For a recent biomedical overview, which also contains references to the Dioscuri, see Isaac Blickstein, 'Superfecundation and Superfetation', in *Multiple Pregnancy: Epidemiology, Gestation and Perinatal Outcome*, ed. Isaac Blickstein and Louis G. Keith (Abingdon, 2005), pp. 102–7.

8 Aristotle, 'History of Animals', 7.585a15–16.

9 See Thomas K. Johansen, 'Myth and Logos in Aristotle', in *From Myth to Reason? Studies in the Development of Greek Thought*, ed. Richard Buxton (Oxford, 1999), p. 291.

10 Aristotle, 'History of Animals', 7.585a13–15.

11 See Pindar, *The Odes of Pindar*, trans. C. M. Bowra (London, 1969), pp. 39–59; Apollodorus, *The Library of Greek Mythology*, trans. Robin Hard (Oxford, 2007), 2.4.8; Hesiod, *The Shield, Catalogue of Women, Other Fragments*, vol. II, ed. and trans. Glenn W. Most (Cambridge, MA, 2007), pp. 49–53. A reference to Heracles and Iphicles is also repeated in Roman texts, for example Pliny, *Natural History*, vol. II, trans. H. Rackham (Cambridge, MA, 1942), 7.43.

12 See for example Wilhelm Nestle, *Vom Mythos zum Logos: Die Selbstentfaltung des griechischen Denkens von Homer bis auf die Sophistik und Sokrates* (Stuttgart, 1940).

13 Metaphysics 1000a5–18, in *The Complete Works of Aristotle*. See Armand Marie Leroi, *The Lagoon: How Aristotle Invented Science* (London, 2014), pp. 41–4.

14 Aristotle, 'The Generation of Animals', in *Complete Works of Aristotle*, ed. Bates, 772a30–772a37.

15 Ibid., 772b13–25. See also Véronique Dasen, *Jumeaux, jumelles dans l'antiquité grecque et romaine* (Zurich, 2005).

16 Judith Halberstam, *Skin Show: Gothic Horror and the Technology of Monsters* (Durham, NC, 1995), p. 27.

17 Hippocrates, *Regimen I, Nature of Man Regimen in Health. Humours. Aphorisms. Regimen 13. Dreams. Heracleitus: On the Universe*, vol. IV, trans. W.H.S. Jones (Cambridge, MA, 1931), 1.30.

18 The Hippocratic writings are frequently attributed to the physician known as Hippocrates of Cos (*c*. 460–*c*. 370 BCE), although evidence suggests they were written by a collective of writers. For the most part I refer to the corpus of writings in this chapter.

19 Hippocrates, *Generation; Nature of the Child; Diseases 4; Nature of Women and Barrenness*, vol. X, ed. and trans. Paul Potter (Cambridge, MA, 2012), 10.540–41.

20 Jacques Jouanna, *Hippocrates*, trans. M. B. Devouise (Baltimore, MD, 1999), pp. 274, 276.

21 Iain M. Lonie, *The Hippocratic Treatises: 'On Generation', 'On the Nature of the Child', and 'Diseases VI'* (Berlin, 1981), p. 255. Also see J. S. Kirk and J. E. Raven, *The Presocratic Philosophers: A Critical History with a Selection of Texts* (Cambridge, 1957), pp. 54–60.

22 See Emily Martin, 'The Egg and the Sperm: How Science Has Constructed a Romance Based on Stereotypical Male–female Roles', *Signs*, XVI/3 (1991), pp. 485–501.

23 See Helen King, *Hippocrates' Woman: Reading the Female Body in Ancient Greece* (London, 1998), p. 27.

24 Hippocrates, *Generation*, 10.541–542.

25 Hippocrates, *Places in Man. Glands. Fleshes. Prorrhetic 1–2. Physician. Use of Liquids. Ulcers. Haemorrhoids and Fistulas*, ed. and trans. Paul Potter (Cambridge, MA, 1995), 8.584.1.

26 A definition given in Nancy Segal, *Entwined Lives: Twins and What They Tell Us about Human Behavior* (New York, 2000), p. 225.

27 Ian Hacking, 'Kinds of People: Moving Targets', *Proceedings of the British Society*, CLI (2007), p. 288. Italics in original.

28 Geoffrey C. Bowker and Susan Leigh Star, *Sorting Things Out: Classification and Its Consequences* (Cambridge, MA, 1999).

29 Hacking, 'Kinds of People', p. 305.

30 Mary Midgley, *The Myths We Live By* (Abingdon, 2011), p. 1.

31 Ibid., p. 4.

3 TWINS ARE DANGEROUS

1 The extent to which Marie de France's 'Lai le Fresne' is a 'romance' in the generic and critical sense is discussed by Elizabeth Archibald, *'Lai le Freine*: The Female Foundling and the Problem of Romance Genre', in *The Spirit of Medieval English Popular Romance*, ed. Ad Putter and Jane Gilbert (Harlow, 2000), pp. 39–55.

2 Marie de France, 'Lay le Freine', in *The Middle English Breton Lays*, ed. Anne Laskaya and Eve Salisbury (Kalamazoo, MI, 1995), pp. 65–74 (ll. 68–72).

3 John Boswell details the history of child abandonment in the Middle Ages: 'between 1195 and 1295 at least thirteen different councils in England alone passed legislation directly or indirectly bearing on the

abandonment of children.' See *The Kindness of Strangers* (New York, 1990), p. 322.

4 See Francis J. Child, *The English and Scottish Popular Ballads*, vol. II (Boston, MA, 1883–6), II.63–83, and Erik Kooper, 'Multiple Births and Multiple Disaster: Twins in Medieval Literature', in *Conjunctures: Medieval Studies in Honor of Douglas Kelly*, ed. Douglas Kelly, Keith Busby and Norris J. Lacy (Amsterdam, 1994), pp. 253–70.

5 See Kooper, 'Multiple Births', pp. 256–60.

6 Ibid., p. 260.

7 Harriet Hudson, ed., *Four Middle English Romances: Sir Isumbras, Octavian, Sir Eglamour of Artois, Sir Tryamour* (Kalamazoo, MI, 1996), https://d.lib.rochester.edu, accessed 13 August 2020. Line references cited in the text.

8 See Monica H. Green, *Making Women's Medicine Masculine: The Rise of Male Authority in Pre-modern Gynaecology* (Oxford, 2008).

9 Muscio's *Gynaecia* is an interpretation of Soranus' *Gynecology*, trans. Owsei Temkin (Baltimore, MD, 1956), p. xlv. The specific details of Muscio's life are unknown but it is generally held that he translated the text in North Africa in the fifth or sixth century. See Monica H. Green, 'From "Diseases of Women" to "Secrets of Women": The Transformation of Gynaecological Literature in the Later Middle Ages', *Journal of Medieval and Early Modern Studies*, XXX/1 (2000), p. 8.

10 Monica H. Green, 'The Sources of Eucharius Rösslin's "Rosegarden for Pregnant Women and Midwives" (1513)', *Medical History*, LIII/2 (2009), pp. 167–92.

11 'On Difficulties of Birth', trans. Ron Barkai, Bibliothèque nationale, Paris, ms Heb. 1120 ff. 66v–67r.

12 *Medieval Woman's Guide to Health: The First Gynecological Handbook*, ed. Beryl Rowland (London, 1981), p. 133.

13 Ibid., pp. 134, 135.

14 Ibid., p. 87.

15 For more on *figura infirmitatum* and their impact on anatomical illustration, see Andrea Carlino, *Paper Bodies: A Catalogue of Anatomical Fugitive Sheets, 1538–1687*, Medical History 19, trans. Noga Arikha (London, 1999), pp. 75–81.

16 See Joan Cadden, *The Meanings of Sex Difference in the Middle Ages: Medicine, Science, and Culture* (Cambridge, 1993), p. 35.

17 Galen, *On the Usefulness of the Parts of the Body: De usu partium*, 2 vols, trans. Margret Tallmadge May (Ithaca, NY, 1968), II.625.

18 Fridolf Kudlien, 'The Seven Cells of the Uterus: The Doctrine and Its Roots', *Bulletin of the History of Medicine*, XXXIX/5 (1965), pp. 415–23.

19 Edward Reichman, 'Anatomy and the Doctrine of the Seven-chamber Uterus in Rabbinic Literature', *Hakirah*, 9 (2010), p. 249.

20 Hugh of Caumpeden, British Library, London, Landsdowne mss 793.

21 Albertus Magnus, *On Animals: A Medieval Summa Zoologica*, vol. II, trans. Kenneth F. Kitchell Jr and Irven Michael Resnick (Baltimore, MD, 1999), II.1309, 18.58.

22 Ibid., II.1311, 18.63

23 Ibid., II.1315, 18.71; II.1316, 18.72.

24 Ibid., I.825, 9.132–3. Here I have also been guided by the summary offered by J. M. Thijssen in his 'Twins as Monsters: Albertus Magnus's Theory of the Generation of Twins and Its Philosophical Context', *Bulletin of the History of Medicine*, LXI/2 (1987), p. 246.

25 See Angela M. Lucas, *Women in the Middle Ages: Religion, Marriage and Letters* (Brighton, 1982), p. 18.

26 Quoted in R. C. Finucane, *The Rescue of the Innocents: Endangered Children in Medieval Miracles* (London, 1997), p. 18.

27 Quoted in Peter Biller, *The Measure of Multitude: Population in Medieval Thought* (Oxford, 2000), p. 368.

28 Pliny the Elder, *Natural History: Book 7*, trans. Mary Beagon (Oxford, 2005), p. 67.

29 See ibid., p. 69.

30 Robert Wood, *Death before Birth: Fetal Health and Mortality in Historical Perspective* (Oxford, 2009), pp. 96–8.

31 K. E. Olsen and L.A.J.R. Houwen, 'Introduction', in *Monsters and the Monstrous in Medieval Northwest Europe* (Leuven, 2001), p. 8.

4 TWINS ARE GLOBAL

1 Orthographic practices of the period meant that Hamnet and Hamlet could be written interchangeably.

2 All quotations from Shakespeare's plays refer to texts collected in *The Norton Shakespeare: Based on the Oxford Edition*, ed. Stephen Greenblatt, Walter Cohen, Jean E. Howard and Katharine Eisaman Maus (New York, 1997).

3 See Robert S. Miola, *Shakespeare and Classical Comedy* (Oxford, 1994), p. 21.

4 As Miola puts it, 'Shakespeare multiples rather than divides: he doubles the number of identical twins and nearly triples the incidents of error from seventeen to fifty.' Ibid., pp. 22–3.

5 Coppélia Kahn, *Man's Estate: Masculine Identity in Shakespeare* (Berkeley, CA, 1981), p. 201.

6 Titus Maccius Plautus, 'The Menaechmi', in *Four Comedies*, ed. and trans. Erich Segal (Oxford, 1996), pp. 75–130.

7 Lorraine Daston and Katharine Park, *Wonders and the Order of Nature, 1150–1750* (New York, 1998), p. 204.

8 *The Oxford English Dictionary*, 2nd edn (Oxford, 1989), *s.v.* 'Monster'.

9 Plato, *Symposium*, trans. Robin Wakefield (Oxford, 1994), 188e–190a, 190d.

10 See Hannah Arendt, *The Human Condition*, 2nd edn (Chicago, IL, 1998).

11 See Roberto Esposito, *Persons and Things: From the Body's Point of View*, trans. Zakiya Hanafi (Cambridge, 2015), pp. 24–33.

12 See Pablo Joseph de Arriaga, *The Extirpation of Idolatry in Peru*, trans. L. Clark Keating (Lexington, KY, 1968).

13 Alexei Siverstev, 'The Gospel of Thomas and Early Stages in the Development of the Christian Wisdom Literature', *Journal of Early Christian Studies*, VIII/3 (2000), pp. 319–40.

14 These estimates are given by the online resource www.slavevoyages.org/assessment/estimates, accessed 27 May 2019.

15 See Eric Williams, *Capitalism and Slavery* (Chapel Hill, NC, 1944).

16 See Stefania Capone, 'Yoruba Religion', in *The Encyclopedia of Latin American Religions*, ed. H.P.P. Gooren, https://doi.org/10.1007/978-3-319-08956-0_561-1, accessed 4 April 2020.

17 This convergence has never been even or stable but is a dynamic part of both history and everyday life, a tension between colonized and colonizers that has transformed over time. See Andre Droogers, 'Syncretism: The Problem of Definition, the Definition of the Problem', in *Dialogue and Syncretism: An Interdisciplinary Approach*, ed. Jerald D. Gort, Hendrik M. Vroom, Rein Fernhout and Anton Wessels (Grand Rapids, MI, 1989), pp. 7–25.

18 See Mikelle S. Omari-Tunkara, *Manipulating the Sacred: Yorùbá Art, Ritual, and Resistance in Brazilian Candomblé* (Detroit, MI, 2000).

19 See Padraic X. Scanlan, 'The Colonial Rebirth of British Anti-slavery: The Liberated African Villages of Sierra Leone, 1815–1824', *American Historical Review*, CXXI/4 (2016), pp. 1085–113.

20 On the missionary work of Samuel Ajayi Crowther, based on Henry Venn's principles (Church Missionary Society), see Jehu J. Hanciles, *Euthanasia of a Mission: African Church Autonomy in a Colonial Context* (Santa Barbara, CA, 2002), pp. 30–31.

21 Ibid.

22 Their company were women accused of witchcraft, those sick with leprosy and others condemned for being abominable. Elizabeth Isichei, *A History of Christianity in Africa: From Antiquity to the Present* (Grand Rapids, MI, 1995).

23 G.O.M. Tasie, *Christian Missionary Enterprise in the Niger Delta, 1864–1918* (Leiden, 1978), p. 36.

24 T.J.H. Chappel, 'The Yorùbá Cult of Twins in Historical Perspective', *Africa: Journal of the International African Institute*, XLIV/3 (1974), p. 250.

25 Ibid., p. 257.

26 Elisha P. Renne, 'The Ambiguous Ordinariness of Yorùbá Twins', in *Twins in African and Diaspora Cultures: Double Trouble, Twice Blessed*, ed. Philip M. Peek (Bloomington, IN, 2011), p. 308.

27 Chappel, 'The Yorùbá Cult of Twins', p. 259.

5 TWINS ARE BIRDS

1 Jane Belo, *Traditional Balinese Culture* (Columbia, NY, 1970),
p. 5.

2 As a friend, collaborator and former student of Margret Mead
and Gregory Bateson, Belo was part of a small group of ethnographers,
photographers and ethnomusicologists who would produce *Trance and
Dance in Bali* (1951), an early example of ethnographic film-making.

3 Belo, *Traditional Balinese Culture*, p. 3.

4 Ibid., p. 8.

5 Elizabeth Piontelli, *Twins in the World: The Legends They Inspire and
the Lives They Lead* (London, 2008); Helen L. Ball and Catherine M.
Hill, 'Reevaluating "Twin Infanticide"', *Current Anthropology*, XXXVII/5
(1996), pp. 856–63.

6 W.H.R. Rivers, *The Todas* (London, 1906), p. 480.

7 For instance Edgar Thurston, *Omens and Superstitions of Southern
India* (New York, 1912), p. 54; J. G. Frazer, *Totemism and Exogamy:
A Treatise on Certain Early Forms*, 4 vols (London, 1910), vol. II,
p. 122; Isaac Schapera, 'Customs Relating to Twins in South Africa',
Journal of the African Society, XXVI (1927), pp. 117–37. For broader
and more recently published overviews see Gary Granzberg, 'Twin
Infanticide: A Cross-cultural Test of a Materialistic Explanation',
Ethos, 1/4 (1973), pp. 405–12; Ball and Hill, 'Reevaluating "Twin
Infanticide"'.

8 Walter E. A. van Beek and Thomas Blakely, 'The Innocent Sorcerer:
Coping with Evil in Two African Societies, Kapiski and Dogon',
in *African Religion: Experience and Expression*, ed. Thomas Blakely,
Walter E. A. van Beek and Dennis L. Thomson (Oxford, 1994),
pp. 196–228. See also Steven van Wolputte, 'Twins and
Intertwinement: Reflections on Ambiguity and Ambivalence in
Northwestern Namibia', in *Twins in African and Diaspora Cultures:
Double Trouble, Twice Blessed*, ed. Philip M. Peek (Bloomington, IN,
2011), p. 66.

9 Leroy Fernand, Taiwo Olaleye-Oruene, Gesina Koeppen-Schomerus
and Elizabeth Bryan, 'Yoruba Customs and Beliefs Pertaining to
Twins', *Twin Research*, VI/ 2 (2002), pp. 132–6.

10 T.J.H. Chappel, 'The Yoruba Cult of Twins in Historical Perspective',
Africa: Journal of the International African Institute, XLIV/3 (1974),
pp. 250–65. Scholars such as Elisha Renne are now tracing how, with
the increased influence of Christianity and modern medicine, twins
are finding new forms of cultural 'ordinariness'. See Elisha P. Renne,
'The Ambiguous Ordinariness of Yoruba Twins', in *Twins in African
and Diaspora Cultures*, ed. Peek, p. 310.

11 Marilyn Hammersley Houlberg, 'Íbejí Images of the Yoruba', *African
Arts*, VII/1 (1973), p. 23.

12 Babatunde Lawal, 'The Oneness of Twoness: Poetics of Twin Figures (*Ère Ìbejì*) among the Yoruba', in *Twins in African and Diaspora Cultures*, ed. Peek, p. 85.

13 Philip M. Peek, 'Introduction', in *Twins in African and Diaspora Cultures*, ed. Peek, p. 13.

14 Ibid.

15 Giorgio Agamben, *Profanations*, trans. Jeff Fort (New York, 2007), p. 74.

16 Houlberg, 'Íbejí Images of the Yoruba', p. 23.

17 See Elisha Renne, 'Twinship in an Ekiti Yoruba Town', *Ethnology*, XL/1 (2001), pp. 66–9.

18 Quoted in Houlberg, 'Íbejí Images of the Yoruba', p. 22.

19 Renne, 'Twinship in an Ekiti Yoruba Town', p. 69.

20 Babatunde Lawal, 'The Oneness of Twoness', p. 84.

21 Houlberg, 'Ibeji Images of the Yoruba', p. 26.

22 Renne, 'Twinship in an Ekiti Yoruba Town', p. 67.

23 Robert Farris Thompson, *Black Gods and Kings: Yoruba Art at UCLA* (Bloomington, IN, 1976).

24 Houlberg, 'Ibeji Images of the Yoruba', p. 22.

25 See Renne, 'Twinship in an Ekiti Yoruba Town', pp. 72–3.

26 See Houlberg, 'Ibeji Images of the Yoruba', p. 26; C. Angelo Micheli, 'Double Portraits: Images of Twinness in West African Studio Photography', in *Twins in African and Diaspora Cultures*, ed. Peek, pp. 137–59.

27 Susan Cooksey, 'Twins, Couples, and Doubles and the Negotiation of Spirit–human Identities among the Win', in *Twins in African and Diaspora Cultures*, ed. Peek, pp. 116–36; Misty L. Bastian, '"The Demon Superstition": Abominable Twins and Mission Culture in Onitsha History', *Ethnology*, XL/1 (2001), pp. 13–27; Adeline Masquelier, 'Powers, Problems, and Paradoxes of Twinship in Niger', *Ethnology*, XL/1 (2001), pp. 45–62.

28 Adeline Masquelier, 'Powers, Problems, and Paradoxes', pp. 52, 51.

29 Imani Roach, 'Ibeji', in *The Oxford Companion of African Thought*, 2 vols, ed. Abiola Irele and Biodun Jeyifo (Oxford, 2010), vol. II, p. 474.

30 Quoted in and trans. Lawal, 'The Oneness of Twoness', p. 89.

31 Houlberg, 'Ibeji Images of the Yoruba', p. 23.

32 Jan-Lodewijk Grootaers, 'Snake, Bush, and Metaphor: Twinship among Ubangians', in *Twins in African and Diaspora Cultures*, ed. Peek, p. 194.

33 Ibid., p. 190.

34 Susan Diduk, 'Twinship and Juvenile Power: The Ordinariness of the Extraordinary', *Ethnology*, XL/1 (2001), p. 33.

35 E. E. Evans-Pritchard, 'Customs and Beliefs Relating to Twins among the Nilotic Nuer', *Uganda Journal*, III (1936), p. 236.

36 E. E. Evans-Pritchard, 'Lévy-Bruhl's Theory of Primitive Mentality', *Bulletin of the Faculty of Arts, Cairo University*, II (1934), p. 32.

37 E. E. Evans-Pritchard, *Nuer Religion* (Oxford, 1956), p. 132.

38 Ibid., p. 142.

39 Wendy James, *The Ceremonial Animal* (Oxford, 2003), p. 7.

40 Claude Lévi-Strauss, *Totemism*, trans. Rodney Needham (London, 1964), p. 78, italics removed.

41 Ibid., p. 80.

42 Ibid., p. 81.

43 Ibid., p. 89. 'With' is added because the adjectival plural of the French expression *bonnes à penser* is difficult to translate and because 'good to think' is grammatically awkward in English. See Edmund Leach, *Claude Levi-Strauss* (New York, 1970), p. 31.

44 Bastian, '"The Demon Superstition"', p. 14.

45 Victor Turner, *The Ritual Process: Structure and Anti-structure* [1969] (Piscataway, NJ, 1997), p. 45.

46 Ibid.

47 Ibid., p. 47.

48 Philip M. Peek, 'Introduction: Beginning to Rethink Twins', in *Twins in African and Diaspora Cultures*, ed. Peek, p. 23.

49 Elisha P. Renne and Misty L. Bastian, 'Twinship in Africa', *Ethnology*, XL/1 (2001), p. 7.

50 Diduk, 'Twinship and Juvenile Power', p. 30.

51 Walter E. A. van Beek, 'Forever Liminal: Twins among the Kapiski/ Higi of North Cameroon and Northeastern Nigeria', in *Twins in African and Diaspora Cultures*, ed. Peek, p. 180.

52 Van Beek and Blakely, 'The Innocent Sorcerer', pp. 196–228. See also Van Wolputte, 'Twins and Intertwinement', p. 66.

6 TWINS ARE EXPERIMENTS

1 Alireza Moayyeri, Christopher J. Hammond, Deborah J. Hart and Timothy D. Spector, 'The UK Adult Twin Registry (TwinsUK Resource)', *Twin Research and Human Genetics*, XVI/1 (2014), pp. 144–9.

2 Francis Galton, *Probability, the Foundation of Eugenics: The Herbert Spencer Lecture Delivered on June 5, 1907* (Oxford, 1907), p. 13. For more on Galton's politics see Maurizio Meloni, *Political Biology: Science and Social Values in Human Heredity from Eugenics to Epigenetics* (London, 2016).

3 See John C. Waller, 'Commentary: The Birth of the Twin Study – A Commentary on Francis Galton's "The History of Twins"', *International Journal of Epidemiology*, XLI (2012), p. 917.

4 Thought to have entered the English language in Shakespeare's *The Tempest* ('a born devil, on whose nature nurture can never stick', 4.i.188–9), Galton's first use of the phrase 'nature and nurture' occurred in 1874, a year before he published his work on twins in *Fraser's Magazine* in 1875, when expressing interest in the 'energy, intellect,

and the like' of other fellows of the Royal Institution. See Francis Galton, 'On Men of Science, Their Nature and Nurture', *Notices of the Proceedings at the Meetings of the Members of Royal Institution of Great Britain, with Abstracts of the Discourses Delivered at the Evening Meetings*, VII, 1874–5 (London, 1875), pp. 227–36.

5 Francis Galton, 'The History of Twins as a Criterion of Nature and Nurture', *Fraser's Magazine*, XII (1875), p. 566.

6 An innovator in biometrics as well as qualitative methods, Galton says he received 'around eighty' responses to his 'circulars of inquiry' (ibid., p. 566), though papers held in the Galton Archive, University College London, suggest he received more. See Nicholas Wright Gillham, *A Life of Sir Francis Galton: From African Exploration to the Birth of Eugenics* (Oxford, 2001), p. 193.

7 Galton, 'The History of Twins', p. 574.

8 Tinca J. C. Polderman, Beben Benyamin, Christiaan A. de Leeuw, Patrick F. Sullivan, Arjen van Bochoven, Peter M. Visscher and Danielle Posthuma, 'Meta-analysis of the Heritability of Human Traits Based on Fifty Years of Twin Studies', *Nature Genetics*, XLVII (2015), pp. 702–9.

9 Yoon-Mi Hur and Jeffrey M. Craig, 'Twin Registries Worldwide: An Important Resource for Scientific Research', *Twin Research and Human Genetics*, XVI/1 (2013), p. 11.

10 Galton, 'The History of Twins', p. 575.

11 However, behaviour geneticist Nancy Segal regrets using the expression 'nature versus nurture' in her early work and now prefers either 'Nature–Nurture or Nature and Nurture, because it is widely appreciated that the two effects work together and are separable only in a statistical sense'. Her studies on twins depend upon the detailed manufacture and public dissemination of this statistical separation. See Nancy Segal, *Born Together – Reared Apart: The Landmark Minnesota Twin Study* (Cambridge, MA, 2012), p. 96.

12 Hermann Werner Siemens, *Die Zwillingspathologie* (Berlin, 1924).

13 For the continued promotion of such a view, see one of the leading textbooks on the field of behaviour genetics, Robert Plomin, John C. DeFries, Gerald E. McClearn and Peter McGuffin, *Behavior Genetics*, 5th edn (New York, 2008), p. 79.

14 Laura C. Ball and Thomas Teo, 'Twin Studies', in *The International Encyclopedia of the Social Sciences*, 2nd edn, ed. William A. Darity Jr (New York, 2008), p. 473.

15 Respectively: G. Miller et al., 'The Heritability and Genetic Correlates of Mobile Phone Use: A Twin Study of Consumer Behaviour', *Twin Research and Human Genetics*, XV (2012), pp. 97–106; S. Ooki, 'Genetic and Environmental Influences on Finger-sucking and Nail-biting in Japanese Twin Children', *Twin Research and Human Genetics*, VIII (2005), pp. 320–27; Andrea Burri et al., 'A Multivariate Twin Study

of Female Sexual Dysfunction', *Journal of Sexual Medicine*, IX (2012), pp. 2671–81; Meike Bartels and Dorret. I. Boomsma, 'Born to Be Happy? The Etiology of Subjective Well-being', *Behavior Genetics*, XXXIX (2009), pp. 605–15; Dorret. I. Boomsma et al., 'Genetic and Environmental Contributions to Loneliness in Adults: The Netherlands Twin Register Study', *Behavior Genetics*, XXXV (2005), pp. 745–52; Catherine Haworth et al., 'The Heritability of General Cognitive Ability Increases Linearly from Childhood to Young Adulthood', *Molecular Psychiatry*, XV (2010), pp. 1112–20.

16 See Jay Joseph, 'The Use of the Classical Twin Method in the Social and Behavioral Sciences: The Fallacy Continues', *Journal of Mind and Behavior*, XXXIV/1 (2013), pp. 1–40; Callie H. Burt and Ronald L. Simons, 'Pulling Back the Curtain on Heritability Studies: Biosocial Criminology in the Postgenomic Era', *Criminology*, LII/2 (2014), pp. 223–62.

17 For a useful discussion of how 'sharing' genes has been distorted in scientific communications, see Barry Barnes and John Dupré, *Genomes and What to Make of Them* (Chicago, IL, 2008), pp. 98–9.

18 Jay Joseph, *The Gene Illusion: Genetic Research in Psychiatry and Psychology under the Microscope* (London, 2004), p. 344.

19 See Heinrich Wilhelm Poll, 'Über Zwillingsforschung als Hilfsmittel menschlicher Erbkunde', *Zeitschrift für Ethnologie*, XLVI (1914), pp. 87–105.

20 See James Braund and Douglas G. Sutton, 'The Case of Heinrich Wilhelm Poll (1877–1939): A German-Jewish Geneticist, Eugenicist, Twin Researcher, and Victim of the Nazis', *Journal of the History of Biology*, XLI (2008), pp. 1–35.

21 Quoted ibid., pp. 21–2.

22 Sheila Faith Weiss, 'The Loyal Genetic Doctor, Otmar Freiherr von Verschuer, and the Institut für Erbbiologie und Rassenhygiene: Origins, Controversy, and Racial Political Practice', *Central European History*, XLV (2012), pp. 631–68.

23 Otmar Freiherr von Verschuer, 'Twin Research from the Time of Francis Galton to the Present-day', *Proceedings of the Royal Society of London. Series B, Biological Sciences*, CXXVIII/850 (1939), p. 79.

24 Ibid.

25 Horatio H. Newman, Frank N. Freeman and Karl J. Holzinger, *Twins: A Study of Heredity and Environment* (Chicago, IL, 1937), p. 19.

26 Ibid., p. 22.

27 See Sheila Faith Weiss, 'Race Hygiene in Germany', *Osiris*, III (1987), p. 230. For how twin research was used to establish the evidential basis for policies of genetic hygiene in a number of national contexts, see Volker Roelcke, 'Eugenic Concerns, Scientific Practices: International Relations and National Adaptations in the Establishment of Psychiatric Genetics in Germany, Britain, the USA, and Scandinavia 1910–1960',

in *Baltic Eugenics: Bio-politics, Race and Nation in Interwar Estonia, Latvia and Lithuania*, ed. Björn M. Felder and Paul J. Weindling (Amsterdam, 2013), pp. 301–34.

28 This 'specific-protein' project, funded by the German Research Council, would also extend twin research of Verschuer's in the genetic pathology of tuberculosis. See Hans-Walter Schmuhl, *The Kaiser Wilhelm Institute for Anthropology, Human Heredity and Eugenics, 1926–1945: Crossing Boundaries* (Berlin, 2008), pp. 60–68.

29 See Robert Jay Lifton, *The Nazi Doctors: Medical Killing and the Psychology of Genocide* (New York, 1986), pp. 347–53. See Carola Sachse and Benoit Massin, *Biowissenschaftliche Forschung an Kaiser-Wilhelm-Instituten und die Verbrechen des NS-Regimes: Informationen über den gegenwärtigen Wissensstand* (Berlin, 2000); Schmuhl, *The Kaiser Wilhelm Institute*, pp. 362–70; Achim Trunk, 'Two Hundred Blood Samples from Auschwitz: A Noble Laureate and the Link to Auschwitz', in *The Kaiser Wilhelm Society under National Socialism*, ed. Susanne Heim, Carola Sachse and Mark Walker (Cambridge, 2009), pp. 120–44.

30 See Segal, *Born Together – Reared Apart*.

31 For a partial history of MISTRA, see ibid.

32 For a description of how MISTRA used the media as a recruitment tool see ibid., p. 33; Segal explains how, in 1989, their team captured a broad national audience on ABC's *Nightline* that used twins to 'plainly state one of the key findings of our paper [published in *Science* in 1990]', p. 104.

33 Ibid., p. 100.

34 Thomas J. Bouchard Jr, David T. Lykken, Matthew McGue, Nancy L. Segal and Auke Tellegen, 'Sources of Human Psychological Differences: the Minnesota Study of Twins Reared Apart', *Science*, CCL/4978 (1990), pp. 223–8.

35 For a wider discussion, formed around twin data, about how the genetics of intelligence may deepen the need for progressive social policy, see Kathryn Ashbury and Robert Plomin, *G Is for Genes: The Impact of Genetics on Education and Achievement* (Chichester, 2014).

36 Lawrence Perlman, 'Memories of the Child Development Center Study of Adopted Monozygotic Twins Reared Apart: An Unfulfilled Promise', *Twin Research and Human Genetics*, VIII/3 (2005), pp. 271–81.

37 For a further example see Mary Leonard, 'Problems in Identification and Ego Development in Twins', *Psychoanalytic Studies of the Child*, XVI (1961), pp. 300–320.

38 Donald Winnicott, 'Review: Twins: A Study of Three Pairs of Identical Twins: By Dorothy Burlingham (London, 1952)', in *The Collected Works of D. W. Winnicott*, vol. IV: *1952–1955* (Oxford, 2016), www.oxfordclinicalpsych.com, accessed 27 December 2019.

39 For an example of an ahistorical history of twin research written by twin researchers, see Richard Rende, Robert Plomin and Steven

Vandenberg, 'Who Discovered the Twin Method?', *Behavior Genetics*, xx/2 (1990), pp. 277–85; see also Thomas Teo and Laura C. Ball, 'Twin Research, Revisionism and Metahistory', *History of Human Sciences*, xx/5 (2009), pp. 1–23.

40 See Francesca Cassata, *Building the New Man: Eugenics, Racial Science and Genetics in Twentieth-century Italy*, trans. Erin O'Loughlin (Budapest, 2011).

41 Kevin Smith, John R. Alford, Peter K. Hatemi, Lindon J. Eaves, Carolyn Funk and John R. Hibbing, 'Biology, Ideology, and Epistemology: How Do We Know Political Attitudes Are Inherited and Why Should We Care?', *American Journal of Political Science*, cvi (2012), p. 12; Plomin, DeFries, McClearn and McGuffin, *Behavior Genetics*, p. 38. The notion that twin research forms a 'natural experiment' connects it to John Snow's epidemiological studies of the 1850s, when Snow observed the randomized effects of differing water quality in two London boroughs. His observations allowed him to deduce the source and spread of cholera through the contaminated water. Natural experiments are prized as a gold standard among health and evolutionary scientists for their scale and variety of time, place and observed specimen, since they allow for experimental conditions that cannot be generated in field or laboratory conditions and can reveal end results of ecological and evolutionary processes over long durations. The claim that twin research constitutes a form of 'natural experiment' emboldens these designs and situates them within a canon of triumphant life-saving and life-preserving discoveries, rendering the randomized distribution of genetic difference between monozygotic and dizygotic twins akin to the randomized distribution of contaminated water in Victorian London.

42 Quoted in Aaron Panofsky, 'Behavior Genetics to Postgenomics', in *Postgenomics: Perspectives on Biology after the Genome*, ed. Sarah Richardson and Hallam Stevens (Durham, nc, 2015), p. 164.

43 Segal, *Born Together – Reared Apart*, p. 62; Nancy Segal, 'Twins: The Finest Natural Experiment', *Personality and Individual Differences*, xlix (2010), p. 317.

44 Tim Spector, *Identically Different: Why You Can Change Your Genes* (London, 2012), p. 21.

45 Quoted in Lucy Jolin, 'Nature's Control Group', *In Touch*, xxii (2013), pp. 20–23.

46 Isabelle Stengers, *Power and Invention: Situating Science*, trans. Paul Bain (Minneapolis, mn, 1997), p. 88.

7 TWINS ARE MADE

1 Sarah Franklin, *Biological Relatives: ivf, Stem Cells, and the Future of Kinship* (Durham, nc, 2013), p. 34.

2 'Frozen Test-tube Embryos Raise Hot Debate', *New Scientist* (18 June 1981), p. 747.

3 Susan Bewley and Jeremy T. Wright, 'Maternal Death Associated with Ovum Donated Twin Pregnancy', *Human Reproduction*, VI (1991), pp. 898–9.

4 Ruth Deech and Anna Smajdor, *From IVF to Immortality: Controversy in the Era of Reproductive Technology* (Oxford, 2007), p. 21.

5 This description provided draws on two sources: Deech and Smajdor, *From IVF to Immortality*, pp. 17–20; and Jane Maienschein, *Embryos under the Microscope: Diverging Meanings of Life* (Cambridge, MA, 2014), p. 5.

6 For reasons connected to demographic change and regulations described later in this chapter, overall birth rates for twins in the USA appear to have stopped growing in the years 2014–18 and are in decline among some age and ethnicity groups. See Joyce A. Martin, Brady E. Hamilton and Michelle J. K. Osterman, 'Three Decades of Twin Births in the United States, 1980–2009', *NCHS Data Brief*, LXXX (Hyattsville, MD, 2012), pp. 1–8; Joyce A. Martin and Michelle J. K. Osterman, 'Is Twin Childbearing on the Decline? Twin Births in the United States, 2014–2018', *NCHS Data Brief*, CCCLI (Hyattsville, MD, 2019), pp. 1–8.

7 All figures taken from Table 3, 'Maternities with Multiple Births (Numbers and Rates): Age of Mother, 1940–2013: England and Wales, 2014', in *Office for National Statistics, Birth Characteristics in England and Wales: 2014* (London, 2015).

8 Martin, Hamilton and Osterman, 'Three Decades of Twin Births', p. 5.

9 David Adamson and Valerie Baker, 'Multiple Births from Assisted Reproductive Technologies: A Challenge that Must Be Met', *Fertility and Sterility*, LXXXI/3 (2004), p. 517.

10 Saswati Sunderam, Dmitry M. Kissin, Sara B. Crawford, Suzanne G. Folger, Denise J. Jamieson, Lee Warner and Wanda D. Barfield, 'Assisted Reproductive Technology Surveillance: United States, 2012', *Morbidity and Mortality Weekly Report*, LXVI/6 (2015), p. 9.

11 Judith Hall, 'Twinning', *The Lancet*, CCCLXII (2003); D. M. Campbell, A. L. Campbell and I. MacGillivray, 'Maternal Characteristics of Women Having Twin Pregnancies', *Journal of Biosocial Sciences*, VI/4 (1974), pp. 463–9.

12 See Amy E. Sparks, 'Culture Systems: Embryo Culture and Monozygotic Twinning', in *Embryo Culture: Methods and Protocols*, ed. Gary D. Smith, Jason E. Swain and Thomas B. Pool (New York, 2012), p. 389.

13 Jenna Healey, 'Babies in Your 30s? Don't Worry, Your Great-grandma Did It Too', *The Conversation*, www.theconversation.com, 19 December 2014.

14 Martin and Osterman, 'Is Twin Childbearing on the Decline?'

15 Hall, 'Twinning', p. 737.

16 M. G. Bulmer, *The Biology of Twinning in Man* (Oxford, 1970), pp. 74–83; I. Macgillivray, M. Samphier, J. Little, M. Ian, M. C. Dorris and T. Barbara, 'Factors Affecting Twinning', in *Twinning and Twins*, ed. Ian MacGillivray, Barbara Thompson, and D. M. Campbell (New York, 1988), pp. 67–97.

17 Martin, Hamilton and Osterman, 'Three Decades of Twin Births', pp. 3–4.

18 Prices quoted in Marcia C. Inhorn, *Cosmopolitan Conceptions: IVF Sojourns in Global Dubai* (Durham, NC, 2015), p. 105.

19 Debora L. Spar, *The Baby Business: How Money, Science, and Politics Drive the Commerce of Conception* (Cambridge, MA, 2006), p. xii.

20 Ibid., p. xiii.

21 See Andrea Fumagalli, 'Twenty Theses on Contemporary Capitalism (Cognitive Biocapitalism)', *Angelaki: Journal of the Theoretical Humanities*, XVI/3 (2011), pp. 7–17.

22 See Bronwyn Parry, 'Narratives of Neoliberalism: "Clinical Labour" in Context', *Medical Humanities*, XLI/1 (2015), pp. 32–7.

23 Spar, *The Baby Business*, p. 33.

24 Parry, 'Narratives of Neoliberalism: "Clinical Labour" in Context', p. 34.

25 Quoted ibid., p. 34.

26 Melinda Cooper and Catherine Waldby, *Clinical Labor: Tissue Donors and Research Subjects in the Global Bioeconomy* (Durham, NC, 2014), pp. 49–50.

27 Ibid., p. 60.

28 The expression is Joseph Galliano's: 'A New Kind of Family', *The Guardian*, 13 August 2003, www.theguardian.com, accessed 19 November 2015.

29 For an ethnographic description of reproduction without sex and sex without reproduction among lesbians in California, see Laura Mamo, *Queering Reproduction: Achieving Pregnancy in the Age of Technoscience* (Durham, NC, 2007).

30 For a critical appraisal of this expression with respect to popular use and twin research, M. Susan Lindee, *Moments of Truth in Genetic Medicine* (Baltimore, MD, 2005), pp. 123–54.

31 Segal, *Entwined Lives*, p. 225.

32 While gamete donation and gestational surrogacy may be available in California, the use of donor gametes is tantamount to adultery within societies governed by Islamic law and children thus born risk being viewed as 'biotechnological bastards'. Inhorn, *Cosmopolitan Conceptions*, pp. 162–3.

33 Twins Trust, 'Same Sex Parents of Twins, Triplets or More', www.twinstrust.org, July 2015.

34 Franklin, *Biological Relatives*, p. 22.

35 The President's Council on Bioethics, *Human Cloning and Human Dignity: An Ethical Enquiry* (Washington, DC, 2002), p. 103.

36 Marcia Inhorn and Frank van Balen, 'Interpreting Infertility: A View from the Social Sciences', in *Infertility around the Globe: New Thinking on Childlessness, Gender, and Reproductive Technologies*, ed. Marcia C. Inhorn and Frank van Balen (Los Angeles, CA, 2015), p. 8.

37 Spar, *The Baby Business*, p. 31.

38 Inhorn, *Cosmopolitan Conceptions*, pp. 108–9.

39 Cited ibid., p. 108.

40 For examples of couples who actively seek IVF twins through international travel clinics in Dubai, see ibid., pp. 101, 119, 145.

41 Lori B. Andrews, *The Clone Age: Adventures in the New World of Reproductive Technology* (New York, 1999), pp. 52–3.

42 R. B. Newman and B. Luke, *Multifetal Pregnancy: A Handbook for Care of the Pregnant Patient* (Philadelphia, PA, 2000).

43 Adamson and Baker, 'Multiple Births', p. 517.

44 Association of Clinical Embryologists, Bliss, British Fertility Society, British Infertility Counselling Association, Donor Conception Network, Endometriosis UK, Fertility Friends, Human Fertilisation and Embryology Authority, Infertility Network UK, Miscarriage Association, Multiple Births Foundation, National Gamete Donation Trust, National Perinatal Epidemiology Unit, Royal College of Nursing, Royal College of Obstetricians and Gynaecologists, Royal College of Paediatrics and Child Health, and Surrogacy UK, 'Multiple Births from Fertility Treatment in the UK: A Consensus Statement', *Human Fertility*, XIV/3 (2011), p. 151.

45 Peter Braude, *One Child at a Time: Reducing Multiple Births after IVF*, Report of the Expert Group on Multiple Births after IVF (October 2006), p. 25.

46 Ibid.

47 Ibid., p. 24.

48 Yacoub Khalaf, 'IVF Twins: Fulfilling Dreams or Turning Them into a Nightmare?', lecture given at Double Take: Twins in Genetics and Fertility Treatment, at the Institute of Child Health, University College London, 4 December 2013.

49 Bart C.J.M. Fauser, Paul Devroey and Nick S. Macklon, 'Multiple Birth Resulting from Ovarian Stimulation for Subfertility Treatment', *The Lancet*, CCCLXV/9473 (2005), p. 1813.

50 Braude, *One Child at a Time*, p. 24.

51 Ibid., pp. 26–8.

52 Susan Bewley, Philippa Moth and Yacoub Khalaf, 'A Complicated IVF Twin Pregnancy', *Human Reproduction*, XXV/4 (2010), pp. 1082–4.

53 Ibid., p. 1083.

54 *Report of the Committee of Inquiry into Human Fertilisation and Embryology* [1984] (London, 1988), p. 30.

55 See www.oneatatime.org.uk.

56 Human Fertilisation and Embryology Authority, *Multiple Births from Fertility Treatment*, p. 5.

57 See P. O. Karlstrom and C. Bergh, 'Reducing the Number of Embryos Transferred in Sweden: Impact on Delivery and Multiple Birth Rates', *Human Reproduction*, XXII (2007), pp. 2202–7.

58 Human Fertilisation and Embryology Authority, *Improving Outcomes for Fertility Patients: Multiple Births* (London, 2015), pp. 7, 17.

59 Inhorn, *Cosmopolitan Conceptions*, p. 191.

60 Ibid., p. 190.

8 TWINS ARE PERFORMERS

1 Miranda Thompson, 'Becoming a Damien Hirst Exhibit', https://mirandalikes.wordpress.com/tag/twins, accessed 21 September 2016.

2 Ibid.

3 Tracy Valcourt, 'Pop Life: Art in a Material World', *Border Crossings*, XXIX/3 (2010), pp. 139–41.

4 Damien Hirst, 'Damien Hirst Seeks Identical Twins', www.youtube.com, accessed 21 September 2016.

5 Adrian Dannatt, 'Life's Like This and Then It Stops', *Flash Art*, XLI (2008), p. 185.

6 Hirst, 'Damien Hirst Seeks Identical Twins'.

7 Ibid.

8 *Oxford English Dictionary*, 2nd edn (Oxford, 1989), *s.v.* 'performance'.

9 Ibid.

10 For an overview of this broader use of 'performance', see James Loxley, *Performativity* (London, 2007).

11 Erving Goffman, *Asylums: Essays on the Social Situation of Mental Patients and Other Inmates* (New York, 1961), p. 95.

12 For what Goffman calls 'back regions' and 'front regions' see *The Presentation of Self in Everyday Life* (New York, 1959), pp. 66–86.

13 Thompson, 'Becoming a Damien Hirst Exhibit'.

14 Elizabeth A. Stewart, *Exploring Twins: Towards a Social Analysis of Twinship* (Basingstoke, 2000), p. 156.

15 Dona Lee Davis, *Twins Talk: What Twins Tell Us about Person, Self, and Society* (Athens, OH, 2014), p. 286.

16 Ibid., p. 3.

17 Ibid., p. 107.

18 Stewart, *Exploring Twins*, p. 156.

19 Kate Bacon, *Twins in Society: Parents, Bodies, Space and Talk* (Basingstoke, 2010), pp. 19–50; Stewart, *Exploring Twins*, p. 129; Davis, *Twins Talk*, pp. 34–5.

20 Davis, *Twins Talk*, pp. 62–3.

21 For a further example see Alexander Ward, 'Women Gives Birth to Twins with Different Fathers', *The Independent*, 11 May 2015, www. independent.co.uk, accessed 24 November 2015.

22 Wilma Stuart, quoted in 'My Ordeal, by Mother Who Had Black and White Twins', www.dailymail.co.uk, 30 May 2006.

23 Ann Curry, 'The World's Least Alike Twins', www.nbcnews.com, 29 September 2005.

24 Ibid.

25 Judith Butler, *Bodies that Matter: On the Discursive Limits of 'Sex'* (London, 1993), p. 2.

26 Steven Connor, 'Polyphiloprogenitive: Towards a General Performativity', 16 April 2013, http://stevenconnor.com, accessed 15 September 2016.

27 Ibid.

28 A point raised in my review of Dona Lee Davis's *Twins Talk*: William Viney, '*Twins Talk: What Twins Tell Us about Person, Self, and Society* by Dona Lee Davis, Athens: Ohio University Press, 2014. 312 pp', *American Anthropologist*, CXVIII/3 (2016), pp. 658–9.

29 Judith Butler calls this foreclosure 'radical erasure'. See Butler, *Bodies that Matter*, p. 8.

30 Hillel Schwartz, *Culture of the Copy: Striking Likenesses, Unreasonable Facsimiles* (New York, 1996).

31 Taylor Lorenz, 'Twinfluencers Are Taking Over the Internet: Why So Many YouTubers and Instagram Stars Are Twins', www.theatlantic.com, accessed 12 August 2019.

32 David Segal, 'Double Exposure', *Washington Post*, 12 May 2005, www.washingtonpost.com, accessed 1 October 2016.

33 Teri J. Edelstein, Sally Ruth May and James N. Wood, *The Art Institute of Chicago: The Essential Guide* (Chicago, IL, 2013), p. 297.

34 There are a growing number of such films, including *Sisters* (1973, dir. Brian De Palma and released as *Blood Sisters* in the UK), where Margot Kidder plays Danielle Breton and Dominique Blanchion; *Big Business* (1988, dir. Jim Abrahams), a modern screen adaptation of Shakespeare's *The Comedy of Errors* in which Bette Midler plays Sadie Shelton and Sadie Ratliff, and Lily Tomlin plays Rose Ratliff and Rose Shelton; *Double Impact* (1991, dir. Sheldon Lettich), featuring Jean-Claude Van Damme as Chad and Alex Wagner; *The Parent Trap* (1998, dir. Mark Waters) with Lindsay Lohan as Hallie Parker and Annie James; *The Prestige* (2006, dir. Christopher Nolan), with Christian Bale as Alfred and Freddy Borden; and *Legend* (2015, dir. Brian Helgeland), in which Tom Hardy plays Reggie and Ronnie Kray.

35 For introductions to *Dead Ringers* within the wider context of Cronenberg's work, consider William Beard, *The Artist as Monster: The Cinema of David Cronenberg*, 2nd edn (Toronto, 2006); and Scott

Wilson, *The Politics of Insects: Cronenberg's Cinema of Confrontation* (London, 2011).

36 See 'A Strange Case of Two Brothers', *Wilmington Morning Star*, 15 August 1975, https://news.google.com, accessed 17 October 2016.

37 As title designer Randall Balsmeyer recalls, 'we put together a sort of art sequence that alternated between twins being considered sort of unnatural monsters in the Dark Ages, as well as images of medical instruments.' See Will Perkins and Randall Balsmeyer, 'Dead Ringers (1988)', www.artofthetitle.com, 31 August 2016.

38 Quoted in Wilson, *The Politics of Insects*, p. 134.

39 David Cronenberg and Serge Grünberg, 'The Coronation: *Dead Ringers*', in *David Cronenberg: Interviews with Serge Grünberg* (London, 2006), p. 98.

9 TWINS ARE WORDS

1 Denise Riley, *Impersonal Passion: Language as Affect* (Durham, NC, 2005), p. 1.

2 See Steven Connor, *Dumbstruck: A Cultural History of Ventriloquism* (Oxford, 2000), p. 6.

3 Having trained as a philosopher, first under the tutelage of Gaston Bachelard at the Sorbonne, and later at the University of Tübingen, Tournier worked as a radio journalist and translator before writing *Vendredi ou les Limbes du Pacifique* (1967; trans. *Friday, or The Other Island*, 1969) and *Le Roi des aulnes* (1970; trans. *The Ogre*, 1972). For readers who are unfamiliar with his work, Mairi Maclean provides a useful overview in her book *Michel Tournier: Exploring Human Relations* (Bristol, 2003), pp. 1–28, as does Tournier in his autobiography, *Le Vent Paraclet* (Paris, 1977).

4 René Zazzo, *Le Paradoxe des jumeaux: précédé d'un dialogue avec Michel Tournier* (Paris, 1984), pp. 45–70.

5 More can be added about the structural qualities of the novel that does not have an immediate bearing on the presentation of twinning. For more on the structure of *Gemini*, see David Gascoigne, *Michel Tournier* (Oxford, 1996), pp. 14–18.

6 Jean Paul, *Blumen-, Frucht- und Dornenstücke, oder Ehestand, Tod und Hochzeit des Armenadvokaten F. St. Siebenkäs* [1796], in *Sämtliche Werke*, ed. Norbert Miller (Darmstadt, 2000), 1.2:66. See Dimitris Vardoulakis, *The Doppelgänger* (New York, 2010), p. 249, n. 4.

7 Jean-Paul Sartre, *Being and Nothingness*, trans. Hazel Barnes (New York, 1992), pp. 340–58.

8 Michel Tournier, *Gemini*, trans. Ann Carter (London, 1981), p. 11.

9 Tournier, *Le Vent Paraclet*, p. 189. The translation is found in Juliana de Nooy, *Twins in Contemporary Literature and Culture: Look Twice* (Basingstoke, 2005), pp. 1–2. My italics.

10 Tournier, *Gemini*, p. 196.

11 Ibid., p. 143.

12 Ibid., p. 12.

13 Ibid., p. 52; and see René Zazzo, *Les Jumeaux, le couple et la personne* [1960] (Paris, 2015). For more recent studies that have explored whether this phenomenon is an impairment or developmental issue, noting how mono- and dizygotic twins acquire language in different ways, see Dorothy Bishop and Sonia Bishop, '"Twin Language": A Risk Factor for Language Impairment?', *Journal of Speech, Language, and Hearing Research*, XLI/1 (1998), pp. 150–60; Bruna Zani, Maria Grazia Carelli, Beatrice Benelli and Elvira Cicognani, 'Communicative Skills in Childhood: The Case of Twins', *Discourse Processes*, XIV/3 (1991), pp. 339–56.

14 Tournier, *Gemini*, p. 133.

15 Ibid., p. 52, italics in original.

16 'Twin Girls Invent Own Language', *San Diego Union*, 5 July 1977; 'Education: Ginny and Gracie Go to School', *Time*, 10 December 1979, http://content.time.com, accessed 20 October 2019.

17 Jeanne-Pierre Gorin, 'Jeanne-Pierre Gorin by Lynne Tillman', *BOMB*, 1 April 1988, www.bombmagazine.org, accessed 20 October 2019.

18 Ibid.

19 See Mel Y. Chen, *Animacies: Biopolitics, Racial Mattering, and Queer Affect* (Durham, NC, 2012), p. 2.

20 Karen Thorpe, 'Twin Children's Language Development', *Early Human Development*, LXXXII/6 (2006), pp. 387–95.

21 Ibid.

22 The distinction is from Mark Freeman, 'Charting the Narrative Unconscious: Cultural Memory and the Challenge of Autobiography', *Narrative Inquiry*, XII/1 (2002), p. 296.

23 Caitríona Ní Dhúill, 'Moments Narratable and Non-narratable: Mundanity and Biography', Narrating Time Seminar, Durham University, 23 January 2014, unpublished. Later revised as Caitríona Ní Dhúill, 'Indigestible Biographies: Limits to the Narrative Processing of Life', in *Narrative im Bruch: Theoretische Positionen und Anwendungen (Broken Narratives)*, ed. Anna Babka, Marlen Bidwell-Steiner and Wolfgang Muller-Funk (Gottingen, 2016), pp. 223–38.

24 Gérard Genette, *Narrative Discourse Revisited*, trans. Jane E. Lewin (Ithaca, NY, 1988), p. 147. See Brian Richardson, 'The Implied Author: Back from the Grave or Simply Dead Again?', *Style*, XLIV/1 (2011), p. 5.

25 Roland Barthes, 'From Work to Text', in *Debating Texts*, ed. Rick Rylance (Toronto, 1987), p. 120.

26 Pamela Spiro Wagner and Carolyn Spiro, *Divided Minds: Twin Sisters and Their Journey through Schizophrenia* (New York, 2005), p. 97.

27 Ibid.

28 Ibid., p. 98.

29 Ibid., p. 182.

30 Ibid., p. 288.

31 Ibid., p. 145.

32 Ibid., pp. 146–7.

33 Nancy M. Docherty, Maddalena DeRosa and Nancy C. Andreasen, 'Communication Disturbances in Schizophrenia and Mania', *Archives of General Psychiatry*, LIII/4 (1996), pp. 358–64. Nancy C. Andreasen and William M. Grove, 'Thought, Language, and Communication in Schizophrenia: Diagnosis and Prognosis', *Schizophrenia Bulletin*, XII/3 (1986), pp. 348–59.

34 Michael Bury, 'Chronic Illness as Biographical Disruption', *Sociology of Health and Illness*, IV/2 (1982), p. 169.

35 Wagner and Spiro, *Divided Minds*, p. 184.

36 Ibid., p. 269.

37 Ibid., pp. 274–5.

38 Ibid., p. 253.

39 Ibid., p. 263.

40 Sean Gallagher, 'Pathologies in Narrative Structures', in *Narrative and Understanding Persons*, ed. Daniel D. Hutto (Cambridge, 2007), p. 222.

41 Ibid., p. 198.

42 Ibid., p. 195.

43 Ibid., p. 314.

44 Ibid., p. 315.

45 Alex Lewis and Marcus Lewis, *Tell Me Who I Am: Sometimes It's Safer Not to Know* (London, 2013), p. 117.

46 Ibid., p. 138.

47 Ibid., p. 149.

48 Ibid., p. 234, p. 139.

49 Ibid., pp. 234–5.

50 Sidonie Smith and Julia Watson, *Reading Autobiography: A Guide for Interpreting Life Narratives* (Minneapolis, MN, 2001), p. 37.

51 Ibid., p. 257.

52 Ibid., p. 287.

53 Andy Clark and David Chalmers, 'The Extended Mind', *Analysis*, LVIII/1 (1998), p. 8.

54 Ibid., p. 17.

55 Ibid., p. 18.

56 Dona Lee Davis, *Twins Talk: What Twins Tell Us about Person, Self, and Society* (Athens, OH, 2014), p. 27.

57 Jeremy Seabrook, 'Twins', *Granta*, XCV (2006), pp. 193, 196.

58 Ibid., p. 206.

59 Ibid., p. 196.

60 Ibid., p. 205.

61 *The Oxford English Dictionary*, 2nd edn (Oxford, 1989), *s.v.* 'Twin'.

FURTHER READING

Bacon, Kate, *Twins in Society: Parents, Bodies, Space and Talk* (Basingstoke, 2010)

Ball, Helen, and Catherine Hill, 'Twin Infanticide Revisited', *Current Anthropology*, XXXVIII/5 (1996), pp. 856–63

Ball, Laura C., and Thomas Teo, 'Twin Studies', in *The International Encyclopaedia of Social Sciences*, 2nd edn, ed. William A. Darity (New York, 2008), pp. 473–5

Barnes, Barry, and John Dupré, *Genomes and What to Make of Them* (Chicago, IL, 2008)

Bastian, Misty L., '"The Demon Superstition": Abominable Twins and Mission Culture in Onitsha History', *Ethnology*, XL/1 (2001), pp. 13–27

Bewley, Susan, Philippa Moth and Yacoub Khalaf, 'A Complicated IVF Twin Pregnancy', *Human Reproduction*, XXV/4 (2010), pp. 1082–4

Bishop, Dorothy, and Sonia Bishop, '"Twin Language": A Risk Factor for Language Impairment?', *Journal of Speech, Language, and Hearing Research*, XLI/1 (1998), pp. 150–60

Blickstein, Isaac, 'Superfecundation and Superfetation', in *Multiple Pregnancy: Epidemiology, Gestation and Perinatal Outcome*, ed. Isaac Blickstein and Louis G. Keith (Abingdon, 2005), pp. 102–7

Braude, Peter, *One Child at a Time: Reducing Multiple Births after IVF*, Report of the Expert Group on Multiple Births after IVF (October 2006)

Burlingham, Dorothy, 'The Fantasy of Having a Twin', *Psychoanalytic Study of the Child*, I (1945), pp. 205–10

Burt, Callie H., and Ronald L. Simons, 'Pulling Back the Curtain on Heritability Studies: Biosocial Criminology in the Postgenomic Era', *Criminology*, LII/2 (2014), pp. 223–62

Bynum, Carolyn Walker, *Metamorphosis and Identity* (New York, 2001)

Cadden, Joan, *The Meanings of Sex Difference in the Middle Ages: Medicine, Science, and Culture* (Cambridge, 1993)

Chappel, T.J.H., 'The Yoruba Cult of Twins in Historical Perspective', *Africa: Journal of the International African Institute*, XLIV/3 (1974), pp. 250–65

Chatwin, Bruce, *On Black Hill* (London, 1982)

Chen, Mel Y., *Animacies: Biopolitics, Racial Mattering, and Queer Affect* (Durham, NC, 2012)

Dasen, Véronique, *Jumeaux, jumelles dans l'antiquité grecque et romaine* (Zurich, 2005)

Daston, Lorraine, and Katharine Park, *Wonders and the Order of Nature, 1150–1750* (New York, 1998)

Davis, Dona Lee, *Twins Talk: What Twins Tell Us about Person, Self, and Society* (Athens, OH, 2014)

De Nooy, Juliana, *Twins in Contemporary Literature and Culture: Look Twice* (Basingstoke, 2005)

Diduk, Susan, 'Twinship and Juvenile Power: The Ordinariness of the Extraordinary', *Ethnology*, XL/1 (2001), pp. 29–43

Duffin, Jacalyn, *Medical Saints: Cosmas and Damian in a Postmodern World* (Oxford, 2013)

Evans-Pritchard, E. E., 'Customs and Beliefs Relating to Twins among the Nilotic Nuer', *Uganda Journal*, III (1936), pp. 230–38

Farmer, Penelope, *Two, or The Book of Twins and Doubles: An Autobiographical Anthology* (London, 1996)

Franklin, Sarah, *Biological Relatives: IVF, Stem Cells, and the Future of Kinship* (Durham, NC, 2013)

Galton, Francis, 'The History of Twins as a Criterion of Nature and Nurture', *Fraser's Magazine*, XII (1875), pp. 566–76

Gross, Kenneth, 'Ordinary Twinship', *Raritan*, XXII/4 (2003), pp. 20–39

Hacking, Ian, 'Kinds of People: Moving Targets', *Proceedings of the British Society*, CLI (2007), pp. 285–318

Hall, Judith, 'Twinning', *The Lancet*, CCCLXII (2003), pp. 735–43

Harris, Rendell J., *The Cult of the Heavenly Twins* (Cambridge, 1906)

Hur, Yoon-Mi, and Jeffrey M. Craig, 'Twin Registries Worldwide: An Important Resource for Scientific Research', *Twin Research and Human Genetics*, XVI/1 (2013), pp. 1–12

Kristóf, Ágota, *The Notebook, The Proof, The Third Lie: Three Novels* (New York, 1997)

Midgley, Mary, *The Myths We Live By* (Abingdon, 2011)

Peek, Philip M., ed., *Twins in African and Diaspora Cultures: Double Trouble, Twice Blessed* (Bloomington, IN, 2011)

Piontelli, Elizabeth, *Twins in the World: The Legends They Inspire and the Lives They Lead* (London, 2008)

Renne, Elisha P., 'Twinship in an Ekiti Yoruba Town', *Ethnology*, XL/1 (2001), pp. 63–78

Roy, Arundhati, *The God of Small Things* (London, 1997)

Schwartz, Hillel, *The Culture of the Copy: Striking Likenesses, Unreasonable Facsimiles* (Cambridge, MA, 1997)

Seabrook, Jeremy, 'Twins', *Granta*, XCV (2006), pp. 191–207

Segal, Nancy L., *Born Together – Reared Apart: The Landmark Minnesota Twin Study* (Cambridge, 2012)

—, *Twin Mythconceptions: False Beliefs, Fables, and Facts about Twins* (Cambridge, MA, 2017)

Smith, Kevin, et al., 'Biology, Ideology, and Epistemology: How Do We Know Political Attitudes are Inherited and Why Should We Care?', *American Journal of Political Science*, LVI/1 (2012), pp. 17–33

Spiro, Pamela Wagner, and Carolyn S. Spiro, MD, *Divided Minds: Twin Sisters and Their Journey through Schizophrenia* (New York, 2006)

Stewart, Elizabeth A., *Exploring Twins: Towards a Social Analysis of Twinship* (Basingstoke, 2000)

Teo, Thomas, and Laura C. Ball, 'Twin Research, Revisionism and Metahistory', *History of Human Science*, XXII/5 (2009), pp. 1–23

Thijssen, J. M., 'Twins as Monsters: Albertus Magnus's Theory of the Generation of Twins and Its Philosophical Context', *Bulletin of the History of Medicine*, LCI/2 (1987), pp. 237–46

Thorpe, Karen, 'Twin Children's Language Development', *Early Human Development*, LXXXII/6 (2006), pp. 387–95

Tournier, Michel, *Gemini*, trans. Ann Carter (London, 1981)

Turner, Victor, *The Ritual Process: Structure and Anti-structure* [1969] (Piscataway, NJ, 1997)

Wiseman, T. P., *Remus* (Cambridge, 1995)

Zazzo, René, *Le Paradoxe des jumeaux: précédé d'un dialogue avec Michel Tournier* (Paris, 1984)

ACKNOWLEDGEMENTS

This book is indebted to the hearsay, fear and fascination that follow human twins. I cannot accept full responsibility for all that this book gathers in its pages. Meanings given to twins are the work of many hands. There are writers that labour with the idea that their work should be secret until revealed in print, like an illusionist's trick guarded by an oath of secrecy. But the struggles I have had with this book have been widely shared. I was fortunate to have the generous support of other writers and researchers with whom I could share my ideas, who helped me think and think more clearly about twins as a topic. They often guided and corrected my work and they showed me how twins had either passed through or become part of their own.

This book has benefited from many 'do-you-know' conversations: have you heard about this story? Do you know this twin study? Have you seen this artwork, read this novel or seen this performance? Do you know these twins? And did you know I'm a twin, too? And while I benefited from the deep expertise and knowledge of my colleagues, I also had these wonderful encounters with strangers, whose thoughts and feelings, rebukes and recommendations were invaluable for broadening my horizons and reminding me that the interest I had in this book's subject was neither original nor unique to me; almost everyone I met seemed to know something, or want to know something, about twins.

During the years I was employed at Durham University I was fortunate to have a great number of colleagues who offered me their insight, guidance, kindness and encouragement. Felicity Callard (now at University of Glasgow) and Angela Woods became wonderful friends and advisers, introducing me to the principles and practice of critical medical humanities research. I feel so fortunate to have met them and to have had the opportunity to learn from their example. I was also very fortunate to work with Corinne Saunders and to benefit from her generosity and advice throughout my time at Durham. I owe a great debt of gratitude to other researchers who were based at Durham University's Institute of Medical Humanities: Jane Macnaughton, Martyn Evans, Sarah Atkinson, Andrew Russell, Mary Robson, Marco Bernini, Pat Waugh, Arthur Rose (now University of Bristol), Charles Fernyhough, Ben Alderson-Day, Hilary Powell, Victoria Patton, Jan B. W. Pedersen (now University College Diakonissestiftelsen), Jenny Laws, Luna Dolezal (University of Exeter) and Ben Kasstan (University of Sussex). Their leadership of, and contribution to, the institute's vibrant research environment has been a constant source of inspiration to me. They gave me opportunities to trial early versions of this book and to benefit from their experience and insight. I also wish to thank Ivana Petrovic (University of Virginia) and Barbara Graziosi (Princeton University) for their comments and encouragement. I have also received invaluable support and professional guidance from colleagues in the Department of English Studies. My special thanks to Marc Botha, Tim Clark, Jason Harding, David Herman, Simon James, Alastair Renfrew and Mark Sandy. Another member of the Department of English Studies deserves special thanks: Elizabeth Archibald read and commented on parts of this book and welcomed me to St Cuthbert's Society, Durham.

I wish to thank colleagues from the Northern Network for Medical Humanities Research for regular opportunities to learn about medical humanities research in the United Kingdom. I have had the good fortune to meet scholars who (either in person or online) have given me their time and perspective. Thank you to Dominic Berry, Jeff Craig, Des Fitzgerald, Greg Hollin, Alice Leonard, Brigitte Nerlich, Martyn Pickersgill, Massimo Mangino, Robert Plomin and Hannah Priest. I also want to thank Juliette Harris and her colleagues at TwinsUK for allowing me to join their Volunteer Advisory Panel (2014–15). I was given invaluable opportunities to present early versions of this research at the National University of Ireland, Maynooth; University of Nottingham; University of Leeds; University of Sheffield; Lund University; and Birkbeck, University of London. Thank you to Margaret O'Neill and Christopher Stokes, Andy Goffey, Stuart Murray, Robert McKay and John Miller, Kristofer Hansson and Lisa Mullen for organizing these events. I also want to thank four twins – James Hoctor, Michele Wysocki, Alison Cool and Ron Levao – who, like me, are twins researching aspects of twinning. I want to thank them for sharing their ideas, encouragement and feedback.

This book was made possible through a Leverhulme Early Career Fellowship at Durham University ('The Wonder of Twins', ECF-2013-466). I also received funding as a Postdoctoral Research Fellow in the Centre for Medical Humanities, as part of the Centre's Wellcome Trust Strategic Award (WT086049). I am grateful to both funders for their financial support.

Thanks to Michael Leaman, Alex Ciobanu, and colleagues at Reaktion Books for editorial input, their professionalism and attention to detail. And I am so grateful to Anne Meadows at Granta Books, who challenged and inspired me to rethink and rewrite this book. Thanks to Anne Beech for helping me through the fine print. Fragments of this project have appeared in existing publications. Thanks to Joe Brooker, John Cromby, Brian Dillon, Jörg Heiser, Jenny Higgie and Maurizio Meloni for publishing these. My heartfelt thanks to Hugh and Lotte Shankland, who, when I was writing this book, gave me a home from home. Finally, I want to thank my British and Italian families. Your love and patience have made all this possible.

PHOTO ACKNOWLEDGEMENTS

The author and publishers wish to express their thanks to the below sources of illustrative material and/or permission to reproduce it. Some locations of artworks are also given below, in the interest of brevity:

Photo Stuart Atkins/Shutterstock: 9; Bibliothèque nationale de France, Paris: 13 (Ms. Lat. 11229), 14 (Ms. Lat. 16169); © Damien Hirst and Science Ltd., All Rights Reserved, DACS/Artimage 2021 (photo Mark Niedermann): 16; Erik Overbey Collection, Doy Leale McCall Rare Book and Manuscript Library, University of South Alabama, Mobile, AL: 6; Galleria Borghese, Rome: 10; photo Lynn Hilton/Shutterstock: 20; photo Marvin Joseph/The Washington Post via Getty Images: 17; Koninklijke Bibliotheek van België, Brussels (Ms. 3701-15): 12; from William Lilly, *Monarchy or No Monarchy in England* (London, 1651): 5; Musei Capitolini, Rome/photo Marie-Lan Taÿ Pamart: 2; Rijksmuseum, Amsterdam: 1; from Eucharius Rösslin, *Der schwangeren Frauen und Hebammen Rosengarten* (Strasbourg, 1513): 4; Andrea Sabbadini/Alamy Stock Photo: 3; Wellcome Collection, London (CC BY 4.0): 11, 15.

INDEX

Illustration numbers are indicated by *italics*